Intellectual Skywriting

Philip Nobile

Intellectual Skywriting

Literary Politics & The New York Review of Books

CHARTERHOUSE  New York

INTELLECTUAL SKYWRITING
COPYRIGHT © 1974 BY PHILIP NOBILE

Portions of this book appeared in different form in *Esquire*.

Library of Congress Catalog Card Number: 72-84218
MANUFACTURED IN THE UNITED STATES OF AMERICA
ISBN: 0-88327-013-7

Designed by Bob Antler

Illustrations by Grandville

Acknowledgments

ome people were more indispensable than others in the making of this book. They are Mike Curtis of *The Atlantic*, who encouraged me throughout the early stages; Tom Ferrell and Harold Hayes of *Esquire*, who did the same during the later stages; Don Congdon, my agent, whose constancy never flagged; John Herlihy, my friend and aide-de-camp for a dozen years; Jack Deedy, sidekick and sounding board, in whose company I have always taken direct pleasure; H. B., who waited; and my editor, Richard Kluger, whose advice I keenly appreciated.

I must also mention some former teachers who have influenced this writer more than they perhaps realize—John Kirvan of the Paulist Fathers, Dr. Edward Callahan of Holy Cross, Dr. John Lavely of Boston University, and Albert Dondeyne of the University of Louvain.

George Frazier of *The Boston Globe*, Justus George Lawler of the late *Jubilee* magazine, James O'Gara of *Commonweal*, Bob Hoyt, the former editor of *The National Catholic Reporter*, and Jim Andrews and John McMeel of Universal Press Syndicate I thank for reasons they must realize.

And then there is Maureen, who bore two children, too many lost weekends, and me while this book was a-borning all over the house. True grit.

To my dear father
Dominic Nobile
1914-1962

Contents

Prologue

I n the opening frames of the film *Bob & Carol & Ted & Alice*, Bob and Carol pay a visit to a Big Sur sensitivity farm. As they race their sports car through the mountains to the strains of the "Hallelujah Chorus," the scene zooms ahead to their weekend destination. The camera picks up three sensational female nudes offering their breasts up to the sun, lingers pruriently, and then turns to a naked old boy ensconced in a hot bath. Oblivious of the flesh around him, the gentleman is reading a paper of some sort. It turns out to be a copy of *The New York Review of Books*. Of course, *The New York Review of Books*. What other journal would the average, self-respecting, educated everyman rather be caught reading in 1969? In other times, in other movies, *The Smart Set, The American Mercury, The New Republic*, or *Partisan Review* would have been appropriate props. But *New York Review* was the hot intellectual magazine of the Sixties, and director Paul Mazurski chose his symbol well.

The New York Review of Books debuted as a Manhattan-based book review during the city's 1963 newspaper strike. The phenomenal reception accorded its two experimental issues suggested that a new high-cult review of books just might survive

3

amidst entrenched competition from the *Times*, the *Herald Tribune*, and *Saturday Review*. Against all reasonable expectations, *New York Review* did better than survive. It flourished—first, as a literary proposition dedicated to selected important books and infused with liberal politics, and later, as a less literary and more politicized platform of the radical Left. In both stages, the *Review* counted on a salon-full of recognizable names and impeccable reputations.

The switch from *belles lettres* to the barricades was on in mid-decade when the country went to war, the blacks went to burn, and the students went to riot. Reacting to this national coming apart, New York intellectuals went to the mattresses. Crisis politics cracked up friendships and loosened long-standing alliances among the local intelligentsia. Because *New York Review* and many of its writers sided with the radical wings of the multiple-front Movement, it lost the allegiance of several previous sympathizers. Irving Howe, a then frequent contributor to *NYR*, summed up the mounting anti-*Review* sentiment in the October 1968 *Commentary*. Howe, the editor of *Dissent*, found the *Review* guilty of abandoning its early premises and letting critical standards fall.

> More precisely, what the *New York Review* has managed to achieve—I find it quite fascinating as a portent of things to come—is a link between campus "leftism" and East Side stylishness, the worlds of Tom Hayden and George Plimpton. Opposition to communist politics and ideology is frequently presented in the pages of the *New York Review* as if it were an obsolete, indeed a pathetic, hangover from a discredited past or worse yet, a dark sign of the CIA. A snappish and crude anti-Americanism has swept over much of its political writing . . . And in the hands of writers like Andrew Kopkind (author of the immortal phrase, "morality . . . starts at the barrel of a gun") liberal values and norms are treated with something very close to contempt.

Thus it became the accepted fashion to chide the *New York Review* for its fashionability. Hostile judgments on this score were rendered in *Time, Antioch Review,* and *Dissent. Esquire* went so far as to remark: ". . . from among their authors the next Stalin and his speechwriters will emerge" (May 1971).

The *Review's* notoriety was such that even Spiro T. Agnew could get a laugh at its expense. During a 1970 mid-term campaign stop in Wilmington, Delaware, the former V.P. paused to give Republicans everywhere an elitism quiz. "The elite consists of raised-eyebrow cynics," he told his audience at St. Mark's High School, "the anti-intellectual intellectuals, the pampered egotists who sneer at honesty, thrift, hard work, prudence, common decency, and self-denial." Just to be sure no GOP types fitted these categories, he deadpanned a self-testing questionnaire designed to weed out the secret effete. The sixth question Agnew asked was: "Does it make you feel warm and snugly protected to read *The New York Review of Books?*" (*The New York Times,* October 15, 1970).

Agnew insinuated himself into literary politics earlier the same year when he complimented such high-caliber New York intellectuals as Sidney Hook and Irving Kristol on their conservative views on higher education.[1] Long before the Vice President became a household epithet, Hook and Kristol were *personae non gratae* at the *Review.* And both, characteristically, signed a Professors for Nixon ad in 1972 (*The New York Times,* October 15, 1972). Kristol, Henry Luce Professor of Urban Values at New York University and co-editor with Daniel Bell of the quarterly *The Public Interest,* was even mentioned by Evans and Novak as a likely White House aide, that is, "a broad gauge advisor on domestic policy," in the second administration of Richard M. Nixon (The *Chicago Sun-Times,* November 19, 1972).

1. Speech given at Republican statewide fund-raising dinner in Des Moines, Iowa, April 14, 1970.

Apparently, the ideological split between the Right and Left factions of the liberal New York intellegentsia had arrived at the point where the first Nixon Administration looked upon the former as friend and the latter as foe. The *Review*'s arch-rival in the Right faction is *Commentary* magazine. *Commentary*'s rightward turn, unthinkable in the mid-Sixties, became inevitable in the early seventies as its editor grew fearful of the Left. Ironically, when Norman Podhoretz took over *Commentary* in 1960, he deliberately mothballed the endemic hard anti-communism of the magazine and tilted toward the Left. But when the radical Left's critiques of American society stiffened during the escalation of Johnson's war and seemed to him blindly dismissive of the democratic system, Podhoretz recoiled. *Commentary* became a *defensor fidei*, gladly smiting all manner of New Left orthodoxy.

Nixon's syncretist Vice President would even have occasion to cite Podhoretz in his elitist-baiting act. On January 19, 1972, he told a Cleveland gathering of the Printing Industries Association of Northern Ohio that Podhoretz and he were one on the subject of repression. "The editor of *Commentary* magazine recently examined the charge that we are living in a repressive society and concluded, as others have, that the charge is totally absurd. In analyzing this rhetorical attack on America, he wrote: 'Never has there been so much talk of repression, but never has there been so great a degree of civil freedom, probably in the history of the world, as exists in the United States today'" ("Issues," *Commentary*, December 1971).

Inevitably, the *New York Review* was subjected to *Commentary*'s scrutiny. Dennis Wrong's article, "The Case of the *New York Review*" (November 1970), detailed what Podhoretz called *NYR*'s "*trahisons* . . . against the defining values of the intellectual life." In the staunch opinion of the editor of *Commentary*, the *New York Review* had metamorphosed into a monger of crises and an enemy of democracy. Had he thought of the phrase before Tom Wolfe, Podhoretz would have delighted in calling the *Review* "the chief theoretical organ of radical chic," a supremely adhesive insult.

New York Review rode out this dark night of recrimination rather well. While the *Review* refused, for some unfathomable reason, to engage in open combat with detractors, its pages gradually became less and less receptive to free-swinging radicalism. They stopped calling *NYR* "The Parlour Panther" in 1972. For though the magazine's Anglophilia stood fast, its knee-jerk New Leftism had passed, and its politics leaned nostalgically toward Left Center.

The *Review*'s standing may have changed in the hearts of the New York intelligentsia, but it is still very much on their minds. According to a recent study of the most influential magazines among the nation's intellectual elite, the *Review* emerged as the overall winner by far.[2] Fifty per cent of the select sample of 147 writers, professors, and editors polled noted that they read or discuss the *New York Review* regularly. No other magazine could claim even half that figure.

The New York Review of Books has come a fair piece since the first issue was pasted together in Robert Lowell's dining room eleven years ago—from a one-shot literary stunt to the largest circulation and most highly regarded magazine of its kind. This book chronicles its rise, profiles its personalities, records its controversies, and reports on its condition as it reflects the state of the intelligentsia culture.

2. See Charles Kadushin, Julie Hover and Monica Tichy, "How and Where to Find Intellectual Elite in the United States," *Public Opinion Quarterly* (Spring 1971).

1

An Afternoon
at the Office

R obert Benjamin Silvers would rather not talk about *The New York Review of Books*. And he doesn't really have to. Leaning back on a beat-up office chair behind a large wooden desk pillared high with books, Silvers, a devilishly handsome fellow in his mid-forties, slouches in the contented posture of deserved success. As the founding editor (properly co-founding editor with Barbara Epstein) and guiding logos of the premiere literary-intellectual journal in the English-speaking world, he is excellently situated to shrug off troublesome inquiries. After all, the *Review* has never given suck to the publicity machine. Its ascendancy is in no wise owed to the ministrations of the press. A probe of the *Review* just isn't useful to Silvers, and he doesn't mind telling you so. Defending his distaste for interviews, he cites the unhappy experience of cooperating with *Time* on a story that turned out astonishingly nasty toward the *Review*. One thing is made perfectly clear: Bob Silvers will not partake in any trivializing study that cannot possibly be commensurate with the complexity of *The New York Review of Books*.

11

"One's relationship with writers is holy. So much is private," explains Silvers in heavy earnest. "All that matters is what one produces." He adds later, "I put my name on the paper, and the rest I don't care to be known." Modus operandi is likewise forbidden ground. "I hate this idea that you know more by finding out how a paper is run." Then how about a few words on something alien, like Dennis Wrong's piece?

"Inadequate, unfair, and base, not worthy of engaging."

Wrong's hit has fouled the air, and Silvers is in a "You're-not-going-to-have-*New-York-Review*-to-kick-around-any-more" mood. He declines to be quoted, wants nothing attributed, and would like to forget the entire matter. The conversation is declining swiftly when who should walk in on his way home from work but Jason Epstein, husband of Barbara, vice president of Random House and creator *ex nihilo* of the *Review*. And what patriarchal attitudes does the pear-shaped Epstein have toward the magazine many people suspect he surreptitiously controls? "I hardly ever discuss the *Review* with Bob," he says in a why-ask-me tone of voice, "except to comment on an occasional piece." Won't Epstein even comment on the *Review*? "Yes, but only in Bob's presence."

Since the subject is already on the table, the conversation moves quickly to Norman Podhoretz and the motives behind *Commentary*'s ongoing offensive against the *Review* and its contributors. Epstein traces the trouble back to *Making It*, Podhoretz's confession of life in the extended New York intellectual "Family" (an elite array of critics, editors, novelists, and poets that manages the country's high culture) and the dirty little secret of success that carried him through. When Roger W. Straus Jr., president of Farrar, Straus and Giroux, recommended some editorial changes in the book, Podhoretz brought his cherished manuscript over to best friend Jason Epstein at Random. Epstein, one of *Making It*'s main characters, advised his suddenly ex-best friend against publication. "If I were God, I'd drown it in the river," he is supposed to have remarked of the book.

The *Making It* affair, however, is very mild stuff compared to Epstein's ultimate diagnosis of the Podhoretz question. "Of course, you can't use any of this," he insists, as he proceeds with a fascinating armchair psychoanalysis which, if true, makes a good deal of sense (but so does Podhoretz's Freudian interpretation of old buddy Jason). Silvers, too, thinks lowly of Podhoretz, who once offered him a post at *Commentary* in the early Sixties. (According to Midge Decter, Podhoretz's wife, Silvers insisted on becoming "co-editor-in-chief" and so the deal fell through.) He says he hardly knew the man and dismisses him with a continuum of choice pejoratives. These must be New York intellectuals. See how they loathe one another.

Barbara Epstein, a frail blond Gelsomina of a woman, enters Silvers' book-infested sanctum with a copy of next Sunday's *Review*, which she hands over to Jason. Nor is she quite captured by the notion of a portrait of *New York Review*. Predictably, her services are not volunteered.

Does the *Review* drop writers who stray from its version of Left orthodoxy? Dennis Wrong listed several former contributors to the magazine who no longer appear for seeming political reasons. Silvers denies the accusation. "We don't take anybody on and so we don't drop anybody." Nobody?

"You dropped Z——— didn't you?" Jason Epstein kids as he looks up from the *Times*, in which he has been overtly enjoying a bad review of Tom Wolfe's *Radical Chic*.[1] Silvers chuckles. Yes, poor Z———, a specialist in one of the most arcane fields the *Review* has ever covered, has been let go. Everyone in the room laughs as Silvers reads Z———'s last letter, which details his upcoming travels and suggests possibilities for future reviews. Pathetic but funny. "We turn down famous—, er," Barbara Epstein grinningly corrects herself, "well-known writers of commissioned pieces."

1. Reviewed by Thomas Edwards, *The New York Times Book Review*, November 29, 1970.

As far as missing persons go, Andrew Kopkind would be more to the point than Z——— or some of Wrong's infrequently used old Leftists. Kopkind was regularly employed at the *Review* in the late Sixties on topics of great moment like Martin Luther King, Robert Kennedy, and the new politics. But Kopkind had not been seen thereabouts in three years, the prevailing word being that his far-out Leftism is more than the *Review* is willing to bear. Complications again, according to Silvers. He was just on the phone with Andy, and the situation is complicated.

The Epsteins leave, and Silvers continues as tight-lipped as before. He is being difficult, but not impossible. Although the deist editor pose is hard to endure, the quest for anonymity is not. Silvers is an inordinately private person with an almost chromosomal inclination for obscurity. He'd like to help, but he'll be damned if he's going to appear self-seeking.

The would-be interview, peripatetic during its waning minutes, comes to a halt outside the corridor men's room. Silvers stands hunched in solemn thought. Although the questions have been pointed, he senses a certain sympathy. He will be available for all queries of a factual nature and won't interfere with the interrogation of his friends. In a parting bit of advice, he counsels reading several *Review* articles that have been outspokenly critical of Left goings-on—John William Ward's review of *Prison Memoirs of an Anarchist*, J. M. Cameron's supplement "On Violence," Hannah Arendt's article "On Violence," Paul Goodman's essay "Reflections on Racism, Spite, Guilt, and Violence," and a series of pieces by Christopher Lasch, which were collected into his *The Agony of the American Left*. "If the ideas in these articles were taken seriously," Silvers says, "they could have changed the history of the Left."

2

Five Easy Titles:
A Chronicle

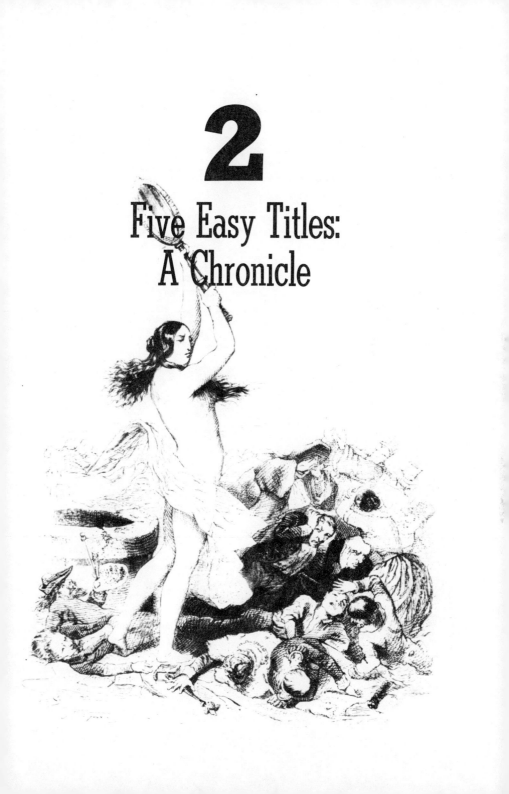

The New York newspaper strike in the winter of 1962–63 was the sufficient, but not the necessary, cause of the *New York Review*. Rather the want of any rigorous American book-reviewing organ comparable to London's *Times Literary Supplement* is what made the *Review* happen. *Saturday Review*, and the Sunday book reviews of *The New York Times* and *Herald Tribune*, the only three native journals whose principle occupation was books, never created a sense of obligation among literary folk. Open contempt may be an apt description of elite attitudes toward the reviewing situation. Witness Edmund Wilson's vicious one-liner: "The disappearance of the *Times* Sunday book section at the time of the printers' strike only made us realize it had never existed."[1]

Saturday Review was dependent on second- and third-rate reviewers and appeared to be no longer "of literature" but of music, travel, racing cars, and cooking. The *Times Book Review*

1. "Every Man His Own Eckermann," *NYR*, September 12, 1963. Wilson was likewise unimpressed with the good old quarterly try: "And those quarterlies are still mostly wandering in the vast academic desert of the structure of *The Sound and the Fury*, the variants in the text of *Billy Budd*, and the religious significance of *The Great Gatsby*."

was believed too soft on books under the benevolent dictatorship
of Francis Brown, who, it is said, operated a surefire system of
choosing wrong and dull reviewers. The *Tribune* section was too
undernourished to make an intellectual dent, although terribly
lively in its later, though now defunct, reincarnation as *Book
Week*. Minor novelist but major highbrow critic Elizabeth Hardwick (formerly Mrs. Robert Lowell), who was to become advisory
editor at *New York Review*, spoke up for her crowd in a 1959
Harper's piece entitled "The Decline of Book Reviewing." "Sweet,
bland commendations fall everywhere upon the scene," she wrote
with excusable hauteur; "a universal, if somewhat lobotomized,
accommodation reigns. A book is born into a puddle of treacle; the
brine of hostile criticism is only a memory." Hardwick's devastating
critique went on to catalogue a syllabus of errors current in the
reviewing industry and wound up with a call for "the great metropolitan publications" to seek first the kingdom of "the unusual,
the difficult, the lengthy, the intransigent, and above all, the
interesting." Some of these seeds fell on good soil. For the *Harper's*
editor who commissioned Hardwick was young Bob Silvers, a few
months returned from a six-year Parisian exile and just starting
his gentlemanly rise in the big city.

Long ago, critic F. W. Dupee, the now-retired Columbia
English professor, felt the need for "a good *Saturday Review* which
would be edited by someone like Lionel Trilling and be filled
with editorials, articles, and reviews." Way back, *Partisan Review*
editor William Phillips used to bring up a similar project in the
presence of potential patrons. Everybody talked about a new book
review, but nobody did anything about it, including Jason Epstein,
that young publishing upstart who, while at Doubleday, singlehandedly begat the quality paperback revolution with Anchor
Books and had moved on to Random House to duplicate his success with the Vintage line. "There's only one person in the country who could do it," Epstein jested with a Simon and Schuster

editor in the late Fifties, "and I'm busy." The *New York Review* would have to wait until Epstein got around to it. But ready or not, the 114-day newspaper blackout beginning late in 1962 provided the perfect cover. All those book advertisements with no place to go. All those readers with no reviews. Power was lying in the streets, and Epstein, literary Leninist that he is, shrewdly picked it up.

A few exploratory meetings were held at the Epsteins' apartment on West 67th Street. Epstein takes up the narration: "We were talking about how pleasant it was to live in New York without newspapers; how, now that there were no newspapers, there didn't seem to be any news either; that things didn't really happen in fact, but happened only in *The New York Times*. A hundred or so pages to accompany the ads, and on Sundays a thousand pages—most of them trivial—had to be concocted. I was especially happy not to have to read *The New York Times Book Review*, that monstrous distorting mirror in which I would find, week after week, the work of tired hacks, lame professors, breezy illiterates. And then it occurred to all of us at once to do a book review of our own." (*A.L.A. Bulletin*, July-August, 1963)

The easy decision was go, at least with a trial issue, and the immediate game plan was simple: concerned critics would work fast and donate their copy; advertising money, newsstand sales, plus a $4,000 loan from Marine Midland Trust would pay the printing costs. But who was going to edit the thing? "We thought and thought who should be editor," Elizabeth Hardwick recalls. Jason's alliance at Random House put him out of the running. Conflict of interest enough that he was in on the deal in the first place. Barbara couldn't handle the job alone, and her name would look suspicious up front anyway. "If there were a natural, inevitable choice, it would have been me," concedes Norman Podhoretz without a glimmer of irony. Of course, Podhoretz was the one. Hadn't he been writing for *Scrutiny*, *Partisan*

Review, Commentary, and *The New Yorker,* doing and undoing reputations with intelligence and attention-gaining flair? "No sooner had my first *New Yorker* piece—a long review of Nelson Algren's novel, *A Walk on the Wild Side*—been published," Podhoretz gushed in *Making It,* "than I found myself transformed overnight into a minor literary celebrity." At thirty, he came to power in his own right as editor of *Commentary.* Memory serves Podhoretz correctly—by natural selection he should have been editor of *NYR.* Over the years, he and Epstein had speculated on "a serious newsprint paper like *The Times Literary Supplement,*" the book review of book reviews published weekly in London, and he was a member of the inner circle that launched the *Review.* Podhoretz was never offered the post exactly, nor did he ask for it, but he is to be believed when he says, "I could have been the editor if I had wanted to." Why didn't he step forward? "I had been involved with Jason on two previous enterprises [Anchor Books and The Looking Glass Library], and I had no reason to believe this one would be more successful."[2] Erik Wensberg, then editor of *Columbia Forum,* a literate and eclectic Columbia community quarterly, was mentioned as a possibility. Bob Silvers eventually got the assignment. As a friend of Jason's, with experience at *Paris Review* and *Harper's* and a reputation for exceeding editorial brilliance, Silvers would do quite nicely. How nicely, no one supposed.

Once the personnel problem was settled, the editorial process began. Reviews were solicited on extremely tight deadlines. Multiple business matters like printing, distribution, advertising, and

2. Business-wise, Anchor Books was an absolute smash, but when Epstein quit Doubleday, his friend and part-time assistant Podhoretz loyally quit with him—despite being offered Epstein's job. After Epstein went to Random House, he set up Looking Glass Library (a line of quality children's books) on the side. Podhoretz was installed as its editor-in-chief and told he would get rich real quick. But Looking Glass did not have the magic of Anchor, and Podhoretz failed to make the big money that Epstein had said they would both earn (cf. *Making It,* pp. 271–72).

the like were attended to in crash fashion by acting-publisher Jason Epstein. After a month of the most excruciating cramming, *The New York Review of Books* sprang forth full grown in February 1963, to the oohs and aahs of an admiring public. "We have all the people," Silvers observed as he showed his handiwork off to Amherst critic Benjamin De Mott in his still unvacated *Harper's* office. He seemed amused and faintly embarrassed by the good fortune of having assembled in a single number of an absolutely new review a roster of the country's finest writers and critics. All the right people meant F. W. Dupee, Nathan Glazer, Paul Goodman, Irving Howe, Alfred Kazin, Dwight Macdonald, Steven Marcus, Norman Mailer, Mary McCarthy, Richard Poirier, Philip Rahv, Susan Sontag, William Styron, Gore Vidal, Robert Penn Warren, *et al.* How did they do it? Mostly through Jason Epstein's well-greased Columbia, Anchor, Random, and *Partisan Review* contacts.

The first issue was unlike anything heretofore in American letters. In a note to the reader on page 2, *NYR* proudly stated its editorial credo:

> *The New York Review of Books* presents reviews of some of the more important books published this winter. It does not, however, seek merely to fill the gap created by the printers' strike in New York City, but to take the opportunity which the strike has presented to publish the sort of literary journal which the editors and contributors feel is needed in America. This issue of the *New York Review* does not pretend to cover all the books of the season or even all the important ones. Neither time nor space, however, have [sic] been spent on books which are trivial in their intentions or venal in their effects, except occasionally to reduce a temporarily inflated reputation or to call attention to a fraud.

What style. What class. What brass.

Accordingly, the initial set of reviews gave books a treatment instead of the accustomed treat. Books were presumed guilty, as Podhoretz put it in his *Show* magazine column of May 1963 on *NYR*, and it was their innocence that had to be proven. This negative cast of mind, so foreign to the reviewing trade, turned up some rare critical specimens. How refreshing it must have been to watch Macdonald rough up Arthur Schlesinger's *The Politics of Hope*, Marcus skewer J. D. Salinger's *Raise High the Roof Beam, Carpenters*, Howe fault *The Partisan Review Anthology*, Vidal lambaste John Hersey's *Here to Stay*, and Jonathan Miller snicker at John Updike's *The Centaur*.

The knack for matching the right reviewer to the right book was apparent from the start: Mary McCarthy on *The Naked Lunch*, Mailer on *That Summer in Paris* by Morley Callaghan, Sontag on *Selected Essays* by Simone Weil, Robert Jay Lifton on *Children of the A-Bomb* by Arata Osada. So also a taste for the academic: Oscar Gass on four studies of Soviet economy, David T. Bazelon on Robert Heilbroner's *The Great Ascent*, Lewis Coser on Fritz Machlup's *Production and Distribution of Knowledge in the United States*.

The showpiece of the first issue and, paradoxically, its most portentous contribution was F. W. Dupee's cover putdown of *The Fire Next Time*. Dupee described Baldwin as a "Negro *in extremis*, a virtuoso of ethnic suffering," "a man whose complexion constitutes his fate," who is "half-inclined to see the Negro question in the light of the Human Condition," and who "wears his color as Hester Prynne did her scarlet letter, proudly." An admirer of Baldwin's earlier *Notes of a Native Son*, Dupee was disappointed in *Fire*, because it had "exchanged prophecy for criticism, exhortation for analysis, and the results for his mind and style are in part disturbing." Baldwin was accused of damaging his cause with rhetorical fireworks and of neglecting to submit the truth of his assertions to the test of social utility. " . . . [I]t is unclear to me," Dupee concluded harshly, "how *The Fire Next Time*, in its madder moments, can do anything except inflame the former [anti-Negro extremists] and confuse the latter [Negroes]." Although Dupee's review seemed the work of a dispassionate old white leftist *in extremis*, it conformed beautifully to every one of Hardwick's canons (the unusual, difficult, intransigent, and interesting) except length.

"I don't regret the evaluation," Dupee admitted in retrospect, "but I do regret that I didn't give myself more space to say what I felt about the black movement. At that point, most of us were alarmed by the Muslims. I was quite wrong in saying Baldwin was a good social critic, but a poor prophet. What was amazing was the number of letters that came in favorable to the review." All this would change, however. As Eugene Goodheart wittily observed in *Dissent* (March-April 1970): " . . . it is as if Baldwin is now reviewing Dupee."

One hundred thousand copies of the first issue of the *Review* were printed, and 43,000 sold. Not bad for an unannounced publication. But the letters, over 1,000 of them, were the best signs of possible afterlife. "Desperately needed"—Ronnie Dugger, editor of the liberal *Texas Observer*. "I found myself reading each page"—Harold Matson, veteran literary agent. "I'd love to subscribe"—Bernard Malamud, novelist. "Do keep it up"—Justin O'Brien, the translator of Camus. "You have won an eager subscriber"—C. Vann Woodward, then Professor of History at Johns Hopkins. Jason Epstein was tickled pink by the popular acclaim. He saw his own unhappiness with the day's literary journalism reflected in this glorious backslapping correspondence. If the *New York Review* could flourish, maybe there was hope for the cultural life of the country after all. As Jason Epstein's magazine goes, so goes . . . "How can this slightly blemished but mostly beautiful child be saved?" queried a more pragmatic correspondent. The answer is, was, and always will be, money, just money. A magazine cannot survive issue to issue on the mere hope that income will rise to meet expenditures. It needs capital.

During the remainder of 1963, the *Review* set out in

search of financing. One of the first schemes considered was a strong feeler from then *New Republic* publisher Robert Luce, who suggested the *Review* might work as a literary supplement to his magazine. "I was thinking," Luce recalls somewhat vaguely, "that indeed it might be a good match. Maybe the *Review* could be a supplement. I talked with Bob and Barbara, and they said they wanted to go on. We had one major editorial meeting in New York to discuss who would do what. At that time, the plan was to have a monthly supplement called *The Review of Books*. I even went so far as to have our designer do some mock-ups. But the matter of editorial control got kind of sticky. The negotiations broke down when we couldn't agree on who should be the ultimate editorial arbiter. We weren't willing to relinquish control, and so the alliance never reached the stage of formal presentation."

The idea of a new highbrow review of the quality demonstrated in *NYR*'s first number was not without appeal among the rich and super-rich of literary inclination. "Each person asked people they knew," explains Elizabeth Hardwick. "Our aim was not to have people who would worry about five or ten thousand dollars." Robert Lowell knew Blair Clark. Blair Clark knew Brooke Astor. A. Whitney Ellsworth, who left *The Atlantic* in the spring of 1963 to join the *Review* as publisher, knew his father, Duncan, his stepmother, Helen, his mother-in-law, Mrs. Mary Bingham, and his old Harvard classmate Pierre de Vegh, who knew Richard Shields, the man who married his stepmother after his father died. Without help from their wealthy friends, the *New York Review* could not have gotten by—certainly not at the cost of $13,000 per issue. Who else would have put up the necessary in cold cash for such a shaky proposition? An investors-eyes-only offering memorandum noted that "the Sunday book reviews of *The New York Times* and the *New York Herald Tribune* and, to some extent, the *Saturday Review* all present material similar to that to be published in the *Review*, and there is no assurance that the *Review* will be able to compete profitably with well-established publications of this type." It went on to warn that "investment in the Class B Stock is speculative and should be made only by persons whose financial position warrants taking a risk of this nature. There is no assurance that the Corporation will be able to operate at a profit after its receipt and application of the proceeds received upon the sale of the Class B Stock." By the end of the year, a private sale of 200 Class B shares priced at $1,000-a-share brought The New York Review, Inc. $140,000 from thirteen investors, and *The New York Review of Books* was thereby assured of at least a limited future.

The corporation was headed by a board of six directors. The board divided equally among themselves 201 shares of controlling Class A stock, which had the assigned value of $3. In other words, in exchange for his or her services, each director got 33½ shares for the sum of $.50. The difference between Class A stock and Class B stock lay principally in voting privileges. Except for the right to elect two members to the board of directors (an option never exercised), the Class B stockholders had no other voting rights. According to the offering memorandum, the all-powerful board was to "set the policy and determine the procedures for operating the *Review*."

The memorandum listed the title, function, and vita of the individual board members as follows:

A. Whitney Ellsworth, Publisher and Director, has served as an Editor of the Atlantic for the last four years. Mr. Ellsworth intends to devote full time to the publication of the Review.

Barbara Epstein, Secretary, Treasurer, and Director, will also serve as an Editor of the Review. She has been engaged in the publishing business for a number of years and, during the past five years, has done editorial work for E. P. ,Dutton & Co., McGraw-Hill Publishing Co., Bobbs-Merrill Co., Random House, and the Partisan Review. Mrs. Epstein also intends to devote full time to the publication of the Review.

Jason Epstein, Vice President and a Director, is a Vice President and an Editor of Random House, the Editor of Vintage Books and Modern Library, and the President and Editor of Looking Glass Library. Prior to his association with Random House, he was the founder and Editor-in-Chief of Doubleday Anchor Books. Mr. Epstein will continue in his present employment, and his services to the Corporation will be limited.

Elizabeth Lowell, an Editor and a Director, writes under the name of Elizabeth Hardwick and has been a literary critic for several years. She is also the author of *A View of My Own* and the Editor of *The Selected Letters of William James*. Mrs. Lowell intends to make her services available to the Review on a part-time basis.

Robert Lowell, a Director, has been connected with the literary world for many years, and is a well-known poet. He is the recipient of a Pulitzer prize for poetry and is presently a Visting Professor of English at Harvard College. Mr. Lowell intends to devote only a limited amount of time to the publication of the Review.

Robert Silvers, President, an Editor and a Director, has, for the last five years, served as an Editor of Harper's Magazine and as an Editor of the Paris Review. Mr. Silvers intends to continue his present employment until the Review realizes its minimum capitalization of 60 shares of Class B Stock, following which he will make his services available to the Review on a full-time basis.

The *Review*'s payroll for Ellsworth, Hardwick, Silvers, and Barbara Epstein amounted to less than $16,000 in 1963. If they all had been working full-time that first year, their cumulative salary would have been $33,000. The offering memorandum remembered Lowell and Jason Epstein in the following manner: "Messrs. Epstein and Lowell intend, for the present, to continue contributing their services without compensation. However, for the year beginning January 1, 1964, and thereafter, the Corporation may increase such compensation and provide for compensation to those persons presently contributing their services."

Meanwhile, back in the new editorial rooms at 250 West 57th Street, a large, older office building, preparations for the second issue were jolted by the serious illness of Silvers. He was hospitalized with lung trouble (sarkodosis) and had a bad go of it until Jonathan Miller, friend and physician, corrected the misdiagnosis. *New York Review*, Number 2, a spring and summer books issue, was edited from Silvers' hospital bed. The lead piece was an insufferably pedantic, but crowd-pleasing self-interview by Edmund Wilson, entitled "Every Man His Own Eckermann." There was also Stephen Spender on Hannah Arendt's *Eichmann in Jerusalem*, Arthur Schlesinger on Anthony Crosland's *The Conservative Enemy*, Benjamin De Mott on Richard Hofstadter's *Anti-Intellectualism in American Life*, and contributions from Allen Tate, Truman Capote, Robert Heilbroner, J. F. Powers, *et al.* The *Review* was clearly up to its new old tricks again.

Manifest destiny was everywhere you looked. "The response from readers of the first special issue of *The New York Review of Books* has encouraged the editors to assume that there may be sufficient demand in America to support a literary review of this sort," Silvers and Epstein proclaimed in a declaration of independence. "Regular issues of *The New York Review of Books* will be somewhat shorter . . . The same intellectual quality, however, will be maintained, and the editors will continue to assume that the serious discussion of important books is itself an indispensable literary activity." Regular biweekly publication was heralded for the fall.

By the time the third issue came around in September, the *Review* had settled into its inimitable and immutable ways. Typographer Samuel Antupit renovated Seymour Chwast's and Edward Sorel's original design of convenience by throwing away the column lines, using the rare Egiziano type for thick black headlines, instituting a linear column layout so that one article ended horizontally flush across the page before the other began, and introducing David Levine. Levine, who was then knocking about under a bushel at *Esquire*, signed on as a *literary* caricaturist. It was love at first sight, and this marriage would be for keeps. Old fashioned (no copyright) engravings were also sprinkled in here and there. The grotesqueries of the tragic nineteenth-century French caricaturist J.-J. Grandville would arrive shortly— as soon as Bowden Broadwater, the recently divorced third husband of Mary McCarthy (after Harold Johnsrud, a playwright and actor, and Edmund Wilson), surrendered his rare copy of *Album des Bêtes* to Barbara Epstein for the greater good. (Grandville scared even Baudelaire, who wrote of his countryman in 1857: "When I open the door of Grandville's works, I feel a certain uneasiness, as though I were entering an apartment where disorder was systematically organized. There are some superficial spirits who are amused by Grandville; for my part, I find him terrifying.")

In the autumn of 1963 *The New York Review of Books* had its negative models. It would not be like *Saturday Review* or the *Times* and *Tribune* Book Reviews. But beyond that, its inner directedness was yet unformed. "We're a national literary magazine publishing literary essays," Elizabeth Hardwick whimsically told a *Newsweek* reporter that September. "We want to cover the current intellectual stream . . . If possible . . . If there is any stream and if there is anyone who wants to cover it." On the latter, Hardwick was not especially encouraging as she raised her highbrow remarking, "I never expected to be doing anything like this! I'm amazed and appalled at people's willingness to write book reviews. It's a form of literary activity that must be done. Somebody must do it." And they did.

*   *   *

The early history of *New York Review* is divided into three periods that adhere pretty much to successive plays on its title—

The New York Review of Each Other's Books, The London Review of Books, and *The London Review of Vietnam*.

The first period, so named by Richard Hofstadter, was historically determined. In very early times, the *Review* had no place to go except to the cheap (five cents a word) and local talent that also happened to be authors or associates of authors of the sort of books to which the *Review* was devoted. For the first half-dozen or so issues, the *Review* was a Family publication and therefore prey to consanguineous defects like nepotism, fratricide, and incest, and even a dose of narcissism. Establishment liberals were reviewing one another wholesale. For example, in addition to articles previously cited: Richard Rovere on *The Essential Lippmann*, Midge Decter on Murray Kempton's *America Comes of Middle Age*, J. Robert Oppenheimer on Eugene Rabinowich's *The Dawn of a New Age*, Marion Magid on *The Paris Review Interviews*, Second Series, Elizabeth Hardwick's parody of Mary McCarthy's *The Group*, and so on.

For reasons of respectability, the. *Review* could not continue to feed off its own kind, especially since much of its own kind was identified with *Partisan Review*, font of intelligentsia wisdom since 1934. People were already calling it *"Partisan* in newsprint." "I guess there was a little tension," William Phillips says. "I was more amused. *They* developed the resentment."

To avoid poaching, then, Silvers looked to England. Isaiah Berlin, who was visiting Princeton during the summer of '63, is alleged to have pointed the way. In any case, the British handwriting was plainly on the wall with issue number 5 when no fewer than six abbreviated subjects of the Crown appeared— V. S. Pritchett, G. S. Fraser, A. J. P. Taylor, J. G. Weightman, V. S. Naipaul, and A. Alvarez. Stephen Spender, George Lichtheim, and Malcolm Muggeridge had already been accounted for, and Frank Kermode, Geoffrey Barraclough, Neal Ascherson, W. H. Auden, J. H. Plumb, E. J. Hobsbawm, D. A. N. Jones, Alisdair McIntyre, Christopher Ricks, H. R. Trevor-Roper, Richard Wollheim, and Bernard Bergonzi were not far behind. *The New York Review of Each Other's Books* was dead. Writing in care of the magazine, Silvers requisitioned *New Statesman* regulars under the nose of its literary editor, Karl Miller. The raid was so constant and intense that Miller, presently editor of *The Listener* and recently a contributor to *NYR*, would refer to the Silvers' paper as "the best magazine I ever edited."

Apart from escaping the New York jungle, the *Review* discovered many positive rewards in Britain. More facile in the art of intellectual journalism than their American counterparts, English writers have acquired the virtue of writing fast and on time. "I think they tend to write a good deal better than our scholars and experts," says Elizabeth Hardwick. "English people live more by literary things than we do." Then there's the money angle. The *Review*'s payments, mezzo-mezzo at home at ten cents a word, are princely sums in the sterling area. Since not many American contributors could afford to work so prolifically for the *Review*, nor could the *Review* afford to make it worth their while, cheap labor from Britain was a splendid solution, a master stroke really. "You guys who need the money can write for the *Review*," Miller instructed, according to one of the neediest of his cases, "and you guys who don't, can't."

The *Review* doesn't flaunt its Anglophilia domestically, however. Silvers used to deny it outright. "We really don't have any sense of nationalism," he said to *Time* in 1967. "Check and you'll see we're not that heavily written by the English." On the other side of the Atlantic, however, unbeknownst to its native readers, Silvers played up the foreign influence. *"The New York Review of Books* comes home to England," ran a December 1967 solicitation in *Encounter*. The copy kindly explained:

> *The New York Review of Books* is now on sale at British newsdealers and British bookstores. Which seems natural enough, since someone's always accusing us of being "Anglophiles." That is, paying too much attention to British books and British writers, and in fact letting you do a good bit of our writing for us.
> Pity!

When the topic was broached in later years, Silvers merely insisted the *Review* obtains the best writers it can.

The short reign of *The London Review of Books* (1963–65) coincided with a general mood of optimism in intellectual circles. John F. Kennedy seemed to be a friend, and the accidental president, Lyndon Baines Johnson, was not Macbird, not yet. The age of crisis was just around the corner, but who could then have predicted the procession of university strikes, urban riots, and guerrilla wars that would divide the nation and its critics? At the *Review*, it was a stretch of benign neglect. Probably because no one was watching too closely, JFK got away with murder in its pages. Hardly a demurrer was sounded in the special Kennedy Memorial issue (the *Review*'s ninth) in November of 1963. A species of the *Review*'s unradical politics can be read in Malcolm Muggeridge's outright dismissal (September 26, 1963) of Bertrand Russell's *Unarmed Victory*, in which Russell blamed the United States for precipitating the Cuban missile crisis. (Compare with I. F. Stone's review of Elie Abel's *The Missile Crisis* [April 14, 1966].) And as late as January of 1965, buried though the review was, Robert Heilbroner would put the hatchet to William Appleman Williams' Marxian examination of American society, *The Great Evasion*, for being "vulgar, self-serving, imprecise, and shallow." Heilbroner later regretted these remarks.

These were the salad days at the *Review*, untroubled by controversy and broken friendships. Future antagonists had nothing exceptional to be antagonized about. No line-drawing disputes had driven Family relations off. Irving Howe, Michael Harrington, Daniel Bell, Irving Kristol, Norman Podhoretz, and Diana Trilling, so incongruous now when thought of as contributors, were all in the *Review* then. Even David Levine's caricatures lacked bite. Instead of rivals, *Commentary* and the *New York Review* were ideologically kin and shared a repertoire of writers they share no longer. (Ronald Steel, Hans J. Morgenthau, Murray Kempton, Alfred Kazin, Hannah Arendt, Edgar Z. Friedenberg, F. W. Dupee, among others, dropped out of *Commentary*'s line-up, and an equal number ceased doing business with the *Review*.) *Commentary* was actually farther Left than the early, unconverted *New York Review*. Historian Staughton Lynd started revising history in *Commentary* in 1960 with his article "How the Cold War Began." Hans Morgenthau wrote "Asia: The American Algeria" for Podhoretz in 1961.[3] Influenced by Paul Goodman and *Growing Up Absurd*, a *Commentary* serialization, Pod-

---

3. A prophetic passage from Morgenthau: "The same pattern [placing bets on inefficient corrupt elites versus popular forces, e.g., in China and Laos] has emerged in South Vietnam and is in the process of emerging in Spain. In both countries, we have identified ourselves with a regime that suppresses the opposition and equates it with communism. In consequence, the popular aspirations for change tend to flow into communist channels. The opposition tends to live up to the communist reputation bestowed upon it by the powers that be, and the same polarization of political life which we have noticed in Laos and in China in the last stages of the civil war is taking place in South Vietnam and Spain."

horetz was distancing his magazine from its immediate anti-Stalinist past and moving toward radicalism at the turn of the Sixties. "Why do you have those boring pieces about Vietnam?" Podhoretz remembers being asked by Dwight Macdonald and Robert Lowell before the *Review* itself went *a sinistra*.

The *London Review of Vietnam* build-up was gradual. The subject of Vietnam did not crop up until the second-to-last issue of 1964, when I. F. Stone reviewed Bernard Fall's *Street Without Joy* and Arthur Dommen's *Conflict in Laos*. The cover headline read: "I. F. Stone on the Southeast Asian Mess." The recruitment of Izzy Stone was an important and courageous step in the politicization of *New York Review*. His unrepentant popular-fronting in the 1930's left him a very unpopular man in establishment journalism. The bigger outlets were afraid to touch him, and he had a hard time getting published outside his own flinty, investigative Left-Wing paper—*I. F. Stone's Weekly*[4]—until Silvers petitioned him to review William S. White's authorized biography of LBJ in the summer of 1964.

Stone's ground-breaker was followed in the latter half of 1965 by six other articles and reviews on Vietnam: Joseph Kraft on Jean Lacouture's *Le Viet Nam entre deux paix*; Joseph Kraft, Hans Morgenthau, Bernard Fall, Marcus Raskin in a special supplement entitled "Getting Out of Vietnam"; and a Lacouture article, "The Chance for Peace in Vietnam," reprinted from *Le Nouvel Observateur*. Each in its own way expressed vigorous but still undivisive opposition to the escalating war. Levine gently caricaturized Johnson crying real crocodiles for tears (Levine's favorite political caricature, incidentally, along with a complementary one of a crocodile crying LBJs) and in bed with Soviet boss Leonid Brezhnev.

Although the peace movement was starting to break up into

---

4. The *Weekly* went bi-weekly with the issue of January 22, 1968, and the name was changed to *I. F. Stone's Bi-Weekly*. It is now defunct.

moderate and radical wings, the *Review* had not yet been affected by the split. A year-end piece—a manifesto called "The Vietnam Protest" and signed by Irving Howe, Michael Harrington, Bayard Rustin, Lewis Coser, and Penn Kemble—was the opening salvo in the debate over anti-war tactics that would eventually cleave American intellectuals according to an unfortunate good guy/bad guy dichotomy. "The Vietnam Protest," authored by Howe, warned against an off-putting apocalypticism in the anti-war Left. "Such a policy," he said, "appealing to sectarian ultimism and impatience, is certain to produce a great deal of publicity, but not much public support or political impact." Comforting the Vietcong was not to be tolerated: "This is both a tactical necessity and a moral obligation, since any ambiguity on this score makes impossible, as well as undeserved, the support of large numbers of American people." Civil disobedience ought to be a last resort and not a routine thing. Revolutionary tactics like lying down in front of troop trains were denounced as "self-defeating, since they merely result in a display of impotence and alienate people who might be persuaded to join in a political protest against the Johnson policy." Draft resistance for the individual who is morally opposed to the war was, of course, right and fitting. "It is quite another thing," Howe went on, "to advocate resistance to the draft or efforts to use its provisions for conscientious objection as a tactic for the protest movement. The latter course, we believe, could only lead to disaster, the reduction of what is potentially an expression of popular outrage to an heroic martyrdom by a tiny band of intellectual guerillas." The near-Fulbright peace plan put forward by Howe and his colleagues called for a US bombing halt, a general cease-fire, and a readiness on the part of the US to negotiate with the National Liberation Front and to recognize the right of the South Vietnamese to determine their own future without foreign intervention. Howe's statement not only passed Silvers' liberal inspection, but it also failed to draw fire from the

Review's keenest supporters. The single discouraging word heard
on the Left was spoken by *NYR* outsider Staughton Lynd, then
a professor of history at Yale, who could not stomach Howe's
etiquette. "May I inquire why it is immoral to desire a Vietcong
victory?" he asked. "I had thought that, just as during the American Revolution there were many Englishman who hoped for a
victory by the American colonists, so it would be only natural to
expect that *some* sincere opponents of the Vietnam War should
actively sympathize with the National Liberation Front."

   This was just the sort of response Howe was waiting for.
Now he could put daylight between the "democratic Left" of his
own persuasion and "radicals" like Lynd who " 'refuse to be anti-
communist.' " (The original quote is Lynd's.) Why is it immoral
to be pro-Vietcong? "Because, Mr. Lynd, a victory for a communist or communist-dominated movement means another totalitarian dictatorship suppressing human freedoms. But, writes Mr.
Lynd, the Vietcong is fighting for 'liberty or death.' Alas! Would
that it were so; then our politics could be marvelously simple. If
by 'liberty' Mr. Lynd means the kind of society that exists in North
Vietnam and China, then no matter what their sincerity, heroism,
or intentions, the Vietcong partisans are fighting in behalf of a
totalitarian society." Thus spake "The Vietnam Protest." It is
interesting to note that in late 1965 such a critique could, and
would, be published in the *New York Review*. If the *Review*'s
head was with Howe in 1965, its heart would be keeping other
company in later times.

   Nineteen hundred and sixty-six was the transition year from
the *London Review of Books* to the *London Review of Vietnam*
—unabated Anglophilia plus wartime politics. The indefatigable
Izzy Stone kicked it off with a January essay on American air
power in Vietnam, extrapolating from General Curtis LeMay's
memoir *Mission with LeMay*. Two successive March issues featured
major Vietnam articles by Jean Lacouture and Bernard Fall.

Lacouture reappeared in May with a long review of James Cameron's book *Here Is Your Enemy*, a firsthand account of this British journalist's trip to North Vietnam. In June, there were anti-war poems by Buddhist monk Thich Nhat Hanh and Vietnam pieces by Morgenthau and Kraft. In July, the *Review* printed Senator George McGovern's five-point peace proposal, another sign that the *Review* was not yet considered beyond the pale by consensus-seeking intellectuals (although eyebrows were raised by a September black power statement—"What We Want" by Stokely Carmichael, then National Chairman of SNCC). Nineteen hundred and sixty-six expired with an "untold story" by Mario Rossi of the United States rebuff of U Thant's secret diplomacy to end the war. On the cover of the Christmas issue Levine drew a festive LBJ happily carving the rump of a full-grown pig set on a holiday table with a globe in its mouth. The *Review* had committed its troops; it was in for the duration.

Despite the outward gravity of purpose, *New York Review* was a madcap operation within. When Raymond Shapiro, an ex-lumber executive with more than wood in his head, entered as business manager in 1965, he was astonished to discover that the magazine possessed neither business files nor a business structure. "There was a Toonerville Trolley aspect to the *Review* in those days," he remarks. "We used to have a linotype printer in Milford, Connecticut, and the dummy was sent up there by railroad. We would pay the conductor five dollars to drop it off. But once the dummy got lost and started on its way to Maine. We called every station after Milford. It took five hours to figure it out, but we finally caught up with the dummy outside Boston." A similar disaster was averted when a Milford bank president accidently found a package of *NYR* proofs lying in the snow next to the railroad tracks.

It was crazy Thursday every other week in Milford when

Ellsworth, Epstein, Eve Auchincloss, and Alexandra Emmet drove to the office of *The Milford Citizen* to read page proofs and preside over the rebirth of the magazine. The ladies would amuse themselves en route with gossip about the beautiful people and, according to Auchincloss, "by counting how many fags, Jews, and Englishmen were listed in the table of contents of each issue." The *Review* was a mixed blessing for the busy presses of the then weekly *Milford Citizen. NYR* often fell behind in its payments, and the Thursday group drove the typesetters batty with its eleventh-hour corrections. And even though the *Citizen*'s owner and publisher, Al Stanford, felt impelled to hike his libel insurance to $1 million on the *Review*'s account, he loved almost every minute of the association. For Stanford is not your ordinary small-town newspaper czar. He is a former second vice president of the *Herald Tribune* who said so-long to New York in the Fifties when the owner's son, Ogden "Brownie" Reid, now a Democratic US Representative from Westchester, "came onto the editorial floor with pearl handle revolvers looking for communists." Exhausted in spirit and wind by the *Tribune* ordeal, Stanford came up to Milford to finish a couple of books and sail his boat. (This old salt was a Navy Deputy Task Force Commander in World War II and designed artificial harbors for the D-Day landing.) Since he was already publishing a boating magazine, he did not expect to purchase a newspaper after just one week in town. But he did.

As a weekly, the *Citizen* could farm out its presses on off days to other journals like the *Village Voice* and *The Nation.* Dissatisfied with the contract provisions of the *Bridgeport Herald*, which produced *NYR*'s two special issues, Whitney Ellsworth scoured the metropolitan region for an economical printer. An editor at *American Heritage* recommended his friend Al Stanford. "We reached an agreement," Stanford says in his small partitioned quarters at the prosperous *Citizen*, "and I got sucked in." But the suction wasn't that bad, as Stanford himself admits.

"Whitney is like a hippo going through a swamp. He wanted Times Roman body type because he was under the spell of Antupit, a goddamned typographical genius. I had to import the headline type from Amsterdam, and it had to be hand-set. But we were on an economic honeymoon and delighted to be part of the venture. We were a weekly, then. They came up on Thursday and swarmed all over the composing room. I finally bought Whitney a printer's apron and tweezers, and was he happy! They would send out for grinders and pickles. The place was strewn with hamburgers. There was much laughter and much fun, and we made money out of it."

Stanford's major difference with the *Review* visitors had to do with their indecision. "They could never, never make up their goddamned minds. Their changes seemed frivolous. At the last minute, after everything was locked up and ready to go, they would change a 'which' to 'that.' I would pull Whitney aside and tell him to get the girls to cut the nonsense out. The thing that surprised me was that Whitney always gave in to Barbara. He was deferential to Bob, Barbara, Antupit. But I always thought he had pretty good judgment himself."

The Thursday group's latitudinarianism regarding type came home to roost in the pages of the *Review*. Whether owing to the editors' over-ardent editing in galleys or typographical mistakes or a combination of both, printing errors were frequent. At the end of its letters columns *NYR* would dutifully record the previous issue's casualties. For example: "Owing to an unfortunate printer's mishap, two lines from Alfred Kazin's review of *Henry Adams* in the January 14 issue were supplanted by lines from an entirely different review . . ." (January 28, 1965).

The most embarrassing mistake occurred when Steven Marcus' review of *Madness and Civilization* by Michel Foucault (November 3, 1966) was mangled beyond recognition. Blocks of type were transposed in mid-sentence, thereby creating an enormous communications gap for the author. Silvers was pretty peeved. He considered recalling the issue, but settled for reprinting the correct version of the review in the following number. He also went to the pain of alerting *NYR*'s 45,000 subscribers by postcard of the foul-up. "I'm not sure whose fault it was," comments Stanford. "The pulling of page proofs for these birds was just an invitation to trouble. All you're supposed to do in page proofs is check corrections, but it wasn't real for them until it became a printed page. Eve was the only chance you had for rationality."

New York Review and *The Milford Citizen* amicably split in the fall of 1968 after five years of collaboration. Their incompatability was mutual and unavoidable. *The Citizen* was about to go daily, and the *Review* required more color presswork than *The Citizen* could provide. Now with its own IBM typesetting machine on the premises, *NYR* can stop the press and reset to its heart's content.

The great leap leftward occurred in 1967. The long march from Family literary magazine to quasi-pamphlet of the New Left was finally completed as the *Review* entered its fifth year. Human wave attacks on liberal institutions and personalities would burn most, if not all, of the *Review*'s bridges to its former traditions. Nineteen hundred and sixty-seven was the year *NYR* unhappily gained a sticking reputation for Left-Wing authoritarianism, anti-Americanism, SDS-ism, political faddism, and what would become known as radical chic (after Leonard Bernstein threw a party for the Panthers and Tom Wolfe). How could this have happened to the dearly beloved *New York Review*, which was immaculately conceived as the last best hope for a decent American book review? Why would Diana Trilling feel obliged to announce before assembled guests in her own home that the "*New York Review* is the enemy"?

Bob Silvers gave one plausible explanation of the magazine's evolution to *Time* in November of 1967. (*Time* did not use the quote in its story, however.) From the very first, he explained, the *Review* ran essays, and since about 1964 or 1965 they had been writing about Vietnam. "But what is obvious is that there is a rising sense of crisis among ourselves and our writers and readers," he said. Political commentary has necessarily taken on a "more urgent" nature in response to the situation.

He cited Noam Chomsky, as an example. Chomsky received a most attractive MIT appointment on the strength of his credentials as an expert linguist. "We didn't anticipate that he would emerge as such an outspoken writer on political issues, but that's what happened," Silvers recalled. Even his nonpolitical assignments ended up dealing with politics, because Chomsky was so involved.

"Philip Rahv is another case in point. His political writing had been dormant for years, and now he has felt compelled to come forward in this area. Or Morgenthau. Or Christopher Lasch. You chat with such men to find out what they're interested in," says Silvers, "and the fact is that among intellectuals the political and social questions have become very urgent."

Silvers also remarked to *Time*: "We like important questions being dealt with by experts with strong views. But take a look at the last few issues, and you'll see we are like we have been from the beginning—we just like to have essays on whatever's happening."

And a lot happened in 1967. Almost every article that the *Review* is now famous, or notorious, for was squeezed into that twelvemonth:

JANUARY: "Fulbright: the Timid Opposition" by I. F. Stone, a dissenting opinion on a leading dove, the last of a three-part series. Far from the anti-war zealot that liberals take him for, Fulbright is a "drowsy watchdog" and a "cloakroom crusader" who

was late on Vietnam, the Dominican Republic, and Dean Rusk. In the first installment, a review of Tristam Coffin's biography— *Senator Fulbright: Portrait of a Public Philosopher*—Stone challenged Coffin's description of Fulbright as a modern Prometheus: "Fulbright would never have had done anything so irregular as stealing fire for Man. He would have sent Zeus a carefully prepared but private memorandum suggesting that it would be better to give man fire than risk the tumultuous uprisings sure to be provoked by cold meats on a rumbling stomach" (December 29, 1966). Coffin profiled more of Fulbright's courage in reply and hastened to deflate Stone's lofty notion of senatorial independence: "The Fulbright whom Mr. Stone has driven from his Utopia so ferociously is like the ogre in the nursery rhyme. My impression is that Mr. Stone believes he planned the Brinks robbery and selected the targets in Vietnam personally" (March 9, 1967).

FEBRUARY: "The Responsibility of Intellectuals" by Noam Chomsky, a documented indictment of American mandarins and an exhortation to American intellectuals to examine their conscience regarding Vietnam. "It is the responsibility of intellectuals to speak the truth and expose lies." Some peers Chomsky found wanting were Walt Rostow, Henry Kissinger, Irvihg Kristol, McGeorge Bundy, Herman Kahn, Daniel Bell, and that self-confessed liar about the Bay of Pigs landing Arthur Schlesinger. (Cf. *New York Times*, November 25, 1965.) Chomsky concluded his *J'accuse* with the story of a death-camp paymaster who, when told the Russians would hang him, asked, "Why should they? What have I done?" Intellectuals, he said, should ask themselves the same question "as we create, or mouth, or tolerate the deceptions that will be used to justify the next defense of freedom." None of the gentlemen on Chomsky's list defended themselves in *NYR*'s letters column. But Schlesinger and Kristol would have their innings in reviews of Chomsky's *American Power and the New Mandarins*, in which "Responsibility" was reprinted.

APRIL: "Report from Vietnam" by Mary McCarthy. The first in a series of behind-the-lines dispatches began with the words: "I confess that when I went to Vietnam early in February I was looking for material damaging to the American interest and that I found it, though often by accident or in the process of being briefed by an official."

APRIL: "The CIA and the Intellectuals" by Jason Epstein. A whistle-blowing exposé of liberal anti-communist attitudes of the Fifties and Sixties, following in the wake of *Ramparts'* startling revelations (from the National Student Association to *Encounter* magazine) of the CIA's covert funding of student and cultural organizations. Epstein, who owned up in a footnote to taking a couple of rides on the CIA gravy train (to Acapulco and Nigeria), speculated on the effects of CIA corruption among New York intellectuals.[5] Out of an original harmony of shared opposition to communism during the Fifties, two factions emerged in the early Sixties. The Left faction (including Epstein himself) was surprised "to find that the country seemed to have fallen into a frenzy of self-destruction, tearing its cities apart, fouling its landscapes, poisoning the streams and skies, trivializing the edu-

---

5. Epstein doesn't indicate in the article whether he realized who was paying his expenses at the time.

cation of its children, and not for substantial human happiness, which could never have been advanced by these factors, but for higher profits and rapidly increased economic growth." The poor were getting poorer "as the middle class grunted its way upward," and Vietnam was just another example of this "Philistine expansionism."

The Right faction saw defects in the American system, "but they were not problems of substance—problems within the national will, so to speak—but of technical maladjustment." What motivated the Right? Epstein wondered if it wasn't "their own arrival, from the sidewalks of New York and Chicago, to tenured positions in respected universities, to distinguished lectureships and invitations to dine and dance at the White House." The CIA was not so much a corrupter of the Right faction, which "did not need to be bought off," as it was "an accessory after the fact." Actually, Epstein hedged on that judgment. "It needed only to be supported in what it was convinced was a virtuous and necessary enterprise. That it could travel in style while defending the interests of mankind was so much to the good, but its members would probably have sustained their convictions even if they had been operating out of a cellar on Bleecker Street. Or would they have? *Weren't there at least some for whom the official limousines, the lectureships, the grants, and other allowances gave proof in the Calvinist sense of the predestined rightness of their choice?*" (Emphasis added.)

Epstein discreetly mentioned no names—except Irving Kristol, former co-editor of *Encounter*, whom he characterized as an archetype of the Right faction (read Daniel Bell, Sidney Hook, and that sort). Kristol's anti-communism was so hard in the Fifties, Epstein argued, that Kristol "found it possible to suggest that Joe McCarthy was something of a necessary evil, willing to do a dirty job which responsible citizens lacked the courage or insight to take on . . ." Epstein had in mind an article Kristol wrote for *Commentary* ("Civil Liberties, 1952: A Study

in Confusion," March 1952) when he was managing editor of that
magazine. While critical of McCarthy's methods, Kristol put his
foot in his mouth with the following remark: "For there is one
thing that the American people know about Senator McCarthy:
He, like them, is unequivocally anti-communist. About the spokes-
men for American liberalism (Henry Steel Commager, etc.), they
feel they know no such thing. And with some justification." One
violation of the intellect could lead to another. Thus Epstein posed
the highly damaging question: "Was not Kristol's form of anti-
communism [. . .] likely to deaden the mind and feelings, so
that when the war in Vietnam fell into our laps, some of us would
have grown too rigid to feel the stupidity and arrogance from
which it evolved and which continues to sustain it?"

Oddly, no Right or Left factionist responded to Epstein's
debatable article in *NYR*.

Politics apart, Kristol thought it was in bad taste. "I didn't
like it," Kristol comments in retrospect. "It was disingenuous. If
Epstein had reached the conclusion that he had been wrong in
the 1950's he should have written an article explaining how and
why. Instead he wrote an article attacking everyone else for having
been wrong in the 1950's. Poor Dan Bell did nothing. He attended
some conferences which, unknown to the participants, were CIA-
sponsored or inspired. But everyone did. He was just one among
thousands."

Kristol suggests that John Thompson, an English professor
at Stony Brook and a former frequenter of *NYR*, was troubled
by the article—as well he might. For Thompson was a stalwart
drinking companion of Epstein's as well as his travel agent when
Thompson worked as the executive director of the CIA-connected
Farfield Foundation. He has nothing to say of this period, however. "You can read the article yourself," he replied to the
author. "I don't go for that interviewing shit."

Thompson didn't go for Dwight Macdonald's inquiries, either,
when he asked him point blank if government money were behind

his foundation, "His reaction was not reassuring," Macdonald wrote in his *Esquire* "Politics" column (June 1967). "After an attempt at bluff evasion—'Come on, Dwight, you can't be serious!' —he burst into what seemed to me forced laughter and denied the charge, but with so ambiguous a nuance that I couldn't tell whether *he* was being serious or whether he was making a disclaimer that any sophisticated person would know to be moral pro-forma."

Norman Podhoretz gave just about every intellectual in town his or her chance to complement or rebut Epstein in the September *Commentary*. An issue-length symposium entitled "Liberal Anti-Communism Revisited" tried to get at the bottom of his divisive thesis. Presumably sticking up for the Right faction, Diana Trilling, who is also the wife of Lionel Trilling, laced into Epstein's political distinctions with a fury: "The difference between Left and Right, Mr. Epstein explains, is determined by the quality and force and direction of our cultural awareness. Depending on how we respond to the poisoning of our streams and skies we will take either a Left- or a Right-Wing position on—say—the Vietnam war. Whoever abhors polluted air and desecrated landscapes will have adequate ground on which to judge American foreign policy. He will recognize it in all its 'Philistine expansionism.' What further guide to decision in foreign affairs does anyone need?"

What Trilling despised about Epstein's view was that it rendered "meaningless and unnecessary *any* judgment upon communism" vis-à-vis one's status on the Left, although it insisted on "an extreme avowal of one's hatred and contempt for America," if one were to be considered properly a person of the Left. This being so, Trilling put the following question to Epstein:

If the nature and degree of one's non-communism are of no account whatsoever, and all that does count is one's opposition to America, what reason can there be not to throw in one's lot with the most powerful and best-defined opposition to America, communism? Why should one not be a communist?

JUNE: "Waiting for Lefty," Andrew Kopkind's review of *R.F.K.: The Man Who Would Be President* by Ralph de Toledano. Kopkind dismissed the author's one-note attack and sprinkled around some not unkind remarks about the Senator, who was just coming out of the regular Democratic closet. But Bobby, as beatific as he appeared to cultists, couldn't hack real reform. "For Kennedy would impose his own kind of elitist reform before any independent forms of social reconstruction could begin . . . [and] in the end Kennedy will not remake the society, either by his personality or with his programs, and we will have need again of a saving remnant." David Levine's companion caricature—hawk face, dove body, and duck feet—was worth more than Kopkind's 1,000 words.

AUGUST: "Holy War" by I. F. Stone, a review of Sartre's *Les Temps Modernes* symposium, "*Le Conflit israélo-arabe,*" in which Stone argues against hard-core Zionism and Jewish exclusivism in Israel and suggests a fair deal for Israeli Arabs, maybe even an Arab state on the West Bank. "If in this account," Stone wrote, "I have given more space to the Arab than the Israeli side, it is because as a Jew, closely bound emotionally with the birth of Israel, I feel honor-bound to report the Arab side, especially since the US press is so overwhelmingly pro-Zionist." The trouble with Israel was that it had been treating its Arab minority badly, which consequently made peace with its Arab neighbors all the more difficult. To show Israel's intransigence toward the Arabs, Stone quoted an exchange between Sidney Gruson of *The New York Times* and Israeli General Moshe Dayan on *Face the Nation* (June 11, 1967):

> *Gruson*: Is there any possible way that Israel could absorb the huge number of Arabs whose territory it has gained control of now?
> *Dayan*: Economically, we can; but I think that is not in accord with our aims in the future. It would turn Israel into either a bi-national or poly-Arab-Jewish state instead of the Jewish state. We can absorb them, but then it won't be the same country. [. . .] We want a Jewish state like the French want a French state.

Stone recommended that Jews outside Israel stay where they were born and thereby allay Arab fears of a huge Jewish immigration to the Promised Land. He also urged the establishment of an Arab state on the West Bank that would be linked with Israel and perhaps Jordan in a confederation. Such Israeli concessions were necessary if the Middle East were to be denuclearized. "Otherwise, the Arab-Israeli conflict may some day set off a wider final solution." What the Arabs, the aggressors in the Six-Day War, were to concede, Stone failed to say.

Pro-Zionist Jews considered Stone's piece a real stinker. In reference to Stone's honor-boundness to report the underpublicized Arab side, Martin Peretz observed in *Commentary* (September 1967): "One would think that a writer's compulsion would be to tell the truth, regardless of whether it had been aired or not." It appeared odd to Peretz that Stone's traditional tolerance for "this communist government or that third world despotism" shrank before Israel, doubly ironic because Israel alone in the Middle East had an active communist politics. "It seems that the Left," Peretz wrote, suggesting the basic objection of Zionists to Stone, "so patient with the political grotesqueries of its favored nations, would only be satisfied with an absolutely unflawed Israel, which would mean also an Israel willing to surrender its national existence."

In a long letter to *NYR* (September 28, 1967) James Michener went for the *cojones* after polite nods to Stone's facts, reasoning, and calm. "Yet the end result of his essay was palpably anti-Zionist, probably anti-Israel, and potentially anti-Jewish. When I put the article down I had the feeling that Miss Hannah Arendt had written it, but that Mr. I. F. Stone had signed it." (Arendt, of course, retired the Pharaoh's trophy for her 1963 book *Eichmann in Jerusalem: A Report on the Banality of Evil*, in which she dared to float an unspeakable revision of holocaust history. If Jewish officials had not cooperated so well with their Nazi executioners, Arendt wrote, "there would have been chaos and plenty of misery, but the total number of victims would hardly have been between four and a half and six million people.") "The same people who abused the Jews for not having resisted Hitler," Michener continued, "now abuse them for having resisted Nasser too much. Apparently, those critics want the Jew to carry with him a moral micrometer to measure how far he is allowed to go in resisting extinction: enough to preserve his reputation among warlike nations, but not so far as to save his life or make anyone angry."

According to an editorial note, I. F. Stone was ill and unable to reply. He never would in the *Review* and, except for a single review, *NYR* cut and ran from the Middle East until October 1971.

AUGUST: "Soul Power" by Andrew Kopkind, a review of Martin Luther King's *Where Do We Go from Here: Chaos or Community?* which included Kopkind's memorable slogan— "Morality, like politics, starts at the barrel of a gun." King's non-violence, according to Kopkind, ain't going to work no more in white America. Kopkind gave up on King as he gave up on Robert Kennedy. Nice talk, but no commitment to radical change outside existing structures. "What is hardest now to comprehend —remembering the *Time* covers and the Nobel award—is King's irrelevancy. [. . .] This summer, King is *shuffling* between Chi-

ago and Cleveland." (Emphasis added.) Completely down on
liberal reform, Kopkind seemed to champion riot: "At least we
know now that even if all Martin Luther King's programs were
enacted, and all [Detroit Mayor] Jerome Cavanaugh's reforms
were adopted, and the Great Society as it is described materialized
before our very eyes, there would still be the guerrillas."

Lewis Coser, then a Brandeis professor, member of *Dissent*'s editorial board, and a disenchanted former contributor to
the *Review*, wrote in to remind Kopkind and the editors that
Kopkind's slogan was "but a restatement of the *Der Stürmer* doctrine, 'When I hear the word culture I draw my revolver.' "
Another correspondent protested: "Somehow I've heard that voice
before, and no matter how righteous its indignation against
immortality, its fascist accent scares me" (October 26, 1967).

Professing surprise at these attitudes, Kopkind replied: "Do
you mean morality *doesn't* grow out of the barrel of a gun? [. . .]
It seems to me that notions of morality, as of politics and everything else, grow out of existing institutional relationships—that
is, how power is organized in a society."

AUGUST: "The Occupation of Newark" by Tom Hayden.
Hayden had been doing community organization work in the
city for four years and was in the perfect position to write an
inside story of Newark's July riot. The final section of his report
—"From Riot to Revolution"—was full of revolutionary understanding and sympathy:

> The riot is certainly an awkward, even primitive, form of
> history-making. But if people are barred from using the
> sophisticated instruments of the established order for their
> ends, they will find another way. Rocks and bottles are only
> the beginning, but they get more attention than all the reports
> in Washington. [. . .] The riot is not a beautiful and romantic
> experience, but neither is the day-to-day life from which the
> riot springs.

[. . .] These tactics of disorder will be defined by the authorities as criminal anarchy. But it may be that disruption will create possibilities of meaningful change.

Like Kopkind, Hayden had revolution on his lips.

AUGUST: The ultimate shock: that Molotov Cocktail diagram on the cover of the Kopkind-Hayden issue. Long after the *New York Review* expires, it will be remembered, like Ralph Branca, for a single pitch. The day the editors tossed a Molotov Cocktail on their cover (August 24, 1967) was the day they lost the pennant. Many fans, especially those who look on from the center sections, will never forgive or forget.

To Irving Howe, the how-to drawing symbolized a wayward trend at the *Review*: "The whole idea of radical chic was embodied in that cover." Michael Harrington saw the cocktail recipe as a "loud editorial." "What the *Review* was saying here, which coincided with certain articles they were publishing on crucial political questions, was that the use of revolutionary violence for social goals at this time in this society is justified. It certainly wasn't opposition to Molotov Cocktails that led them to run the drawing there. At best it was a joke and a very stupid one." David Levine wouldn't have had anything to do with such incendiary art, since "it might have fallen into wrong hands."

Loyalists in the left-field seats are more tolerant of the home team's miscues. "After all," Murray Kempton observed, "those weren't A-bomb secrets on the cover—and besides, the *Review* got complaints from Newark that its formula didn't work." According to Ellsworth, it wasn't the cover that got the *Review* into trouble, but the combination of the cover and Andrew Kopkind's neo-Maoist saying about morality and guns, which appeared in the same issue headlined, incidentally, "VIOLENCE AND THE NEGRO."

The *cause célèbre* began rather innocently when Tom Hayden brought along a rough pencil sketch of a Molotov Cocktail and its ingredients with his article on the Newark riots. The impression was that the sketch had been used as a visual aid during the uprising. Perhaps this revolutionary relic would make for an interesting illustration. Artist Lemuel Line was called in to try a more worthy rendition. "Line's copy was so fantastically drawn," recalls then assistant editor Rhoma Paul, "that it looked like an eighteenth-century engraving. Bob and Barbara must have decided that it was too beautiful to languish inside."

Line does not suffer any Hiroshima pilot complex for his middleman's role. Although he felt queasy initially, his doubts gave way when he was assured by Barbara Epstein that anyone who wanted to get this information could obtain it readily from other sources. "As an artist, I come into this conflict quite often," Line confesses. "I just finished doing some induction posters for the Army. You're really playing a part in getting boys into the service, but . . ."

Finally, whether the Molotov Cocktail cover was intended to be a statement *against* violence (as Elizabeth Hardwick contends) or for violence (as Harrington & Co. argue), it was at least an inadvertence of the sort that the *Review* has been careful not to repeat.

SEPTEMBER: "The Case for Garrison" by Richard Popkin, philosophy professor at the University of Santa Clara and author of the ingenious JFK assassination study *The Second Oswald*, originally published in *New York Review*. The case for Garrison??? New Orleans' District Attorney Jim Garrison wasn't always considered the tinhorn sheriff we know him to be today. When he announced in February 1967 that he had "positively solved the assassination of John F. Kennedy," there were many in the press who believed he just might have something. Fred Powledge spoke highly of Garrison in the *New Republic* (June 17, 1967),

Playboy interviewed him (September 1967) and *Ramparts* put him on its cover (January 1968). *New York Review* had especially good reason to get into the act—Popkin, who wowed Silvers earlier with the Oswald *Doppelgänger* theory (July 28, 1966), was on the scene in New Orleans, assisted by Silvers' good friend and assassination buff Jones Harris.

Popkin's endless apologia defended Garrison against the carping criticism of *The New York Times*, NBC, and doubting experts. Despite the unsavory line-up of witnesses paraded out by the DA, Popkin believed where there was assassination smoke, there had to be fire. "So, at this stage of the affair," wrote Popkin prior to the trial of chief suspect Clay Shaw, "there does not seem to be good cause for concluding that there is no evidence and no case."

Sylvia Meagher, author of *Subject Index to the Warren Report and Hearings and Exhibits* and *Accessories After the Fact*, objected strenuously to Popkin's brief (December 7, 1967). She had helped Silvers check out *Second Oswald* in manuscript form, but wasn't buying the professor's theories this time. "I am willing to wait with Professor Popkin for the trial, but since the *known* evidence on Mr. Garrison's side [the Russo/Bundy testimony, the "code," and the Baton Rouge rendezvous] is, at best, vulnerable, I find no basis for assuming that the still-submerged evidence will be convincing or conclusive." Meagher was also unhappy with "the imputation that anyone who disavows Garrison is to be lumped with NBC or the other news media who are notorious for their hysterical and unashamed commitment to the Warren Report . . ." The final sentence of her letter was deleted by the editors. It read: "One is not obliged to take sides in a gang war in which both sides have only contempt for truth."

NOVEMBER: "An Exchange on the Left" between Irving Howe (editor of *Dissent*) and Philip Rahv (co-founder and then on the editorial board of *Partisan Review*). An affair of honor precipitated by Rahv's October slap of Howe's *Dissent*-ish anthology *The Radical Imagination*. Howe thrusts: "And now, after nearly twenty years of planful circumspection, appears Philip Rahv, offering Michael Harrington and myself Little Lessons in Leninism [. . .] Rip Van Winkle wakes up and fancies himself at the Smolny Institute." Rahv parries: "Irving Howe seems to be very angry. Too bad. [. . .] Can it be that he is infuriated with them [the young people of the New Left], because they refuse to accept him as the *éminence grise* of American radicalism?"[6] The moderate and radical wings of the New York Left move farther and irreconcilably apart.

NOVEMBER: "Vietnam: Solutions" by Mary McCarthy. Schlesinger, Goodwin, Galbraith, Fulbright really don't object to Vietnam, suggests McCarthy. "Or not enough to stop thinking in terms of 'solutions,' all of which imply continuing the war by slightly different means . . ." It suffices for the peace movement to push for immediate unilateral withdrawal. *How* that can be accomplished is the concern of the war makers, not the war protesters. "The country needs to understand that the war is wrong, and the sole job of the opposition should be to enforce the under-

6. Perhaps Rahv was alluding to a passage in Howe's *Partisan Review* article "Radical Questions and the American Intellectual (Spring 1966), in which Howe criticized younger radicals for their immaturity: "But now there is beginning to appear in the graduate schools and near the student and civil rights movements a younger generation of intellectuals and semi-intellectuals, perhaps not as well-equipped dialectically as the older leftists, semi-leftists and ex-leftists, and certainly not as wide-ranging in interest or accomplished in style, yet endowed with a self-assurance, a lust for power, a contempt for, and readiness to swallow up, their elders which is at once amusing, admirable, and disturbing. Thinking of themselves as 'new radicals,' these young people see as one of their major tasks the dislodgement of the old ones; and they are not inclined to make precise distinctions as to differences of opinion among the old ones. It seems clear to them that a good many radicals of the Thirties have grown tired, or dropped out, or, in some instances, sold out."

standing and to turn it, whenever possible, into the language of action."

It was Diana Trilling, for the Right faction again, who deplored the subliminal anti-Americanism of the McCarthyist Left faction ("On Withdrawing from Vietnam: An Exchange," January 18, 1968): "Certainly Miss McCarthy's refusal to deal with a communist victory in South Vietnam as any kind of threat to the values she would wish to see multiplied in the world characterizes the preference of the American intellectuals for addressing a single moral culprit, America. But this is a game we play. Most of us [the Right faction of the liberal intelligentsia] know better."

McCarthy stuck it to Trilling, remarking she'd rather be a live Solzhenitsyn than dead-sure Kristol—or Glazer—or Podhoretz-type: "I reject Mrs. Trilling's call to order. The imminent danger for America is not of being 'taken in' by communism (which is what she is really accusing me of—that I have forgotten the old lessons, gone soft), but of being taken in by itself. If I can interfere with that process, I will. And if, as a result of my ill-considered actions, world communism comes to power, it will be too late then, I shall be told, to be sorry. Never mind. Some sort of life will continue, as Pasternak, Solzhenitsyn, Sinyavski, Daniel have discovered, and I would rather be on their letterhead, if they would allow me, than on that of the American Committee for Cultural Freedom."

DECEMBER: "On Resistance" by Noam Chomsky, an up-from-dissent call for discreet, nonviolent, civilly-disobedient resistance, or otherwise an implication of "complicity in what the Government does." Chomsky labels the Pentagon "the most hideous institution on earth" and Mike Mansfield "an American intellectual in the best sense, a scholarly, reasonable man—the kind of man who is the terror of our age."

There would be other coffin-sealing *causes célèbres* the next year—Edgar Z. Friedenberg's review of *Making It*, Ronald Steel's "Letter From Havana," Jason Epstein's articles on the New York schoolteachers' strike, Dwight Macdonald's "Open Letter to Michael Harrington," but 1967 was the year of the *Review*'s Great Refusal, the year they told liberals, social democrats, intellectuals, Jews, Kennedy people, Martin Luther King people, and hordes of their own people to, in effect, stifle themselves—and didn't seem to give a damn.

The *Review* beat its plowshares into swords with such abandon that there were no immediate misgivings about the new course. In the fall of 1967, *NYR* rubbed the *défi* in with a prankish advertising campaign that deliberately traded on the paper's reputed contrariness. "*The New York Review of Books* has been called cliquish, intellectual, opinionated, and snobbish. For $7.50 a year you can be too," said the boldest of the advertisements under a photograph of a Roman statue (in profile) to whose aquiline nose was adjoined a real thumb forming that timeless gesture of nose-thumbing contempt. If the visual was cute, the text was cuter:

> For $7.50 a year you can be feared and envied. . . . Imagine the reaction of your Jewish friends—any of your friends for that matter—as you quote I. F. Stone's critique of Zionism in his article on Sartre's important symposium, *"Le Conflit israélo-arabe."*
>
> Or, if you want to bring a Molotov cocktail to your next cocktail party, arm yourself with Tom Hayden's "The Occupation of Newark," in which the Establishment's version of what went on there is blown to bits by fact after carefully aimed fact. (*The New York Times Book Review*, October 1, 1967, p. 49.)

"They had some shitty attitudes," remarks Charles Burch, the former head of the short-lived Angelus Advertising Agency, which handled the audacious *NYR* account. "They seemed to feel that the principal appeal for the *New York Review* was to have it on your coffee table. Readers don't necessarily read it for the writing or for the purposes of the authors. They could put it on their coffee tables and even quote it at parties. When Silvers and Ellsworth said that crap about their audience, we saw a way to make humor out of it."

The forty-year-old Burch, a finely muscled gay activist, began to have serious doubts about his clients' philosophy after the Molotov Cocktail cover. "They giggled about that cover," he recalls. "They didn't see it as something like *Steal This Book* or *The Anarchist's Cookbook*. It was a piece of artwork intended to titillate people who would never make a bomb. It was a ripping off of the black revolution. They were just trying to be groovy, and I hated them from then on."

Burch got his motivational cues during briefings from Ellsworth and Silvers. "I took all the stuff they didn't want to say publicly and said it. All good advertising is finding out what the hell the clients have nightmares about and make them come true. I used what could be taken for anti-Semitism there because I was really ready for controversy. They said, 'Wow, a lot of Jews will burn up when they read this.' "

And how did the *Review* get away with it? Magnificently. Radical politics was big box office in the late Sixties, and the *Review*'s receipts swelled accordingly. What it lost from the old order, it gained with the new. Without subscribing to the thesis that the *Review* carefully gauged its politics to the times (and the money), the fundamental truism—that no independent, for-profit magazine wilfully cooperates in its own downfall by forcing on its audience what it doesn't want—seemed to apply.

The *Review*'s gross success, mind you, is not simply the saga of an *ancien régime* publication which turns its back on its origins and finds health and happiness in embracing the revolution. This crude rendering of the *Review*'s young life passes over an accounting of the financial side of the business. Good little and middle-sized magazines come and go, speaking of debts and creditors. Quality does not guarantee longevity. The odds on bringing off a journal like *New York Review* were abysmally low. Cracked John Fischer, editor-in-chief of *Harper's* at the time of *NYR*'s founding: "The *Review* has the chance of a twelve-foot sloop in a hurricane." But *New York Review* prevailed, and in three years—that is, before its revolution—it was in the black. (In contrast, *Commentary*'s trip toward solvency took over twenty years.)

The principal architect of this business feat is A. Whitney Ellsworth, the *Review*'s thirty-six-year-old publisher. Ellsworth was once the *Review*'s twenty-seven-year-old publisher. That was in the spring of 1963, soon after he decided to quit the staff of *The Atlantic* and seek a position on Jason Epstein's new magazine. Ellsworth had admired the *Review*'s first issue from afar. "It included authors I appreciated, but couldn't get for *Atlantic*."

Apparently, Ellsworth's tastes were different from those of Edward Weeks, *The Atlantic*'s proper Bostonian editor since 1938 (although Weeks cannot recall any specific policy fights). This divergence was natural enough. Weeks, almost forty years Ellsworth's senior, was on the verge of retirement in 1963 and could hardly be expected to yield to an untutored assistant, however bright. Ellsworth presumably coveted Weeks's chair. His ambition at Harvard, where he was chairman of *The Advocate*, the college's literary magazine, was to become editor of *The Atlantic*, he confided to a Harvard professor. He was indeed cut from *Atlantic* timber—the correct family, schooling, and bearing. Many thought he was being groomed for the job, since there were no other candidates on the premises.

The would-be successor got his start on *The Atlantic* after Weeks picked him out of a litter of summer trainees when he was still at Harvard. Part of the training involved hunting out

good manuscripts that had been pre-selected by the staff and planted in piles of unsolicited dreck. "Whitney was just an absolute star," Weeks recalls. "His reports were so alert, bright, and perceptive. He made such an impression that we asked him to stay longer." After a postgraduate tour of duty with the US Army, Ellsworth returned to *The Atlantic* in 1959. He lived on Beacon Hill—a short walk across the swan-filled Boston Gardens to *Atlantic*'s stately mansion on Arlington Street—with his bride, the former Sallie Bingham (of the Louisville Binghams), whose prize-winning short stories he had published in *The Advocate*. Sallie was Jonathan (*Death at an Early Age*) Kozol's girl at Radcliffe, but married Ellsworth a few months after graduation. (They were divorced in 1965.)

If tradition had ruled, Ellsworth's wish would have come true. "The young man who was showing promise usually moved up," Weeks commented. "[James T.] Fields worked with [James] Russell, [William Dean] Howells worked with Fields, then [Thomas Bailey] Aldrich was around the office a lot." Weeks himself moved over from Atlantic Monthly Press to succeed Ellery Sedgwick. "If the successor had come from within, it would have been Whitney." Ellsworth had everything going for him except the accident of birth. He was born too late. "If he had been a bit older when I retired, I think he might have been made editor-in-chief. If the choice had been entirely up to me, he would have been one of the top two or three choices. But the proprietors, the Danielson family, had already met Bob Manning. It's silly that there should be such an arbitrary thing as age when you're dealing with a man as clever as that."

Down in New York on an editorial trip in March, Ellsworth expressed his marvel over *New York Review* to Jason Epstein. But no offer was extended in return. Fed up with Boston and *The Atlantic* situation, Ellsworth started job-hunting in New York that April. A friend of his, whose wife was Silvers' secretary, kept telling Ellsworth that there was nothing available at the *Review*, that they didn't even know whether it would continue. Ellsworth, as he remembers it, made such a bore of himself nonetheless that Epstein invited him over to his apartment for drinks. Epstein was seated when Ellsworth arrived. Looking up, Epstein said to him straightway, "Do you want to be publisher?" Publisher? Ellsworth had something more like managing editor in mind, but if it meant employment with the glamorous *Review*, publisher he would be. "Yes," he replied. "Then you are," said Epstein, and it was done.

Although KING has been painted in large black letters on Ellsworth's office door, there is nothing imperious within. His quarters are small, dingy, and cursed by a crosstown view of New Jersey as seen through a glass darkly. The publisher himself is a tall, pleasingly plump gentleman with curly blond hair and a round, smooth-skinned face of perpetual youth. Surely the least hierarchical of the *Review*'s hierarchy, Ellsworth is an easy fellow to get along with—as several past and present associates attest. Like Boston Blackie, he is in a manner of speaking "a friend of those who have no friends [at the *Review*], an enemy of those who make him an enemy." Although Ellsworth weighs his words, he displays far less uptightness under interrogation than his colleagues. Everything is on the record, and there are no mealymouthed circumspections.

*   *   *

The shortage of Jewish money behind the *Review* is often remarked upon. Murray Kempton doesn't understand how it has managed to function without the kind of patronage the American Jewish Committee has perennially lavished on *Commentary*. Norman Podhoretz, on the other hand, is suspicious of the WASP patriciate types who have hitched their bank accounts to the *Review*'s naysaying. "If our backing is non-Jewish," Ellsworth rebuts, "it's purely by chance. Jewish investors discussed the stock offering with us at least, and one wasn't interested." Two were, however. Walter Pincus and Philip Stern by name. The Jewish question aside, the *Review* has been fortunate in attracting an almost ideal set of benefactors. For the most part, they are stinking rich, approved by the Social Register, friends or friends of friends of the *NYR* principals, and dedicated to a policy of non-interference in the internal affairs of the *Review*.

When the *Review* almost went broke in 1965, the thirteen original investors plus two new ones came through with a major refinancing, totaling $59,845. At the same time, the corporation was changed over to a limited partnership (The New York Review, a Limited Partnership) for tax purposes. (In 1972, the *Review* would revert to corporate status for the same reason. NYREV, Inc., an ur-corporation, now sits atop the *NYR* empire.)[7] New York Review, Inc., representing the six directors, became the General Partner. The fifteen investors, who agreed to keep their money in the till until December 31, 1970, became the limited partners. Whence this largesse? Why wouldn't the *New York Review* Fifteen have to "worry about five or ten thousand," as Hardwick hoped? Let us see. (The following figures in parentheses correspond to the total individual investment of each shareholder in the *Review* partnership as of 1965, excepting small sums of earned but unextracted interest. One partnership share cost $1,000.)

Brooke Astor ($35,000) was the third and last wife of the late Vincent Astor, great-grandson of fur trader John Jacob Astor. Her husband's personal worth (circa 1957) was reputed by *Fortune* to be between $100 and $200 million. Mrs. Astor withdrew from the partnership, however, in October 1969—two months before the five-year waiting period was up. Her limited partnership shares were divvied up among the *NYR* upper management.

---

7. A partnership, as opposed to a corporation, permits the investor to write off losses in the partnership (applied pro rata) against personal income. This arrangement is obviously to the advantage of investors in yet-to-be-profitable enterprises. However, once the business begins to show a steady profit it is to the investors' advantage to incorporate because the corporate tax rate is lower than the personal tax rate.

Mary Stevens Baird ($3,000), one of the two new patrons, is Ellsworth's aunt on his deceased mother's side. The Stevens family is old New Jersey stock (the Stevens Institute of Technology) and once owned the district that is now Hoboken.

Mrs. Mary C. Bingham ($10,000), former mother-in-law of Ellsworth, is married to Barry Bingham, editor and publisher of the *Courier Journal* and Louisville *Times* of Louisville, Kentucky. Mr. Bingham was a commander in the US Navy (Pacific Theater) during World War II and was decorated Commander in France's Legion of Honor and Britain's Order of the British Empire. In 1956, Bingham worked as the National Chairman of Volunteers for Stevenson and Kefauver.

Blair Clark ($25,000) describes himself as a "journalist" in his *Who's Who* biography. For the past thirty years he has labored successively as reporter for the *St. Louis Post Dispatch*, publisher of the *New Hampshire Sunday News*, editorial writer for the *Boston Herald Traveler*, foreign correspondent and vice president of CBS News, and associate publisher of the *New York Post*. Clark's inheritance was tied to Coats & Clark, Inc., a merger of two old and venerable thread companies, the Clark half of which was once presided over by his grandfather. He was listed by The Citizen's Research Foundation as having given $75,000 in political contributions in 1968, the year he managed Eugene McCarthy's trot for the Democratic nomination.

Duncan S. Ellsworth ($25,000) was the father of Whitney. The senior Ellsworth led an amazingly graceful life as philanthropist, great white hunter, and patron of the arts. He prepped at Eton, served with an ambulance corps in Northern Italy during the Great War, and graduated from Harvard in 1922. He accompanied wildlife expeditions around the world and brought back specimens for the American Museum of Natural History. He was elected President of Manhattan's posh River Club, an office he held from 1937 to 1953, and owned stock in the exclusive Okeetee Club in Jasper County, South Carolina. For the twenty-five years preceeding his death in 1967, Duncan Ellsworth was a partner in the now defunct insurance brokerage firm of Freeborn and Company.

Mrs. Helen Ellsworth ($10,000), the second wife of Duncan Ellsworth and Whitney's stepmother, was left her husband's interest in *New York Review.*

John Eyre ($2,000), an Englishman by birth, matriculated with Whitney Ellsworth at Harvard. A former Wall Street broker, Mr. Eyre has dabbled in both theater and restaurants.

S. George Gianis ($6,000) is President of Gianis and Company, a Wall Street brokerage firm, and won't say who lured him into the enterprise.

James Merrill ($10,000), a poet and playwright, won a National Book Award (1967) in poetry for *Nights and Days.* Denis Donoghue reviewed the book in *NYR* (April 4, 1966.) "It seems that the long poem needs an opulent tray of images from which the poet chooses according to a principle known perhaps only to himself. Mr. Merrill's principle is clear enough, and his tray is richly endowed." Mr. Merrill is the son of the deceased Charles Merrill of the Merrills of Merrill, Lynch, Pierce, Fenner and Smith, and founder of the Ingram Merrill Foundation, which bestows $50,000 each year on deserving writers and artists. In 1972, his foundation granted a cool one million to Hampshire College in Amherst, Massachusetts. Barbara Epstein is said to be the contact here.

Paycol & Co. ($10,000) is a small, secretive partnership that has neither a telephone listing nor its own office. Apparently, the firm conducts business from behind the shield of United States and Foreign Securities in the GM building. Paycol partner Robert F. Quick stated that he could not divulge the nature of the company's transactions.

Walter H. Pincus ($3,000) could be the poorest of the lot.

As a very young man, he was given a modest amount of money upon the dissolution of the family electrical supply business. A former *Washington Post* reporter and editor and publishing freak, Mr. Pincus bought stock when the buying was low in both *The New Yorker* and *New York* magazines. A lawyer friend of Ellsworth's made the connection.

Banque Privée S. A. of Geneva ($5,000) is a blind for somebody who doesn't want anybody to know he or she has cash in *New York Review*. Jacqueline Onassis? Irving Kristol? David Susskind? The secret investor may be Baron Thierry von Zuylen of France and Belgium, a wealthy friend of Silvers from *Paris Review* days. Elizabeth Hardwick informed a *Newsweek* reporter in 1963 that the Baron was a backer, although his name never showed up in the *Review*'s statement of ownership.

Richard Shields ($12,000) is a director of both the Guggenheim Exploration Corporation and the Straus Exploration Company.

Philip M. Stern ($10,000) directs the Philip M. Stern Family Fund and initially bankrolled the Fund for Investigative Journalism. He is a former newspaper editor and Deputy Assistant Secretary of State for Public Affairs in the Kennedy administration, as well as the author of *The Great Treasury Raid, Security on Trial: The Case of J. Robert Oppenheimer,* and *The Rape of the Taxpayer.* His money comes from a Sears & Roebuck fortune.

Pierre de Vegh ($12,000) is the son of the late Imrie de Vegh, an expatriate Hungarian economist who came to this country in 1930 and served in a high post on the War Production Board during World War II. The senior De Vegh, who died in 1962, was founder of the De Vegh Mutual Fund, Inc. and the De Vegh Investigating Company, Inc.

* * *

"Nineteen sixty-six was our growth year," says Ellsworth, "but not much has happened since." Circulation, which had been climbing at an annual rate of 11,000 during the previous four years, and reached 66,000 in 1966, leveled off at 82,000 in 1968. The upward trend in advertising also peaked the same year. While the going was great, Ellsworth was predicting an eventual circulation of 125,000. Now that plateau appears unattainable, unless the *Review* were willing to sink huge sums into promotion and employ marginal mailing lists. Until recently, the *Review* had insisted on full-price subscriptions, proudly eschewing the kind of cut-rate deals which once temporarily bloated the *New Republic*'s circulation to over 190,000. Circulation rose 3,000 in 1969, dipped 1,000 in 1970, and climbed 1,000 in 1971 to 84,000. The purchase of *I. F. Stone's Bi-Weekly*'s list boosted *NYR*'s roll to a record high average of 94,000 in 1972, but by the end of the year circulation had dropped off to just short of 90,000. A mere net gain of 6,000 in 1972 means that not even one of ten *Bi-Weekly* subscribers bothered to switch over to *NYR*.

The *New York Review* has not buried its talents in the magazine. It has diversified instead in allied industries. New York Review Books, the magazine's own book outlet, grew out of *NYR*'s editorial apparatus. If certain material is written for, edited at, and first published in, the *Review*, why then hand over reprint rights to an outside agency? Ellsworth cites the Christopher Lasch articles collected into *The Agony of the American Left* as a *Review* giveaway. Thus the *Review* has published under its own imprint ten pamphlets or softcover books, including Richard Popkin's *The Second Oswald*, Herbert Kohl's *The Open Classroom*, Edmund Wilson's *The Fruits of the MLA*, and I. F. Stone's *The Killings at Kent State*. Random House and Vintage Books handle the distribution. This select and streamlined operation turns a profit.

Review Presentations, Inc., a multi-media lecture bureau designed to hustle highcult on campus, wasn't as lucky. But it certainly seemed like a smashing idea in 1968, when the *Review* was at its cultural apogee. The people that brought you Tom

Hayden, Gore Vidal, and J. H. Plumb in print, would transport the same to you in person through Review Presentations.[8] In addition to a cluster of *NYR* notables, attractions were offered in theater, music, dance, and foreign movies. A letter came in from Alaska saying, "We will be glad to have anyone you send us." Despite class like J. P. Donleavy, the La Mama Repertory Troupe, Bernardo Bertolucci on film, and Sylvia Marlowe on harpsichord, the agency never caught fire. "We were always struggling," admits Mrs. Roberta Gaal, a former vice president of Presentations. "It turned out to be too expensive. Launching a company, making something happen takes money, promotion, telephones . . ." Ellsworth, the road show's impresario, pulled up stakes in 1971. Colleges were cutting back on *divertissements*, and the pure administrative bother of Review Presentations was more than Ellsworth anticipated. "We jumped into it too fast," he explained. "If I had spent more time investigating other lecture bureaus, I would have thought more about it." Financially, the loss accrued to Ellsworth alone. Apart from its good name, the *Review* merely loaned him the grubstake money.

Probably the soundest investment the *Review* ever made was the 1971 acquisition of The Kirkus Service, Inc., publisher of *Kirkus Reviews*. An advance trade-review medium like *Library Journal* and *Publishers Weekly*, *Kirkus Reviews* sends its capsule comments out to 4,400 subscribers—mostly librarians and booksellers. At the time of the purchase, Ellsworth stated no changes were contemplated in Kirkus' operation and that the subsidiary would "remain absolutely independent of the *New York Review*." Occasionally, some Kirkus briefers have found their way into the back of *NYR*. Neither buyer nor seller disclosed the terms of the transaction. When the author asked Kirkus' former owner, Maurice Friedman, merely whom he sold his business to—NYREV, Inc., or New York Review, Ltd.—Friedman refused to answer. "I'm a

---

8. Ellsworth was president of this corporation. Silvers and both Epsteins were vice presidents.

lawyer," he protested, "and it's a private matter. It would be improper for me to say." Shortly thereafter, Ellsworth passed the word to Kirkus that such questions were not to be entertained.

And what of the future? The *Review* has already rejected one conglomerate's offer to buy. "At some point or other," Ellsworth grants, "we're going to have to think about selling the company, or going public, or selling off the stock held by both the managers and the investors. At some point, the editors and myself will probably want to stop doing this and get some return for our investors. There are no present plans, however, and I don't look forward to selling out."

Ellsworth would have no comment on two questions. How much have the *Review*'s benefactors recouped? "You better ask them." And why did zillionaire Brooke Astor, the largest single investor, withdraw from the partnership in 1970? "You better ask her."

A random sampling of the original stockholders produces four different stories. "*New York Review* is one of the poorer investments I've ever made," declares S. George Gianis. "Some-how I was given the impression it would be a good business investment, but I think my chances of getting even are very remote." Gianis specializes in high-risk stocks and considers his association with the *Review* something of a joke. In eight years Gianis has not yet realized $1,000 on an investment of $6,000 or $8,000—he couldn't remember which. "I don't receive the money," he says in an ascending tone of incredulity. "They give me credit, which they keep, and I put it on my tax return." Since there are no stockholders' meetings, he has never conferred with the other investors, whom he describes as being "too free and easy with their dough." Gianis remarks that when his caller first mentioned the *Review*, he thought a deal for his shares was in the offing, a deal he would have been more than ready to ponder.

Gianis could have avoided a $6,000 (his actual investment) misunderstanding if he had consulted before the fact with Walter Pincus. "As publications go, they've done very well," Pincus insists. "They haven't tried to do more than they are. But anybody who went into *New York Review* to make money is a fool and doesn't understand specialty publications. The *Review*'s audience was always limited." Pincus sold his shares in 1973.

Pierre de Vegh has not been pleased by the *Review*'s progress, but since capital gain was not his object, his disappointment is on a higher plane. "I invested in the *Review* because I thought there was the opportunity to have a great intellectual and literary magazine. I can't say that promise has been entirely wasted. It was like this in the beginning, and still is to some extent. Otherwise, the *Review* has become a political magazine. To the degree that they are relevant—in the forced sense of the word—that's too bad. I'm not a radical liberal. When they turn shrill I don't listen. I probably wouldn't invest in it now, but I won't pull out because I don't want to weaken the magazine." But he did pull out in 1973, and Richard Shields went with him.

Blair Clark keeps his threads in one of Manhattan's neatest living modules. The back of his brownstone apartment at 229

East 48th Street helps shield the block-long Turtle Bay Garden, a private oasis of greenery amid the concrete jungle. Clark is a tall, sharp-featured gentleman with silver sideburns and the mien of Walter Pidgeon in his prime. He has been on the phone with Silvers prior to being interviewed and, while cordial, is signally cool. "I'll give you something you can use," he says, after declaring how little he has to volunteer. "Lowell always described my investment as a 'contribution.' "

Why did Clark pitch in with $20,000 the first time around and $5,000 the second? "I just took a look at the project and thought it was a reasonable thing to do. Whitney had good ideas, and Bob was a good editor." Clark pooh-poohs Gianis' pessimism. He contends that if the *Review* ever went public, the investors could get back "x times" their original money. "My own feeling is that we shouldn't look at the *Review* on too short a cycle. It was in the black quickly, and has remained self-sustaining. I neither expect to get rich nor see it go down the drain. I don't know what will happen. And I'm not at all worried." Since Clark was the *Review*'s go-between with Mrs. Astor, is he privy to the reason for her exit? "Yes, I am. But you'll have to find that out for yourself."

It is easier for a rich man to enter the kingdom of heaven than it is for a reporter to gain the ear of Mrs. W. Vincent Astor. Why she took her money and ran from the *New York Review*, however, is no riddle. Marion Javits, the Senator's wife and an acquaintance of widow Astor, passes the incident off as a mere shift in priority. Mrs. Astor, she supposes, was more interested in the ghetto dispensations of the $100 million Vincent Astor Foundation, which performs corporal works of mercy in Harlem and the Bedford-Stuyvesant area of Brooklyn. But $35,000 is hardly a distraction. This couldn't be the reason.

Perhaps Mrs. Astor was reacting to Daniel Moynihan's "benign neglect" memo. "The time may have come," the President's Chrysostom wrote, "when the issue of race could benefit from a period of 'benign neglect.' The subject has been too much talked about. The forum has been too much taken over to hysterics, paranoids, and boodlers on both sides. [. . .] You perhaps did not note on the society page of yesterday's *Times* that Mrs. Leonard Bernstein gave a cocktail party on Wednesday to raise money for the Panthers. Mrs. W. Vincent Astor was among the guests." The *Times* broke the leaked memo on March 1, 1970. Soon afterwards, the paper printed a terse letter from Mrs. Astor dated March 2. She wanted to go on record as an absentee from the Panther fête. "I was invited to the party, as I imagine a whole list of New Yorkers were, but I did not attend." And not so much as a How-do-you-do for the Panther 21 who had been collared for conspiring to blow up Abercrombie & Fitch, among other sites, and detained in jail for almost a year at a bail of $100,000 per. "She does things for liberal causes," observes Charlotte Curtis, the *Times'* society gumshoe and the author of the original Bernstein story, "but she doesn't like being identified with them. She knew there was going to be a trial. She was *sympathetic*. But she was also furious that people thought she was there. All those people panicked. It was a catastrophe. Everybody ran for cover." Mrs. Astor had, in fact, withdrawn her *NYR* assets five months before Moynihan's memo surfaced.

One needn't pry into personal affairs. There was sufficient reason for divorce on the grounds of incompatibility. The lady invested in a class-ridden literary magazine and gradually saw herself backing a bomb-tosser. This was no position for a Nelson Rockefeller Republican to be in. "You're making deductions," says Mrs. Astor's business manager, Leon Bennett, "but you're probably reasonably close."

If there were any doubt about Mrs. Astor's alienation from the *Review*'s orbit, one had only to pick up the *Times* on January 14, 1969, and peruse the eight-column society page story headlined "PRESIDENT AND FIRST LADY GIVEN GALA FARE-

WELL—400 ATTEND PLAZA PARTY." Co-host of this lavish send-off for Lyndon Johnson, and the woman photographed next to him in the receiving line, was Mrs. Astor. Two years later President Nixon would be the one, according to an item in "Suzy Says" (the New York *Daily News*, October 31, 1971):

> President and Mrs. Nixon will attend the Salute to the President dinner at the Americana Hotel Nov. 9. (As the dinner is for President Nixon, it would be pretty pointless if he didn't make it.) The purpose of the affair is to raise early money for Nixon's campaign, and it is just one of 21 dinners in 21 cities on the same night, marking the opening of the campaign. Tickets are $500 each, and for that you get Bob Hope. Doesn't he *ever* give up?
>
> The goings-on will be shown on closed-circuit television, and the governors of New Jersey and Connecticut will be present. You won't believe the list of red-hot Republican women who are out hustling those tickets—Mrs. Ogden Phipps, Mrs. E. F. Hutton, Mrs. Joseph Meehan, Mrs. Virgil Sherrill, Mrs. Herbert Patterson, Mrs. Edmund Lynch, like that. Mrs. Vincent Astor and Mrs. Charles Shipman Payson have taken tables. So have the Clifford Michels. Mary Roebling of New Jersey and the John Morrises. That's what rich friends are for.

Mrs. Astor must have closed her mind on the *Review*. For by the time she withdrew her assets and began feting with Presidents, the *Review* was a different magazine. The revolutionary flowers that bloomed in 1967 were cut down by 1970. *The London Review of Vietnam* ceased as the operative metaphor. The British influence remained in *belles lettres*, and Vietnam did not sink into the horizon, but the escalatory *élan vital* that sparked *NYR* in the middle Sixties was snuffed out. *The New York Review of Books* entered a new period in 1968; its new title became, in effect, *The New York Review of the Rectification of Errors* (1968–70).

The repudiation, or at least the purging, of the immediate

past, began with a rather unprecedented criticism of the *Review*'s
leading firebrand, Andrew Kopkind (unprecedented because
NYR hardly fostered head-on collisions between its political writers). At the end of his chastening supplement on black power
("The Trouble With Black Power") in February 1968, Christopher Lasch recommended an alternative to Kopkind's militancy:

> In the meantime, will events wait for analysis? Immediate
> crises confront us, and there is no time, it seems, for long-
> range solutions, no time for reflection. Should we all take to
> the streets, then, as Andrew Kopkind recommends? In critical
> times, militancy may appear to be the only authentic politics.
> But the very gravity of the crisis makes it all the more impera-
> tive that radicals try to formulate at least a provisional theory
> which will serve them as a guide to tactics in the immediate
> future as well as to long-range questions of strategy. Without
> such a perspective, militancy will carry the day by default;
> then, quickly exhausting itself, it will give way to another
> cycle of disillusionment, cynicism, and hopelessness.

Elizabeth Hardwick balanced the scales again with her elegy on
Martin Luther King in May.[9] King may have "shuffled" for Kopkind, but to Hardwick he seemed "more radical" at the end of
his life. In the next issue, King's philosophy of nonviolence was
redeemed by a Paul Goodman piece on the Kerner Report, which,
in effect, took another slap at Kopkind:

> Finally, it is said that nonviolence might suit the Hindus,
> but it is contrary to American spirit and tradition. Quite the
> contrary. It seems to me to be simply an extension of tradi-
> tional American populism, the democratic process as con-
> ceived by Jefferson that has always revived in times of great
> crisis: acting "illegally" and "petitioning," rousing the gen-
> eral will, protected by the Bill of Rights, with fringes of
> violence, and ending up with important institutional change.

9. "The Apotheosis of Martin Luther King," May 9, 1968.

In every major country in the world, power is terribly deeply entrenched; but America is the most likely place for a non-violent movement toward freedom to succeed.

Since I have this occasion, let me say a word about the death of Martin King. He was a stubborn, reasonable man, and political without being a fink. I do not know any other national leader for whose death I would have wept.[10]

Even Robert Kennedy, thrown on the dustheap of history a year earlier by Kopkind, found salvation in *NYR*. Hans Morgenthau's August obituary spoke eloquently of the assassinated presidential candidate:

> That this voice has been forever stilled is the great loss the country has sustained. Even if Robert Kennedy had lived, it is likely he would not have been nominated in 1968. Yet this passionate voice, contemporary and addressing the future, would have reminded us that there exists an alternative to Humphrey's liberalism of thirty years ago and to the timeless opportunism of Nixon. It would have been proof to those of us who were ready to opt out of the American political system altogether at the beginning of this year, not only that there are alternatives to the obsolete philosophies and policies of the powers-that-be, but that there are men who are willing to search for those alternatives and put them into effect.[11]

In the first month of 1969, cool hand Harvard professor Barrington Moore threw water on the possibility of radical revolution in the United States.[12]

> Hence any such major disruption would very likely result in martial law or worse. Unless events and trends that no one can now foresee intervene to generate both widespread support for a revolutionary break and a more passive willingness

10. "Reflections on Racism, Spite, Guilt, and Violence," May 23, 1968.
11. "On Robert Kennedy," August 1, 1968.
12. "Revolution in America?" January 30, 1969.

to go along with it, any temporary collapse within the next twenty or thirty years would probably have utterly tragic consequences. Even if it succeeds in taking power, a revolution that tries to remold society against the mores and folkways of the mass of the population must turn to terror and propaganda on a gigantic scale in order to stay in control. In America a black dictatorship of the proletariat or even a black and white version—something as far as I am aware no one takes very seriously—might claim to have poetic justice on its side, but practically nothing else. It would almost certainly be a failure.

Moore would be just as sober in a subsequent article on the intoxicating crisis of the students. In "On Rational Inquiry in Universities Today" (April 23, 1970), he philosophized in a key *NYR* hadn't heard much before. For example:

> In the current situation of chronic crisis and intermittent polarization on the campus, and in the country as a whole, what can the professional intellectual do? Especially what can he do if he is an academic intellectual, strongly opposed to the current drift of American society, yet equally strongly committed to certain liberal values, such as rational inquiry, intellectual freedom, tolerance, and civilized discourse, values that some sections of the extreme left now vehemently reject? Does this kind of liberal commitment sooner or later force one inevitably and reluctantly into the arms of those who call the police, and thus not very indirectly into the arms of the military and all those forces responsible for the cruelties that pass under the name of law and order in western civilization?
>
> One answer comes to mind, based on the famous remark attributed to Florence Nightingale: Whatever else hospitals do, at least they should not spread disease. We can paraphrase it thus: Whatever else academic intellectuals do, they should not spread myths.

There was a slight deviation in February 1969, when *NYR* published Jerry Rubin's "A Letter to My Brothers and Sisters in the Movement" (February 13, 1969). With Hannah Arendt's essay "On Violence" coming up soon (February 27, 1969), however, the *Review* could tolerate it. Silvers must have wanted Arendt desperately. Her critique of Left violence was extremely useful to him that year, but he had to break a *Review* canon to get her in. Arendt's piece was already scheduled for the winter issue of Columbia University's School of Foreign Affairs' *Journal of International Affairs*. Silvers had to twist the arms of the student editors to allow for simultaneous publication. They compromised on a shorter version for the *Review* and insisted on the *Journal*'s retention of the original copyright (which was printed at the end of the article in the *Review*).

Another trade-off occurred in 1969. Ronald Steel chose not to probe the hard underbelly of the Panthers in his "A Letter From Oakland: The Panthers" (September 11, 1969). In contrast, Harold Cruse reprimanded Eldridge Cleaver's halfway radicalism in a review of his speeches:[13]

> The problem with Eldridge Cleaver and those of his generation who opt for "political revolution" is that a new set of social and philosophical concepts are [sic] needed to substantiate political activism toward more and specified goals. To say that America is a racist society is not enough—there is more to it than that. If American racism created the institutions, it is now the institutions themselves which legitimize the racist behavior of those who are the products of the institutions. The problem, then, is how to deal *structurally* with these institutions—how to alter them, eradicate them, or build new and better ones? What is the method of social change to follow the demonstrations, the oratory and polemics, the jailings, the agony, and the exiles?

The *Review*'s Rectification of Errors program concluded in the summer of 1970. An anti-violence supplement by British

13. Review of *Eldridge Cleaver: Post-Prison Speeches and Writing*, edited by Robert Sheer, May 8, 1969.

philosopher J. M. Cameron smothered the last embers of *NYR*'s
Molotov cocktail fire (July 2, 1970). Final expiation for past sins
of political adventurism could be read into the *Review*'s giving
cover status to Eugene Genovese's National Petition Campaign.
In a special Cambodia issue headlined "The Crisis" (June 4,
1970), the editors of the *Review* opened their pages to a long
letter from Rochester University's Genovese explaining his
straightforward, inoffensive, end-the-war petition intended for
Congress. The professor who urged a Vietcong victory early in
the war and thereby stirred a statewide controversy while on the
faculty of Rutgers, New Jersey's state university, was now going

down the well-traveled establishment road. How come? He saw war-weary Congressmen as potential allies of the peace movement against the President. "Many radicals understandably gag on such a strategy," he allowed. "Our best young radicals here at Rochester, for example, heatedly and correctly argued that these measures will not in themselves expose the imperialist basis of American policy and may in fact divert the attention of radicals once more into liberal politics. But there is nothing in this or any reasonable alternative strategy that makes such an outcome inevitable. *The hard fact is that the New Left has collapsed, and the Left, Old or New, is in disarray.*" (Emphasis added.)

With the publication of Genovese's petition, *NYR*'s catharsis was complete, and it was ready for new fields. But where? Which way should it go? Silvers told a friend that the *Review* had been through four or five phases and that, at the end of each phase, he wondered about the next. "I know Bob was concerned," the friend says, "where the *Review* would go after Vietnam."

Obviously, the *Review* is bringing the war home. In its latest phase, its title should be *The Neo-Edinburgh Review of Domestic Entanglements* (1970–). *NYR* is harking back to its nineteenth-century origins, to the kind of magazine it was conceived as in 1963, that is, a literary magazine on the British nineteenth-century model, which would mix politics and literature in a tough but gentlemanly fashion. As Silvers mentioned to *Newsweek* in 1965, that is, before the country went haywire: "There's nothing slick or jazzy about us, nothing that couldn't be done in the nineteenth century" (December 27, 1965).

Domestically, the *Neo-Edinburgh Review* is much involved with surveillance. This trend surfaced with Frank Donner's long essay "Spying for the FBI" (April 22, 1971). Ex-agent Robert Wall sang to *NYR* about his life and times gangbusting the Movement (May 4, 1972), and his story made the front page of the *Times*. *NYR* opened ten of its pages to correspondence to and from Harper & Row, the CIA, and Alfred McCoy over McCoy's controversial exposé *The Politics of Heroin in Southeast Asia* (September 21, 1972). Just as *NYR* jumped on the McCarthy bandwagon in 1968, it appeared to be four-square behind the McGovern campaign when it published his tax and income distribution plan during the primaries (July 20, 1972). I. F. Stone cast his McGovern dissent upon the waters, however, when he needled the Left Great Hope on the arms race: "While the Nixon program offers no hope of arms reduction and little prospect even of a freeze in the areas which count, the McGovern program implicitly accepts the same doctrines which have fueled the arms race through several administrations, Democratic and Republican."

In 1973, the *Review* broke into Watergate with a series of pieces by Mary McCarthy, I. F. Stone, Henry Steele Commager, and Kirkpatrick Sale.

NYR may have sold in, but it would never sell out. No matter how far the *Review* had moved toward the political mainstream by 1973, its radicalism has not been entirely eradicated.

Bob Silvers reaffirmed *NYR*'s commitment to the past in February 1972 at a conference entitled "The Media as Indicator of a Changing Society," sponsored by the American Marketing Association. He told the assembly that *NYR* had far more essays on the nineteenth century than on the present. While this is an exaggeration, the *Neo-Edinburgh Review* analogy holds.

The first *Edinburgh Review* commenced publication in 1802. It was, like its American successor, eclectic in its interests and severe in its judgments. The inaugural editorial of *The Edinburgh Review* is remarkably similar to the statement of the editors in the premiere issue of *New York Review*. *The Edinburgh Review* expressed equal disdain for bad books, while speaking for the imperatives of intelligent criticism:

ADVERTISEMENT.

In committing this Work to the judgement of the Public, the Editors have but little to observe.

It will be easily perceived, that it forms no part of their object, to take notice of every production that issues from the Press: and that they wish their Journal to be distinguished, rather for the selection, than for the number, of its articles. Of the books that are daily presented to the world, a very large proportion is evidently destined to obscurity, by the insignificance of their subjects, or the defects of their execution; and it seems unreasonable to expect that the Public should be interested by any account of performances, which have never attracted any share of its attention. A review of such productions, like the biography of private individuals, could afford gratification only to the partiality of friends, or the malignity of enemies.—The very lowest order of publications are rejected, accordingly, by most of the literary journals of which the Public is already in possession. But the Conductors of the EDINBURGH REVIEW propose to carry this principle of selection a good deal farther; to decline any attempt at exhibiting a complete view of modern literature; and to confine their notice, in a great degree, to works that either have attained, or deserve, a certain portion of celebrity. [. . .]

Even with these allowances, perhaps the reader may think, that some apology is necessary for the length of a few articles in the present Number.—If he cannot find an excuse for them, in the extraordinary interest of the subjects, his candour will probably lead him to impute this defect to that inexperience, which subjects the beginning of all such undertakings to so many other disadvantages.

The Edinburgh Review died in 1929, after 127 years of continuous service. It died because it was no longer needed, as the closing statement made plain.

The REVIEW was founded to conduct an active Whig policy, and to the end of its life it has continued to bear the blue and yellow party colours. But the political views that it was intended to support have ceased to play any leading part in the national life. The functions of a quarterly critical journal in 1929 are very different from those required nearly a century and a half ago. Circumstances and conditions have greatly altered. In the early years of the nineteenth century the EDINBURGH REVIEW and its rival the QUARTERLY held the field of criticism. Today the monthly magazines, the extensive daily press, and the B.B.C., compete in offering highly-trained criticism and specialised information in every branch of human knowledge to a wide public.

The Neo-Edinburgh Review of Domestic Entanglements is trying valiantly to ward off an obsolescence of the same sort. Julie Hover and Charles Kadushin predict in *Change* ("Influential Intellectual Journals: A Very Private Club," March 1972) that *NYR* will decline if there is "any sharp decrease in interest among intellectuals in Left politics" and that the more liberal and more pragmatic *Commentary*, "whose editor has a history of moving from one circle to another," would be "the next leading contender for the power position." Norman Podhoretz is supremely confident about the outcome. "If you want to know the truth," he told *The Wall Street Journal* (November 19, 1970), "the truth is, I know I'm going to win."

Maybe. Nonetheless, *The New York Review of Books* has already displayed a marvelous capacity for adaptation in its first decade. There are, you can wager, other easy titles in its future.

3
Members of the Board

The play of power at the *Review* is not all that obvious. Robert Silvers and Barbara Epstein respectively are listed as editors —not co-editors. The only other editorial personnel mentioned, except for two assistant editors who perform strictly mechanical tasks, are advisory editor Elizabeth Hardwick and contributing editor I. F. Stone. Jason Epstein and Robert Lowell, both members of the board, have no official link to the literary operations of the *Review*. Thus two editors of supposedly equal authority and an advisor of uncharted influence direct the *Review* out front, while one of New York's heaviest publishers and the country's most highly regarded poet remain backstage. How does this strange alliance function? Who really runs the show? Actually, the *Review*'s office politics are pretty unbloody. "There was some conflict between Bob and Barbara at the beginning," Hardwick discloses, "but all of that completely died down under pressure of putting things out."

The wording and design of the masthead, for instance, proved to be a sticky wicket for the two principals. Silvers wanted the titular upperhand. Given his previous track record and the gam-

ble of leaving his job at *Harper's*, he seemed to deserve it. Barbara Epstein had nothing to lose except some freelance textbook
editing, which she did in her spare housewifely time. But Epstein,
a nepotist by happenstance, despite her gifts, fought for the
appearance of equality—no missionary positioning on the masthead for this girl. Thus the lateral compromise was struck—their
names would run on the same line marquee-style. Silvers would
be satisfied with his unalphabetical placement before Epstein,
and she in turn would be saved from all too discernible difference or discrimination. Outside agitation from Jason Epstein and
Lowell also seems not to be a factor of great concern now, if it
ever was before. One very informed source advised that the
Review's cultural revolution was fought between Silvers and the
Lowells on one side and the Epsteins on the other. "Lizzie was
more militant, and the Epsteins less so. Then that gave way to a
closer relationship." Here they are then—the major characters in
The New York Review of Books story—in order of their appearance.

*   *   *

"Jason is a caricature of a New York Intellectual," says
Dwight Macdonald. "He's a nineteenth-century entrepreneur, a
robber baron, only his market is not copper, but intellectuals."
Macdonald meant this as a compliment. After all, Epstein was in
his early twenties and fresh out of Columbia when he started the
Anchor Books line for Doubleday and therewith made America
safe for the quality paperback. Before Jason Epstein, the publishing of cheap and popular paperback reprints of classics like *The
Charterhouse of Parma* and current studies like Edmund Wilson's
To the Finland Station was just a gleam in an imaginative editor's
eye. They said it couldn't be done. The idea was in the air, but
no one had ever licked all the distributing, marketing, and consumer problems.

Kenneth McCormick, Doubleday's kindly editor-in-chief

from 1941 to 1971, speaks with unalloyed fondness of his former protégé. "Jason's parents tried to get him into the family textile business, but he had come out of college with a sense of excitement with the scholastic world and an abiding feeling that academia was not served by the world of books. He was convinced that if scholarly books could be purchased for the price of a movie, they'd sell. This was in the back of his head.

"Meanwhile, he was the star graduate of our training program. As he learned his way around, he did a lot of private research on why there couldn't be a quality line of non-mass market books for students interested in reading. He discovered that hardcover books by scholars were written solely for each other. He did homework on figuring out sales, manufacture, promotion, all the while he was ingratiating himself with us as a hard worker.

"One day, he came into my office and said, 'Ken, I wonder if I can walk home with you tonight. I'm going to explode if I don't explain.' As we walked through Central Park that evening, he told me about his idea for Anchor, which would be fashioned after England's Penguin Books, but with unique features. I was absolutely sold by the time I got home. Jason was just out of college, and it would be a marvelous experiment."

So it was. In consultation with two Columbia professors, Andrew Chiappe and Moses Hadas, as to what texts would be most appropriate for college-course bibliographies, Epstein went about buying reprint rights for titles like *The Liberal Imagination* (Lionel Trilling), *Socrates* (A. E. Taylor), *Studies in Classic American Literature* (D. H. Lawrence), and *The Organization Man* (William H. Whyte). Anchor tapped a mother lode that had never been mined before. For example, Yale University Press managed to sell only a few thousand copies of David Riesman's *The Lonely Crowd* in its original hardbound edition. Thanks to Epstein, *The Lonely Crowd* sold a quarter of a million copies as an Anchor paperback. "Jason has the mind of a scholar and the

instincts of a pushcart peddler," observed Joe Marks, then head
of Doubleday's subsidiary rights, "and that's what made Anchor
Books."

The fair-haired Anchor boy also edited Vladimir Nabokov
(*Pnin*) and Edmund Wilson for Doubleday. The former he cor-
ralled himself; the latter switched over from McCormick. "Jason
and Wilson were real pals and traded households," McCormick
says. "I began to feel from Wilson that this arrangement would
work much better." Nabokov and Wilson, literary disputants themselves after Wilson tried to tell Nabokov about Russian verbs,
figured in a dispute Epstein had with the company. He would not
resign on this particular account, but the situation did crystallize
his discontent in the house. "*L'affaire Lolita*" began when Nabokov turned in his X-rated manuscript about the love of a dirty
old man for a fourteen-year-old nymphet. Epstein wanted to
publish it. But from the tip of its management down to its lawyers,
Doubleday didn't have the heart. In 1946, the New York Society
for the Suppression of Vice banned Edmund Wilson's and Doubleday's *Memoirs of Hecate County* as "salacious and lascivious"
literature. The Supreme Court of the land held up the ban on a
four-four split decision. If that was the fate for *Hecate County*, it
made sense to assume *Lolita* would be gang-raped even more
assiduously by deputies of the public morality and outlawed forth-
with by the courts. Doubleday was gun-shy. "If you've done time
for bank robbery, and you're waiting for a bus outside a bank
that's being robbed," explains McCormick in retrospect, "then
you're going to be picked up, innocent or not." So Doubleday
spurned *Lolita* and frosted its editor.

The parting of the ways cannot be linked to any one event.
"Jason was too big for Doubleday," according to then managing
editor Walter Bradbury. "He was a publisher chafing under the
restrictions of being an editor." McCormick traces the difficulty
to Jason's desire for more autonomy and the unwillingness of
Douglas Black, then Doubleday's president, to grant it. "A state

of siege developed between him and Black, who was a very testy guy. They had a square-off, in which Black became increasingly irritated with Jason's arrogance. Jason was immature at the time and was in the exciting process of growing up. It seemed to me that a man in Black's position should have been more understanding of volatile young talent. 'If Jason's getting too big for his pants,' I thought, 'why not give him bigger pants?' Neither man understood the other." Epstein pressed for a higher salary or a share of Anchor's profits, but neither demand was met. After eight years of blazing glory, he resigned from Doubleday in 1958, a week after turning thirty.

His next stop was London, where he stayed with Irving Kristol, who was then one of Allen Dulles's unwitting dupes on the cultural-political monthly *Encounter.* The purpose of the trip was to clinch a deal whereby Epstein and Barney Rosset (the father of Grove Press and *Evergreen Review*) would purchase the American rights to Penguin Books from Penguin's seignorial publisher, Sir Allan Lane. "He was in a state of high excitement," recalls Kristol, "telling everyone it was all set. But he met his match in Lane, who had been the Jason Epstein of his day." The sale was off, and a disappointed Epstein returned home to heed Bennett Cerf's call to Random House, where he repeated his dazzling history by building up Random and Knopf's paperback outlet Vintage Books, solidifying Random's Modern Library, latching on to authors like Paul Goodman, Oscar Lewis, Jane Jacobs, Philip Roth, and lately Gore Vidal, and, in general, by radicalizing the firm's list with titles in glorious tune with the counterculture.

"If Edmund Wilson likes you, you can't possibly help liking him."[1] That was Epstein's estimate of his curmudgeonly friend from Talcottville. This description likewise fits public attitudes toward himself. For Epstein is pound-for-pound one of the less popular individuals in the New York intelligentsia. Yet if you hap-

1. Quoted from "Wilson," by Eleanor Perényi, *Esquire,* July 1963.

pen to be on the receiving end of his affection, he is irresistible.
Poet Frederic Seidel, whose collection *Final Solutions* was edited
by Epstein, sums up Epstein's image when he comments that
"Jason tends to be very keen on you or dismissive." But Seidel
adds: "Jason cuts a lot that way, and I suppose some people
bleed. He may be a louse sometimes, but none of his detractors
is half as good as he is; that energy and intelligence are at a level
where the others in publishing couldn't breathe. And he is *interesting*, his choices are not *à la mode* but really his own. One
thing sets him apart absolutely: He isn't jealous of other people's
success; he doesn't end up being jealous of writers he's discovered
or touted. I can't think of anyone else in New York literary life
you could say that about."

Nonetheless, it would seem that more people have felt dismissed than doted upon by Epstein, and that is perhaps the clue
to why his unpopularity cuts across party loyalties. While Podhoretz's personal enemies are mostly in the Left faction and
politically motivated, Epstein appears to have as many backbiters
among his soul brothers as he does among those in the Right
faction. There is much of Archie Bunker, "the lovable bigot," in
Podhoretz (or "Poddy" as he is affectionately referred to by
Gore Vidal). "There are two kinds of people in this world,"
Podhoretz told Merle Miller, "—those who want to be loved and
those who want to be feared. I want to be loved . . ." Epstein may
be in the opposite camp. (*New York Times Magazine*, March 29,
1972)

Some people think that Willie Morris had Epstein in mind
in his book, *North Toward Home*, where he tells the story of his
first day in New York City (pp. 322–327). Morris had just left
Austin and the Texas *Observer* and was out job-hunting in the
place he called the Cave. The "august American publishing
house" he visited and the "most intelligent editor in New York"
he conversed with are anonymous, but the circumstantial evi-

dence from the company's director ("a man noted for his jokes and puns") to the editor himself (who "had helped start [. . .] an ambitious book review")—all strongly suggest Bennett Cerf's Random House and Jason Epstein.

"What makes you think you want to work in New York?" asks the editor Morris quotes.

"I've got some experience editing and writing, and I guess everybody wants to come to New York for a while," replied Morris.

"It's a horrible place," the editor said, putting the kid right at ease.

Morris inquired about prospects with the new book review. No, they weren't hiring. Did Morris have anything else in mind? Yes, *The New York Times* and *Harper's.*

"Those are two of the most boring publications I know of," the editor said.

"I mentioned two executives from other publishing firms that I might see," Morris continued.

"They're not very intelligent people," the editor said.

"Well, you know, a job's a job."

"I guess so," the editor said, looking again at his watch.

At this point, Morris admits he went into a slow Mississippi boil. The editor "seemed less likable than a boondocks Texas reactionary after a successful vote," and he had to restrain himself from "throwing this little man out of a second-story window into a courtyard."[2]

Philip Roth, who dropped his Random editor Joseph Fox— in a fracas over *Portnoy's Complaint*—for Epstein, won't hear of downgrading his friend. "I should simply like to say," writes Roth, "that my own experience has shown Jason to be honest in his dealings, shrewd in his judgments, and when it has come to criticism of my work, absolutely straightforward about his likes and dislikes. I value him greatly for his editorial candor, his considerable literary taste and understanding, and his high publishing standards, and I hardly believe that I am the only writer published by Random House who feels this way."[3] (Roth left Random House for a sweetheart contract with Holt, Rinehart and Winston in 1972.)

2. Morris denies Jason Epstein was the character in this anecdote. When a copy editor at *The New York Times Magazine* called him to check on this passage in connection with Merle Miller's profile of Epstein and Podhoretz, Morris said the figure was not Epstein but a "composite."
3. Letter to the Editor, *Esquire,* June 1972.

At least one of Epstein's authors, David Rogers, who wrote *110 Livingston Street: Politics and Bureaucracy in the New York City School System*, is rather less enthusiastic about him. It seems that just when Epstein was blossoming as a critic of the said system, in the *New York Review* in 1968, he also happened to be editing Rogers' manuscript at Random. This coincidence caused whispering in the house and consternation in the author. Epstein's literary *chutzpah* is indeed legendary: He is probably the only editor in the history of publishing who ever reviewed a book he himself edited (W. H. Auden's *Dyer's Hand* in *Partisan Review*, Summer 1963) and who ever edited a book he himself had written (*The Great Conspiracy Trial*), setting his own advance, and so on; even Bennett Cerf, Random's founder, discreetly went *extra muros* with his several volumes. But the *110 Livingston Street* affair was *chutzpah* of a different order. For here we had an editor simultaneously treading the same literary ground as one of his authors.

This coevality of interests can be traced back to *New York, N.Y.*, an eight-page tabloid newspaper developed by Epstein and distributed by Random House as a reading tool in local ghetto schools in 1966–67. Although the paper quietly caught on with parents, students, teachers, and principals, the Board of Education cancelled its Random House contract (reported to be in the quarter-million-dollar neighborhood) in March of 1967. As *New York, N.Y.*'s publisher, Epstein was not a little perturbed. The New York City Board told him its hands were tied by a state education regulation and that he should go to Albany. In the capital, he was told to go back to the City Board. Epstein happened to discuss this run-around with someone familiar with Rogers' research and was informed that Rogers could give him the story on the school bureaucracy inch by inch. Having recently completed three years' research on the school system at the Center for Urban Education, Rogers was Epstein's man.

When Rogers offered to show him his 1,500-page manuscript in July of 1967, Epstein eagerly accepted, promising to read it in two days. He liked the work so much that he signed it up for Random House. (He also got *New York, N.Y.*'s contract renewed.) After a major rewrite, the book went to press in March 1968 under the title *110 Livingston Street*, the actual address of the New York School Board's main offices. During this pre-publication period, Epstein decided to voice his opinions on the school bureaucracy and related issues in a series of three *New York Review* articles.[4]

The first piece was a review of the so-called *Bundy Report*, named after Ford Foundation President McGeorge Bundy, who chaired the Mayor's Advisory Panel on Decentralization and authored its findings. Epstein showed the Bundy review to Rogers, who immediately became distressed about what he felt was the similarity of ideas and logic between his manuscript and his editor's.

But Rogers failed to mobilize himself. It was his first book, and he was inordinately grateful to have Epstein as an editor— even though their personal relations had deteriorated. Embittered by this experience, Rogers will say only that he doesn't think his editor knew as much about the school bureaucracy as he himself did, at least not before reading *110 Livingston Street*. "I feel I taught Jason a lot," says Rogers.

Another view of Epstein comes from Abbie Hoffman, former campaign manager for H. Stuart Hughes' 1962 Massachusetts Senate race, zany founder of the Youth International Party, Chicago Seven conspirator, and lately an alleged cocaine pusher. "Jason is the real interesting person in my life," Hoffman quips. Epstein and Hoffman once had a healthy respect for each other's

4. A review of *Reconnection for Learning: A Community School System for New York City* by the Mayor's Advisory Panel on Decentralization of the New York City Schools; McGeorge Bundy, Chairman, June 6, 1968; "The Brooklyn Dodgers," October 10, 1968; "The Issue at Ocean Hill," November 21, 1968.

standing. They both made bread with the Hoffman-Random House production of *Woodstock Nation*. They were in court together in Chicago—Abbie in the dock, Jason in the press section. "Jason was my mentor," says Abbie. "We got very close during the trial. I kept telling him I'm going to write a book you wouldn't publish. On the back cover of the second edition of *Woodstock* it said, 'Steal this book.' He got a kick out of it. But they took it off the third edition. I yelled censorship, and they yelled shoplifting. So it changed from edition to edition."

The book Hoffman wrote and predicted correctly Epstein wouldn't publish was *Steal This Book*, a do-it-yourself manual of rip-offs including instructions on how to shoplift, cheat AT&T, and even how to make your own bomb. With Epstein, *Steal* went over like a lead balloon. "It's only when you tell how to do things that books get banned in the US," Hoffman protests. "You're getting on a different level than theory. We had long, complicated meetings. The title bothered him. And Jason took the position that he would not publish a book with a bombing diagram. But Jason knew I was flexible. I changed things in *Woodstock*. I said to him, 'Jason, look at *New York Review*. You published a diagram of a Molotov Cocktail.' "

Well, that was offbeat, Epstein said.

" 'But there was a bomb diagram in *Woodstock*,' I told him."

That was different, he remembers Epstein saying. "Now I was serious, he said. Kids are going to get in trouble, he said."

" 'I got in trouble reading Michael Harrington,' I said. 'What about your conspiracy? Don't you want kids to act?' "

Hoffman insists *Steal*'s rejection lay in hands higher than Epstein's and that Epstein wouldn't admit he was powerless to ram the book through. He confronted Epstein with his suspicions. Epstein shot back that he was not "a company man" and stated that he didn't want to publish the book.

"It's not your decision," Hoffman replied. "I know it. You know it."

"He and John Simon have that problem," observes Hoffman, explaining the ambivalence inherent in company radicalism.
"Simon would say, 'Don't identify us with the corporation.' I told
him, 'John, you publish J. Edgar Hoover.' "[5]

Christopher Cerf, son of Bennett and formerly an editor at
Random, doubts Hoffman's interpretation of the *Steal* caper.
"Jason wanted to publish it, but really felt someone might blow
himself up after reading it. He took a mildly pro stance, which
eventually turned neutral." Whatever Epstein's reservations about
the book, he was scarcely the only editor in New York who
turned it down. More than a dozen others declined the opportunity, several of them in the belief that it was simply an inept
piece of writing marked by heavy-handed irony and little saving
grace.

When Bennett Cerf asked Ken McCormick if he ought to
hire Epstein, McCormick answered, "Any young man worth anything is brash—hell, you were." Cerf and Epstein got along all
right, but the pair never reached the stage of binding their bleeding thumbs together. Cerf was a rich man's St. Francis, a disciple
of Mammon. He yachted with Frank and Mia and guessed along
with Arlene and Dorothy on the old, long-running *What's My
Line?* panel. He was an unashamed liberal. But anyone who
had put James Joyce through customs and defended *Ulysses* in
court couldn't be all bad in Epstein's eyes. "My father understood
Jason totally as a human being," comments Chris Cerf, who
jumped leagues by going over to The Children's Television Work-
shop in 1970 as editor-in-chief of non-broadcast materials. "They
had good rapport, they were friends, and saw each other socially.
My father got a big kick out of Jason's modus operandi—how he
got authors to come to Random and then got other editors to do
the dirty editorial work. He thought that was delightful. Jason
wasn' t earning his salary on a time basis, but through his
acquaintances and influence."

5. Random House was publisher of Hoover's *Masters of Deceit*.

"He's the only intellectual Bennett Cerf ever understood," is one publishing executive's rendering of the Cerf-Epstein alliance. This understanding, however, did not mean uncritical acquiescence in Random's radicalization under Epstein. "He felt Jason was becoming radical chic," Chris Cerf says, "that the Chicago Seven or Eight were totally wrong. He thought Jason became obsessed with it, and he himself had no taste for publishing these guys. He thought we were doing too much in that direction. He was much more liberal than the rest of the executives there. He saw what a lot of the younger editors were into, but felt we should be doing more right-wing books for the sake of balance. My father lost patience with Jason when Jim Silberman [editor-in-chief of Random House] didn't. People find Jason exasperating at times, but they also regard him as a plus."

"For all Jason's defects and faults and laziness and lack of attention span," remarks author David Halberstam, "he is a diamond. He's sort of like a pitcher who should be a twenty-game winner—he should have a record of twenty and eight but instead it's fifteen and twelve. But you know that every other year or so he'll pitch a no-hitter and do things for Random House that nobody else could do. You know there's a real intelligence there. He's just a hell of a lot brighter and more creative than most people in book publishing."

Is Jason Epstein a radical? Can a man whose "About the Author" note in the back of his book says, "He lives in New York City and Sag Harbor, Long Island," find true love in the revolution? Martin Mayer jibes, "Jason is a sort of primitive New Leftist, a Peppermint Lounge liberal."

The erstwhile cabin cruiser he kept at Manhattan's Seventy-ninth Street boat basin, the European wardrobes, the proper private schools for the kids, the English bootmaker—all seemingly manifestations of unraised consciousness—are classed, in radical parlance anyway, with the problem and not the solution. "What he loved was doing things in style," Podhoretz wrote in *Making*

It, "and like Miniver Cheevy (but not at all growing lean as he
assailed the seasons), he grumbled constantly over the inferior
tools America gave him to work with: The restaurants were
lousy, New York was ugly, the whole country stank. But he did
the best he could with the material at hand." And doesn't Epstein
draw his salary from one of the nation's larger defense con-
tractors (Random House is owned by RCA). So where does he
get off, the murmuring goes, as a big cheese on the radical Left?

"I think his politics are what he says they are," says a friend
who has collaborated with Epstein for a number of years, "but
I'm not certain he didn't arrive at them because they were nice
politics. He loves to be a pessimist. He takes great glee in being
pessimistic about everything." The politics of pessimism. Lugubri-
ous chic.

Epstein sliced off a prime cut of his gloomy *Weltanschauung*
in "Civilization as a Process; Culture as Banal Repetition," an
extraordinarily revealing article written ten years ago for the
American Library Association Bulletin (July–August 1963). The
thirty-four-year-old author was sick unto death with the artifacts
of American civilization. Each morning on his way to work, he
was oppressed by the sight of "so much dead culture"—especially Radio City Music Hall, "where, in the deepest winter and
on the brightest spring mornings, lines of New Jerseyites and
others—thousands of them—stand in rows, uncomfortable,
patient, grinning . . ." As a burnt-out Freudian, he saw the accu-
mulation of culture-killing instinct. Yet there was one tiny ray of
hope for the public, which was "at least as bored with the cultural
products it gets as I am." Shining through the clouds of repression
was the promise of *The New York Review of Books*, already the
talk of the town on the strength of its first two issues. Caution,
however, was the best policy. "It would be absurd, of course, to
generalize from the limited if enthusiastic reaction to *The New
York Review of Books* that America is no longer largely philis-

tine in its tastes, conventional in its responses, and docile under
even the clumsiest persuasion. But it would also be wrong to
assume that America is quite so monolithically committed to its
prevailing cultural patterns as is suggested by the vulgarity of
Lincoln Center and the pathetic dreariness of those lines standing
in the snow before Radio City Music Hall."

Civilized life was still just a bowl of Sysiphean rocks. But
might there not be parts of the world "where the proportion of
established civilization to available instinct is still in favor of
instinct?" Africa perhaps. How about those upfront Nigerian village kids who swarmed around Epstein during his CIA-sponsored
junket to the dark continent? If they could only hang on to their
noble savagery, maybe Nigeria wouldn't have to blow it. But
Epstein's discontent crept back:

> When I returned finally to the capital city at Lagos and to
> my great Hilton-like hotel where the *Daily Mail* and *Time*
> magazine sat absurdly upon the Italian marble tables in the
> cocktail bar, I was dismayed to see a group of African stu-
> dents, not much older than those we had seen in the villages,
> but already covered in dacron. Their button-down shirts em-
> barassed me. I felt an impulse to take my own off, to tell
> them to go back before it was too late. But they were too busy
> winding their cameras, and in any case it *was* too late. The
> process toward civilization is inevitable, after all. There is no
> avoiding it. And one day Africa too will have its version of
> *The New York Times Book Review*—I may even have helped
> indirectly to launch it.

Epstein's praise of instinct and disgust for American civ
reappeared in *The Great Conspiracy Trial*. While writing as an
objective third-person reporter, he let his own world view show in
a passage about the Weatherman ethos. "The Weathermen, on the
other hand, were determined not to argue with a dying culture
but, no matter how feeble their present means, to try to kill it."

Thus Bernardine Dohrn, the hunted Bonnie Parker of the Wea-
ther-people (as they are now called), grooved on the Sharon Tate
murders. "Wild," she said.

What did instinctualist Epstein think? "Perhaps Miss Dohrn
intended no more by these remarks than to illuminate the hypocrisy by which a society deplores the violent murder of an actress,
while collectively it murders Vietnamese and brutalizes its own
poor; so Miss Tate and her friends, being white Americans, got
no more than they deserved, in Miss Dohrn's view. But her celebration of murder also reflects another concern of the Weathermen: that their instinctual sources of aggression have been
illegitimately taxed by a culture that has perverted and collec-
tivized these energies and converted them to purposes of mass
killing, leaving its individual members psychologically feeble and
thus unable to confront their brutal culture with sufficient force.
Hence the echo in Miss Dohrn's manifesto of the passion with
which such writers as the Marquis de Sade and D. H. Lawrence
attacked the institutions of sexual repression within their own
cultures. Like these enthusiasts for sexual self-determination, Miss
Dohrn and her followers may feel that society has stolen from its
members an important part of their instinctual capital and that to
regain these resources is essential not only to their personal survival, but to the survival of the species."

Jeff Shero, an alumnus of SDS and an engaging cowboy
revolutionary, probably dug Epstein more than anybody in the
counter-culture. Epstein befriended him when he migrated to
Manhattan from Texas in 1967. The penniless Shero had an idea
for a right-on underground paper (*Rat*), which he passed on to
Epstein. Epstein not only introduced him to leftish philanthropists,
but lavished upon him the wealth of his own experience in the
politico-literary game. When Shero needed an apartment, Epstein
fixed him up with W. H. Auden's flat. When Shero was scrounging
around for cash to publish the SDS's *Movement Guide to Chi-*

cago, Epstein came up with the money in two days in the form of a Random advance for an anthology of Movement writing.

Shero's enchantment with Epstein's political values waned after they and four young people were busted by state police on a highway outside Poughkeepsie, New York, in the spring of 1969. All six were arrested for the "criminal possession of a dangerous drug" (marijuana) and were kept overnight in jail. At the trial Shero pleaded guilty to possession, and the charges against the other five were dismissed.

"He's powerful and brilliant," says Shero, in a slow, dogged attempt to call back the essential Epstein. "He's not sad so much personally as, given the options he had in his life, he did what he could, but history didn't provide him with enough openings to do what he wanted to do. [. . .] Jason has real values. He respects talent, but can put up with only a certain amount of bullshit. [. . .] Jason and I would talk politics. I was generally optimistic and revolutionary. Jason would tell me I wasn't going to make it, and I'd say, 'Well, Jason, we're going to give it a try.' I'd do my rap about living in the empire, New York is the Rome of the empire, and it's falling apart. Maybe we're the barbarians or the Vietcong of the barbarians, but the third world people are eating this place up, and I'll do the best I can. Jason saw himself going into exile, because what we were doing didn't make sense. He'd say that we have didn't have enough roots or substance. And his judgment was right. My optimism was boyish optimism . . . I've been drunk with him late at night when he goes off by himself down to the wharf, stare at the water, and think about where it's all at. I never had the impression that Jason was superficial. [. . .] He expressed ambiguity about everything. Shit, yeah, he had lots of guilt—torn between what might be done and his sense of the hopelessness of it. [. . .]"

At the core, Shero believes, Epstein is cynical. "The core of that cynicism gives him great insight into the city," he adds, "but at the same time it's corrupting. McGovern could have never come

out of New York. McGovern could only come out of a place like
the Plains, where he had a certain innocence to say, 'Look, I
don't give a shit if I get two percent, I'm going to give it a whirl.'
Jason won't fight; he won't toss himself in all the way and fight
and lose."

Whenever the name of Jason Epstein is raised nowadays,
there you will also hear the name of Norman Podhoretz. Not
since Hemingway lampooned Scott Fitzgerald in *The Short Happy
Life of Francis Macomber* has a literary feud become so public
a property. Peter Steinfels discussed the grudge quotient operating between the lines at *New York Review* and *Commentary* in
his *Commonweal* article "The Cooling of the Intellectuals" (May
21, 1971). "What once could be taken as another family squabble
among Manhattan literati," he divined, "looks more and more
like an indicator of future political alignments." In its paper-of-
record tradition, *The New York Times Magazine* surrendered
ten pages to Merle Miller's blow-by-blow account of the Epstein-
Podhoretz love-hate ("Why Jason and Norman Aren't Talking,"
March 29, 1972). Miller interviewed fifty friends and acquaintances of the pair, but neither principal would speak about the
other for print—not that very much either had to say about the
other would have been printable. Jonathan Black made a mock-
ery of Miller's detail in a *Village Voice* parody entitled "Bob and
Lionel: A Literary Feud" (April 13, 1972):

As reigning editors of their respective journals—the Beth-
Shalom Newsletter and Review (circulation *circa* 4800) and
the Review and Newsletter of St. Sebastian in Extremis (circulation *circa* 4900)—Bob and Lionel pretty much bestrode
the nonhospital world like a colossus. Both are triple Scor-
pios, both were "boy geniuses" at the same agricultural college; they shared the same brain-trust of friends, the same
apartment, and as it turned out, the same wife. Nor was it so
long ago that Bob and Lionel and Brenda conducted an in-

formal nightly salon of dazzling repartee, the keenest of minds and intellects, among the regular guests Maude Brown, whose own hospital newsletter and cancerous wit were often the subject of both serious analysis and well-meant tomfoolery. . . .

Epstein dispatched a letter to Miller (March 28, 1972) saying he was sorry for him and a letter to the *Times Magazine* (April 19, 1972) disputing matters of fact and opinion. Apart from some minor corrections on his weight at Columbia and the unheated condition of his erstwhile boat, what Epstein appeared most ruffled about was Miller's mention of his relationship with the *New York Review.* "What is not minor at all, however—what approaches the gray and ugly margin of slander," he wrote "—is Mr. Miller's suggestion that *The New York Review of Books* is under my influence and not the unique product of its writers and its editors, Robert Silvers and Barbara Epstein. That I could, even if I chose, advise these people how to run their magazine is untrue. Nor is there any truth in Mr. Miller's theory that, since I am married to one of the editors, our thoughts are alike. Had he bothered to read the *Review*—what I have written there and what others have written—he could hardly have made this foolish error."

If Miller erred in this association, then he has company in New York. Charles Kadushin and Julie Hover's article, "Influential Intellectual Journals: A Very Private Club" (*Change,* March 1972), notes that several elite intellectuals mentioned Jason Epstein in their questionnaires as one of the *editorial* powers behind *NYR.*

Miller would seem to have been on solid ground when he observed that Epstein was one of the *Review*'s founders, that his wife and friend are its editors, and that the three of them appear to be in agreement on the larger concerns of the magazine. One wonders how Epstein would have reacted if Miller had been more specific. After all, Epstein signed incorporation papers in 1963, sits on the board of directors, holds one-sixth of the voting stock, hired Silvers and Ellsworth, was a vice president of Review Presentations, edits the books of many prolific *NYR* contributors, distributes *NYR* books at Vintage, and is a top executive at Random House, which, with its subsidiaries Alfred A. Knopf and Pantheon, has great impact on the *Review* in terms of writers used, books reviewed, and advertising bought. While denying that Epstein ever "served as publisher" or was "that involved," even Ellsworth admits to a "consulting role." "Jason keeps abreast of what's going on."

David Halberstam would occasionally tease Epstein about his intimacy with the *New York Review*, and Epstein would very persistently deny Halberstam's implications. "Finally I said," Halberstam relates, " 'Jason, you remind me of some Assistant Secretary of Defense for Public Affairs denying that our bombs are hitting civilians. You do protest too much. Don't tell intelligent people what they know to be true isn't true.' Once or twice when I was in Jim Silberman's office, Jason would come in and, protesting again, say, 'Now about me and *The New York Review of Books* . . .' "

Whatever residual or latent influence Epstein may or may not have over the influential magazine he helped found, he doesn't open the *Review*'s morning mail any more on the way crosstown to Random House—a regimen he followed when the magazine was young. He would often help write headlines in those days and that, too, he has evidently abandoned. One thing is sure: Epstein, called "ten times smarter than Silvers" by a former Random associate, no longer plays Charles Foster Kane to Silvers' Jedediah Leland.

*   *   *

"I feel I play a very negligible editorial role," Elizabeth Hardwick modestly affirms. "Advisory editor is a title they gave me because I don't like to work in an office." Barbara Epstein lives a couple of doors down on West 67th Street, and Hardwick is on the telephone with Silvers during the week, so she keeps in touch for whatever it's worth. "Bob is so alert he's thought of everything before I have."

Hardwick's digs are an objective correlative of literary life at the top. The Smithsonian would be wise to re-create her *Salle de living* for perpetuity, as they have with dwellings of the under-class. This apartment must not be allowed to pass away. Mere nodding acquaintance with periods and *objets d'art* cannot cope with the decorative strata of its interior, which one visitor would place, in the main, somewhere in the nineteenth century. (The exterior is dated by Lowell in the poem "Half a Century Gone," where he describes the building as "the last gasp of true Nineteenth-Century Capitalist Gothic.") Antique woodcuts, crucifixes, and unfamiliar furnishings throw one's calculations off, however, as to the dominant period. The great hall—living room just won't do—is a cavernous, high-ceilinged affair with a huge arching skylight in the rear, a wall of books along one side, and an eight-foot balcony leading to the upper level on the other. The mistress of the house and her visitor converse in the center on opposite ends of a long red couch, intermittently distracted by the meanderings of a quite sociable cat.

Elizabeth Hardwick is a tall, well-proportioned woman who, dressed in a mod purple-striped maxi outfit and splashed with mid-afternoon make-up, appears not the least like the grump on the back cover of *A View of My Own*. Her mid-fifties become her. Possessor of a splendid prose style that is more nineteenth century than modern, Hardwick is a gifted but not prolific writer. Two early novels (*The Ghostly Lover* and *The Simple Truth*) were well received, but she seems to confine herself to just a few essays and reviews a year.

The talk jumps from topic to topic: the *Review*'s editorial selection? "They try not to print articles they don't like." The avoidance of puffs? "The horrors we've been through with bad

reviews of our dear friends. Crews was very snippy on Wilson."[6]
The dearth of younger critics at the *Review*? "They should have
more young people, but where do you find them?" The condition
of fiction reviews and poetry? "I do feel that fiction and poetry

6. See Frederick Crews's review of *The Bit Between My Teeth, A
Literary Chronicle of 1950–1965*, November 25, 1965. Hardwick went to bat
for Wilson in a letter to the editor (December 22, 1965), suggesting Crews
was all wet in both his low assessment of Wilson's literary eminence and his
political thought. Crews replied that Hardwick's letter rested on such poor
reading of his review "that I see nothing to be gained from quarreling with
her. Perhaps she might simply reread my essay unhysterically."

are very much slighted." The *Review*'s politics? "The politics are very sensible. They're violently anti-war, and that's about it. We all stand for the same thing—civilization. We're not hippies." Radical chic? "You live your politics out on a spiritual level. There's no one in the editorial world living the socialist life. During the French Revolution, the upper classes, far from being cut off, were encouraging the people."

For the sake of accuracy, the visitor gathers, Hardwick says that her then husband, Robert Lowell, moved out and is living in England. The matter is not pursued.

When queried about his expatriation by Ian Hamilton in the British periodical *The Review*, Lowell commented, "Why I am in England is mostly personal and wouldn't be correct in an interview. But there are certain common reasons. I'm not here in protest against conditions in America, though here there's more leisure, less intensity, fierceness. Everyone feels that; after ten years living on the front lines in New York, I'm rather glad to dull the glare."[7]

Lowell and Hardwick were divorced in 1973, after twenty-three years of marriage. Lowell, fifty-six, quickly married Lady Caroline Blackwell, a former companion of Bob Silvers, and has a son by her.

The interview goes well. The Hardwick persona, hard-bitten in print, brims over nicely with a comforting Southern accent in person. Blithe-spirited and madcap Elizabeth Hardwick can come on like a blend of Martha Mitchell and Blanche Dubois. Naturally, she is being protective of the *Review*, but not disingenuous. A few months afterward, the visitor attempted to check out the background of certain disclosures made in the interim. The first involved her caning of Lincoln Center's 1967 revival of *The Little Foxes* directed by Mike Nichols (December 21, 1967).

7. This interview with Lowell was reprinted in *Modern Occasions* (Winter 1972).

Lillian Hellman was a dear old friend, and so the vehemence of Hardwick's *NYR* review startled everyone. "It is nearly always said that Lillian Hellman's plays are triumphs of craftsmanship," Hardwick wrote. "Actually, the question of motivation, the construction of a plot, are quite awkwardly managed in most of them. [. . .] A footnote on Mike Nichol's [sic] direction of *The Little Foxes*. It did not seem to me at all interesting or important." In the very next *Review*, Edmund Wilson, no less, extolled the staging of *The Little Foxes* in "An Open Letter to Mike Nichols." And two *Reviews* after that, Penelope Gilliatt, an intimate of both the playwright and director, wrote in to criticize Hardwick: "If a critic happens not to respect the work of someone he is fond of, what's against shutting up? [. . .] The guise of sonorous remoteness that writers sometimes use to betray it [friendship] in print is a board chairman's emotion, and it comes cheap."

Hardwick denied she acted vengefully toward Hellman and dismissed other allegations regarding her opposition to I. F. Stone's entry into the *Review*; the ancient ideological split pitting Silvers, Lowell, and herself against the Epsteins on the political future of the *Review*; the typographical sabotage of William Snodgrass by *NYR* employees for Snodgrass' cloying review of Lowell's play *The Old Glory*; the hatchet job of Richard Gilman's *Confusion of Realms* by Philip Rahv; and the canning of Susan Sontag. The author was not dwelling on these matters morosely. He merely sought Hardwick's comments, because his sources seemed reliable.

Rather than admit that even the editors of *New York Review* may be heir to the effects of original sin, Hardwick adopted a meliorist Nixonian line (Isn't it time we started talking about what's good in *The New York Review*?). To wit, follow-up letter to the author, which said that America was blessed with too few papers of high quality for *NYR* to be subject to such sick speculation regarding which piece was rejected by what editor for what reason. (A tempered response next to her reaction to Merle Miller's piece in the Sunday *Times*. Miller says she woke him up early the following Monday morning with a phone call to tell him he ought to be in jail.)

* * *

Although Barbara Epstein and Silvers jointly share the title of "editors," some billings are more equal than others.[8] In this instance, Epstein, not *il miglior fabbro*, is on the short end. The circumstantial evidence confirms her subordination. Silvers is president of New York Review, Inc., she secretary-treasurer. His office is huge, hers half the size. He has two secretaries, she none. It is in Silvers' presence that Jason insists on talking about the *Review*, not his wife's. Her outpost is the lesser region of literature, not politics, where the *Review*'s action resides. When the paper was printed in Milford, Connecticut, it was Barbara, not Bob, who rode the dummies up there every other week. "Her function is stylistic," observes a former assistant, "arguments between 'which' and 'that'—the image, appearance, sound, and look of the *Review*." How do they accommodate each other?

8. In *Who's Who* Epstein lists herself as "editor" of the *Review*, while Silvers employs the designation of "co-editor.'

"They're equal," insists an advisor of the pair. "Well, no. But Barbara's role is important. There are certain writers he can't get without her. She has more power than people think; she works with Wilson, Auden, Dupee . . ." Actually, Epstein and Silvers are an exceptionally well-knit editorial team. No current or former co-worker who spoke to the author could recall overhearing a single office spat.

Barbara Epstein, forty-five, mother of two, is a quiet, clever, and endearing woman who seems to arouse the higher instincts in man. Martin Mayer remembers her at Radcliffe as "a little ray of sunshine on Cambridge Common." When Epstein was at Doubleday in the early Fifties, she was placed in charge of the American edition of *The Diary of Anne Frank*. She happened to meet Anne Frank's father, who noticed a resemblance between her and his daughter. He commemorated this similitude with the gift of an antique gold pin. Barbara Epstein as Anne Frank . . . The comparison ought not be stretched, but there is a seeming vulnerability about this delicate, girlish woman who sits deep in her office behind the sign "I must soon quit the scene. Benjamin Franklin to George Washington, March 5, 1780" that allows the identification.

* * *

The I Am Who Am of the *New York Review of Books* is none other than Robert Benjamin Silvers, son of a Long Island sales executive; A. B., Chicago, 1947; press secretary to Governor Chester Bowles of Connecticut, 1950; dropout of Yale Law School, Class of 1951; US Army 1952–53; member of the editorial board of *Paris Review*, 1954–; graduate of the Paris Ecole des Sciences Politiques, 1956; associate editor of *Harper's*, 1959–63; co-editor of *Writing in America*, 1960; translator of *La Gangrène*, 1961; co-editor of *The New York Review of Books*, 1963–; member of board, Theater of Ideas.

But who is Robert Benjamin Silvers? Never has so little been known of so much by so many. Incredibly, Dennis Wrong can

write a tome about the *Review* without ever once mentioning his name. A Family critic, who has collaborated with Silvers inside and outside the *Review* for several years, is astounded by the news of Silvers' cultivated eye for women. Not that he thought Silvers had other preferences, but rather that he was, egad! chaste.

Silvers is not an introvert. He turns out for a high percentage of New York's social and political occasions, chairs a Theater of Ideas Symposium here and speaks out at a cold-war panel there. The real Silvers, however, persists as an unknown quantity. He can be quite animated, even effervescent, during working hours, when discussing a current project with an illustrious *Review* contributor and somehow ignore the same man at a party that very evening. "My admiration for Bob is as an editor," says the illustrious contributor, "not as a friend. I very clearly divide Bob as friend and editor. Even Barbara Epstein doesn't understand him." While the latter impression is probably misleading, the implication rings true—Silvers does not open up his heart to the world. "You can get a lot of information from him," observes a colleague of many moons. "He always knows everything, both *au courant* and theory. But having a discussion with him is like having a discussion with Hal the Computer."

If Gay Talese, that connoisseur of human frailty, described Silvers in an *Esquire* story about the *Paris Review* (March 1968) as "a man with no apparent vices except smoking in bed," you can be sure his slate is clean.

A portrait of Bob Silvers is preserved in a photograph accompanying Tom Wolfe's article "Radical Chic" as published in *New York* magazine (June 8, 1970). There he is with a let-them-eat-meatballs-*petites à la Coq Hardi* grin masking a fat jowly face which he is about to fill with one hand, while a brown Omega cigar dangles from the other. His partner in conversation is a high-cheeked beauty who seductively thrusts five inches of bare upper thigh in Silvers' direction. Off in the background, where he belongs, a hairy Panther stares across Leonard Bernstein's crowded room that enchanted evening.

Another portrait of Silvers (*circa* 1963) allegedly hangs in a collection of short stories, *Born Losers*, by British novelist Barbara Skelton, the former wife of critic Cyril Connolly. While some people close to Silvers recognize him in the character of Ben Gold in "Sour Grapes," best-friend George Plimpton denies the resemblance.

Silvers was a child prodigy. He entered the University of Chicago in 1945 at the age of sixteen and graduated, after having numerous requirements waived, two and a half years later. In the fall of 1948, he went up to Yale Law School, but stuck around for three semesters with average grades.

At Yale, Silvers became friendly with Chester Bowles, Jr. He pitched into Governor Bowles' losing gubernatorial campaign in 1950 and was eventually appointed press secretary to the governor for the last few weeks of his term "I've only met him a half a dozen times," said Bowles, when asked about young Bob Silvers.

At the height of the cold war, Silvers served his country in the United States Army, stationed in Paris at (American Congress for Cultural Freedom members, past and present, please note) the SHAPE intelligence library. John P. C. Train, then managing editor of *Paris Review*, a smart little magazine founded by George Plimpton and friends during their lost generation period, introduced Silvers to Plimpton and the *Paris Review* set, which was just coming into its own in the early Fifties. Plimpton and Silvers got along famously as Silvers stepped in and straightened out the unsteady *Paris Review*. "I was impressed by him enormously," observes Plimpton of the friend who would later be best man at his wedding. "The Café Tournon, where we first met, was full of argument then. He was rather shy but formidable and a strong voice amidst all this *Sturm und Drang*. He made the *Paris Review* what it was."

Deactivated from the service in 1953, Silvers stayed on in Paris for another five years, studying, seeing to the *Paris Review*, and doing whatever Americans did there in those days, which included, for Silvers, going to the Ecole des Sciences Politiques, setting up house with Peter Duchin on a Seine River barge perilously anchored at the Porte d'Italie, and dating Joan Fontaine. If GI Bill payments lapse after a year, how did he survive so long abroad? "Lots of little jobs," he replies, smiling at the thought of his secret. One smiles with him. "Little jobs" is just the kind of understatement that a cinema undercover agent might use. Bob Silvers a former CIA operative? *Incroyable!* Bob Silvers, a promising enlistee, leaves Army intelligence and periodically dashes into the cold for his government under the cover of the *Paris Review*. John Train, the original contact man now a financial speculator in New York, refuses to talk. Silvers' *Who's Who* biography shows no visible means of support for the five years in question. It all fits, but the scenario is pure balderdash.

Silvers did have a CIA connection, all right, but nothing so romantic as spying. He became briefly—and almost certainly unwittingly—an accessory in the CIA's cold war against communism by co-editing the World Assembly of Youth's quarterly magazine *WAY Forum* (25 Rue d'Astorg, Paris 8e). His name can be found on Numbers 26 and 27 published in June and December 1957. During Silvers' six-month tenure, *WAY Forum* carried such winning free-world send-ups as "Industrial Work and Leisure in the United States" by David Riesman and Warner Bloomberg, "An Interview with Hagib Bourguiba," "The Case for Kenyan Independence" by Tom 'Mboya, and "Memories of Childhood" by Kwame Nkrumah. According to the legend on *WAY Forum's* subscription blank, the World Assembly of Youth was "an organization through which young people work together on common interests, for freedom, and for social, economic, and political democracy. It promotes international understanding by providing a setting for young people to meet, to consider common problems and to evolve solutions. Through its field staff, publications, mutual self-help programmes, leadership training institute and seminars, and the educational exchange of youth leaders, WAY seeks to strengthen and enrich youth work throughout the world." What the promo did not declare, and probably what Silvers did not realize at the time, was that CIA funny money through grants from its witting conduit, the Foundation for Youth and Student Affairs, was footing the Assembly's bills. (See *The New York Times*, February 16, 1967.) Silvers then must join the line-up of known CIA dupes, which includes many top-seeded New York intellectuals in both the Left and Right factions. Having been co-editor of WAY *Forum* in one's youth is truly nothing to be ashamed of or something one should feel constrained to pass over in one's *Who's Who* biography.

Francine Gray, who writes elegant Movement reportage in the *New York Review*, crossed paths with Silvers briefly in Paris. Her recollection is of an unsettled, twenty-six-year-old displaced American more apt to go to the Comédie Française than to discuss politics. "There was always this aura of brilliance around Bob, although he hadn't accomplished much by that time. People said he had the highest IQ of anyone of his generation. When one met him one found an extremely quiet, diffident, but terribly curious young man. He had no idea of what he wanted to do with his life—like an Arab wandering in the desert with a bag of diamonds on his back.

"He knew everybody in the city, but had no allegiance to anybody. He still retains the friendship of Parisians of *ancien régime* tendencies. Although he has many friends on the Left who are ardent Castroites or whatever, he has never fallen into any category of leftism."

Harper's editor, John Fischer, was on the lookout for new editorial talent in 1958. Francis Plimpton, an upper-crust lawyer and former UN diplomat, as well as George's father, recommended Silvers.[9] After some brief negotiations in Paris, Fisher gained not only an ambitious sub-editor, but a probable successor. "You know I'm not going to be there forever," he said to Silvers. It was an inviting pitch. So the expatriate came home in quest of literary fortune, which, he made certain, would not be long in arriving.

He took a tiny apartment in George Plimpton's building and moved easily into the upper reaches of his good friend's glittering social network. Much has been written of George Plimpton's midwifery in the alliance of intellectuals and the "beautiful people" in the Sixties. He was very thick with the Kennedys until the end of Camelot, when he wrestled down Sirhan Sirhan in the kitchen of the Ambassador Hotel, and knew every writer worth knowing. Podhoretz has compared his return to New York in the late Fifties with De Gaulle's return to France after World War II. In the sober *Public Interest*, Irving Kristol and Paul Weaver pinpointed the editorial circle of *The New York Review of Books* as "an odd almagam of journalists, cultural entrepreneurs, and a healthy slice of café society" whose "central figure is not a Koestler nor an Orwell but . . . George Plimpton" (Summer 1969).

Isn't this a bit much? "No," says Plimpton, lounging in his half court living room, which overlooks the East River for almost a block on East 72nd Street. "This place used to be a spot where *New York Review* and *Paris Review* people used to come in and out. It was Elaine's [an upper East Side watering hole for arrived writers] before there was an Elaine's." It was also where Bob Silvers entertained his own guests.

At *Harper's*, Silvers was in charge of *belles lettres* and, curiously, kept his distance from the political and muckraking streams of the magazine. He introduced faces that were new to

9. The elder Plimpton was also a director of The Foundation for Youth and Student Affairs.

Harper's—like Elizabeth Hardwick, Benjamin De Mott, Mary McCarthy, Paul Goodman, Robert Brustein, Kingsley Amis, Alfred Kazin, and Plimpton—and conceived special supplements on Russia, writing in America, and religion in America. As eligible bachelor and *Harper's papabile*, he was very much in demand in those days. "Really, I need a fourteen-day week to go to all the parties," he complained to a colleague. "Bob can be thrilling company," the colleague went on. "He can be very worshipful and has a sense of who's going to be important." Whenever Jason Epstein's name came up prior to *New York Review*, a Random and *Review* writer recalls, Silvers would say, "Jason's my best friend."

Despite the quality and output of his editing, however, accession to Fischer's chair wasn't in the cards. He just didn't get along with the team. A combination of eccentric working habits (he would disappear for days on a project) and a distressing intellectual arrogance ruined his chances. In editorial meetings, Silvers would utter scathing criticisms of other editors' articles but forbid round-table discussion of his own pieces. If you had to make comments, you could make them in private. "Bob wasn't impressed with his co-editors and seemed to upstage them," remembers a former *Harper's* staffer. The junior editor was particularly restive in the area of literary criticism. He had a heated disagreement with Fischer over the editor-in-chief's column in praise of James Gould Cozzens' atrocious bestseller, *By Love Possessed*, and wrote a memo on the weakness of the deceased Katherine Gauss Jackson's book section. According to the then managing editor, Russell Lynes, Silvers was too highbrow for Fischer. "Jack was probably relieved when Silvers quit, because his idea of the magazine was so different from Silvers'." An outsider who hung around with Silvers while he was at *Harper's* interprets his conduct there as a spillover of nervous energy: "Bob always acted as if he already were editor of the *New York Review*." When Silvers cleaned out his office, Fischer says he at least was sorry to see him go (but not sufficiently sorry to assure that he remain). "If I told Bob he would have been editor at some time in the future, I think he might have stayed. Such was a possibility, but by no means a certainty. I thought he was still a young and relatively undeveloped editor and would have liked him to have had more experience."

Silvers isn't the same editor today that he was at *Harper's*. "Bob has changed," says a friend who has known him since Paris. "Success has been a marvelous thing. It has helped him develop sweetness and generosity." Anyway, at *New York Review*, there were few people to be intellectually arrogant to. Instead of going underground with projects, Silvers punches the clock unmercifully. A regular workaholic, he is at his desk until seven or after nearly every night and hits the office on weekends as well. (Perhaps this is the inspiration for the office graffito, borrowed from the ILGWU subway poster, "If you don't come in on Sunday, don't come in on Monday.") Two secretaries on separate shifts fall behind his marathon pace. "He's a competent and brilliant man," says a depleted ex-secretary, "but an absent-minded professor to work for." But who wouldn't be absent-minded, putting out a paper as fully packed as the *New York Review* every other week? Jealously guarding their editorial prerogatives, Silvers and Epstein haven't hired the kind of help that could ease the load. Eve Auchincloss, who quit the *Review* in 1967 for *Book World*, was the only associate editor it ever had, and even she was no more than a water-bearer. "Title notwithstanding," she says, "all I did was paste up dummies, scale pictures, style copy, and proofread. I had nothing to do with anything involving policy decisions or even decisions about reviewers, books, etcetera."

Obviously Silvers Stylites thrives on this voluntary asceticism, and self-interested *Review* writers wouldn't have him otherwise. He is almost unanimously acclaimed, begrudgingly by enemies and ecstatically by sympathizers, as a master technician. "He's the best literary editor I've ever known, a marvelous reader," attests Alfred Kazin. "He is utterly admirable." Murray Kempton heartily concurs: "Silvers has some of Trilling's critical qualities and an almost novelistic ability to see someone else's point of view. He's also good at keeping me from making a fool of myself in the last three paragraphs."

Silvers' modus operandi, give or take a few variations, is a thing of beauty. First the book or books are posted anonymously to the potential reviewer—a cute piece of psy-war, because the receiver is thrown off balance wondering, "Who sent me this package, and what does it mean?" Then, in the words of an *NYR* critic who has been here before, "an ass-licking letter of fulsome praise" telling you that you are the only one on God's earth capable of reviewing this book and that you'll have as much space as you need. Now Silvers has you where he wants you—in possession of the book (all the better to incite guilt feelings if you're thinking of refusing) and a letter that is difficult to disagree with (since you *are* the best person for the book). While the review is in the writing, Silvers peppers the author with additional books and essays bearing on the subject. A prodigious memory with an instant retrieval system ferrets out tiny bits of related material. If the matter is current events rather than a review, Silvers will be on the phone with useful updates, as he was with Eqbal Ahmad's "Letter to a Pakistani Diplomat" (September 2, 1971). Ahmad, a Pakistani scholar and the "outside agitator" in the Harrisburg Seven conspiracy case, sent Silvers a copy of a letter he had addressed to a countryman critic on his dim view of General Yahya Khan's military intervention in East Bengal. Ahmad wanted to know if Silvers would entertain an article based on the brief note. Silvers figured why not publish the note itself. Ahmad agreed and then took off for Cape Cod on a fundraising tour, content to let the matter go. But not Silvers, who tracked his quarry down at Robert Jay Lifton's duneside summer place in Wellfleet. Was Ahmad aware that such and such had occurred in the meantime? Would he like to add a paragraph? Ahmad is an editor of the Paris-based *Africasia* and knows the journalistic ropes, but this sort of assiduousness he had never seen.

If an author's line is busy, even in Manhattan, Silvers may telegraph him information that might have waited for the morrow. Karl Meyer, former correspondent and editorial writer for the *Washington Post*, still marvels at the telegram Silvers sent him the Sunday after John Kennedy was shot. Meyer had just turned in a review of *The Senate Establishment* by Senator Joseph Clark *et al.* (January 9, 1964), but he was numb that crazy weekend like everyone else and never gave the Clark piece a thought—until, that is, Silvers' wire arrived: "ASSUMING THE REVIEW WILL BE DRASTICALLY REVISED IN VIEW OF EVENTS AND HOPE YOU CAN DELIVER BY WEDNESDAY."

The actual editing of the manuscript is an exercise of devotion—Aschenbach between the candles. Silvers is not a nuts-and-bolts editor like Podhoretz, who, according to tradition, can make a stumblebum read like Macaulay. Silvers suggests revisions in arguments rather than in prose. Consuming himself completely in the labors of other men's minds, he serves by assuring that their ideas are presented clear and distinct in the pages of *New York Review*. In this vocation, he is sainted, his only weaknesses being powerlessness against length and deference toward giants. At last, the exquisitely handled review is delivered to the sender for final inspection. It may even come by motorcycle if you live in the metropolitan area. "Silvers never spares the horses," says I. F. Stone. Or the horsepower. Rarely will there be any major objections at this stage. H. Stuart Hughes blew his stack over editorial changes which Silvers effected in his review of some books on J. Robert Oppenheimer (July 2, 1970). "Often the changes showed he didn't know what he was doing." Silvers capitulated. The original passages were restored. But the Hughes incident was an aberration. When El Exigente approves, the people are usually happy.

Silvers has mellowed some since *Harper's*.

Item: a female caucus at *NYR* badgers him about sending feminist books to male reviewers; he desists and dispatches a batch of fem lib lit to Susan Sontag.

Item: Silvers' secretary objects to the narrow elitist scope of a prison report on Philip Berrigan (not enough on his comrades behind bars), so Silvers grafts on a couple of sympathetic sentences for the downtrodden convicts before consulting the author.

Item: Silvers sends an article by Eugene Genovese to radical feminist Ellen Willis for appraisal. "He was talking about housewives being economic parasites, which is like saying slaves are economic parasites because they stay on the plantation." She gave Genovese a bad mark, and the paper was never published in *NYR*.

Curiosity Silvers has in abundance. He was fascinated by the ongoing debate over the Kennedy assassination. He arranged a Theater of Ideas round table on the subject, attended rap sessions with buddy Jones Harris of the freelance Committee to Investigate Assassinations, and even had a private audience with Lee Oswald's mother. He knew his stuff inside out. "It was just Bob's sort of thing," says one listener of the period. "He could give the most extraordinary spiels." Then, of course, there was Popkin's "The Second Oswald" and "The Case for Garrison" in the *Review*. "This was the only weakness I've seen in Bob as an editor," remarks Plimpton. "He was absolutely preoccupied by the assassination, riveted by it. Having gotten the tiger by the tail, he couldn't let it go."

When Bob Silvers the editor turns into Bob Silvers the lion-hunter after hours, he appears to be mesmerized by celebrity. A well-known New York cartoonist and writer has remarked, "The worst thing I can say about Bob Silvers is that he's the headwaiter of journalism." Or, from another observer, "He has what I call 'Sardi eyes.' " To Marion Sanders, a *Harper's* editor who cut in on Silvers at the wrong time at a party, he said, "Really, can't you see I'm talking to Lionel Trilling?" "It was as if Trilling were a god," Sanders recalls, "and Trilling stood there *like* a god!" A writer of middling renown used to appear fairly often in the *Review*. His dealings with Silvers were cordial, but never warm. Then the writer was elevated to one of New York's most coveted literary posts. Suddenly Silvers was falling over him. But when the post was vacated, Silvers split. The writer was never asked over to the *Review* again.

How lethal are these judgments of character? That depends on what you expect from the editor of the *New York Review*. Personality is beside the point. What should we care if Silvers looks up to heaven every day and thanks God for making him more like his friends George Plimpton, Peter Duchin, Richard Wollheim, Stuart Hampshire, and Jonathan Miller than the rest of men? If he wants to talk to Lionel Trilling without interruption, that's not too much to ask. You don't have to love Bob Silvers to love his magazine. A modicum of disedification goes with the territory. To paraphrase Leo Durocher, nice editors finish last. But a master morality, the elevation of oneself beyond good and evil, is something else.

Some of his contributors suggest that Silvers has difficulty coming right out with negative decisions affecting *Review* writers. "Silvers hates scenes and contretemps," says Murray Kempton, "and avoids direct fights." This abhorrence of confrontation has occasionally led, according to a former *Review* staffer, to his allowing his doubts about a controversial review to be carried under his co-editor's sponsorship.

The notion of Bob Silvers as editorial reed blowing with the *Zeitgeist* also has its revisionary angle. Francine Gray was in Silvers' company when a Left celebrity decreed that he would neither criticize anyone on the Left nor associate with anyone who criticized anybody on the Left. "Bob almost had a fit. I've never seen him so excited or appalled. Bob is very moderate and critical—like a microscope always shifting the focus of the lens.

He doesn't hang on to old columnists, but switches to new ones for fresh analysis."

Isn't that what an editor is supposed to do? Just as Stone clashed with the liberal gilt of *The New York Review of Each Other's Books*, Andrew Kopkind would stick out like a sore thumb in today's calmed-down *Review*. There is nothing less powerful than a fashion whose time has gone. Editors Irving Howe and Norman Podhoretz can better afford to swim against the tide. *Dissent*'s expenses are a pittance compared to the *Review*'s, and *Commentary*'s deficits are in the good hands of the American Jewish Committee. Silvers, on the other hand, must ride the crest of the future wave. It is foolhardy to bracket the *Review* off from the marketplace of the marketplace and wish Silvers had the ideological consistency of Dorothy Day. The *New York Review* pays; Miss Day has to beg for her living.

Discovering Silvers' ideological whereabouts would be simplified if the *Review* only published editorials. But oddly, it does not. *New York Times Book Review* editor John Leonard has "The Last Word" column; Philip Rahv had "This Quarter" in *Modern Occasions*; Norman Podhoretz speaks in "Issues" in *Commentary*; Irving Howe pens his editorials in *Dissent*; and lately William Phillips has been forewording for *Partisan Review*. But Silvers hands us a stone. Research discloses his signature attached to just three works, none involving his own prose. He interviewed Françoise Sagan with Blair Fuller for the *Paris Review*. (Since tape recorders were not quite so portable in the Fifties, the *Paris Review* interviewers used to travel in pencil-pushing pairs.) He translated a short book called *La Gangrène* about the torture of five Algerian political prisoners in Paris in 1958. When *Harper's* ran an excerpt, no translator was listed. The only real piece of prose that can be attributed to Silvers—"A Letter to a Young Man About to Enter Publishing" from *Harper's* "Writing in America" supplement—was signed "Anonymous." When *Writing in America* was brought out in book form

as edited by John Fischer and Robert B. Silvers, Silvers was the
only person absent from the contributor's page.

Why doesn't Silvers write? "I have a sense that he was
uneasy about writing," says Plimpton. "The idea of working with
so many people's brains seems more exciting to him than working
alone." Karl Meyer goes deeper: "Silvers is in the tradition of
great editors like Harold Ross and Henry Luce who, because
they lacked personality themselves, absorbed like sponges everything around them and created an artificial personality." When
the author sought Silvers' explanation, he responded, "Isn't there
always someone better?"

The fatso in the *New York* photo no longer exists in the
natural state. The thin man screaming to break out of chubby
Bob Silvers for forty years emerged in 1970 with the collusion of
How To Stay Fit and Young Over Forty by Leeland Kordell.
A diet of health foods, fruit, and vitamin pills fights a winning
battle against recidivism. He is an aficionado of boxing and talks
a better game of tennis than he plays. "He tends to scramble
around the court," says Plimpton. The new Bob Silvers has
recently immersed himself in an arcane form of high karate taught
by a lone Chinese guru in New York. As for women, the current
interest in a passing parade of aristocratic beauties is Lady Dudley, née Grace Kolin, the elder daughter of Dr. Michael Kolin
of St. Jacob, Dubrovnik, third wife of the late third Earl of
Dudley and former wife of Prince Stanislas Radziwill, who subsequently married Lee Bouvier (sister of Jacqueline Kennedy
Onassis) after her divorce from the late Michael Canfield of the
Harper & Row Canfields, who was afterward wed to Viscountess
Laura Long, the second wife of the third Earl of Dudley.

Thus the enigma of Bob Silvers is not such a conundrum
after all. Or it is? One hears that Silvers is a wizard swimmer,
impervious to tide and temperature. Yet irreconcilable reports
coexist on the fundamental matter of his stroke. Bowden Broadwater's "black shark" is George Plimpton's "dying polar bear."

The Intelligentsia at War

tered. (If they couldn't refer to 1967, or so it seems, *NYR* critics would be out of work.) Allowing for the too synthetic a priori nature of his judgment,[1] and the arbitrary selection of evidence, Wrong put on an exemplary polemic. Laid end to end, his arguments were shrewdly constructed and sometimes irrefutable. But for cross-examination, "The Case" would be open and shut.

Wrong singled out two writers—Noam Chomsky and Edgar Z. Friedenberg—as *loci classici* of everything untoward at the *Review*. Wrong has spoken elsewhere of Chomsky ("Of Thinking and Moralizing", *Dissent*, January-February 1970), so he didn't dwell on the man here. Anyway, since the publication of *At War With Asia*—a series of pieces based on Chomsky's tour of Indochina, much of which appeared in *NYR*—Chomsky is scarcely worth engaging, in Wrong's eyes. "For all their display of the apparatus of careful scholarship, it is hard to see how anyone but the already persuaded could take Chomsky's articles seriously any longer, or even bother to read them for that matter." What hath Chomsky wrought to deserve this terminal reproof? Just a year previously in *Dissent*, hadn't Wrong compared him favorably, despite alleged excesses, to J. Robert Oppenheimer apropos of scientific career and "political sensibility"? Apparently, Chomsky's hasty fall from grace had to do with two mortal sins committed in *At War With Asia*. Wrong ridiculed Chomsky for (1) "suddenly discovering that the 'controlling assumption' behind US misadventures in Southeast Asia is the desire to maintain Vietnam as a market for Japan" and (2) for the exaggeration of the title *At War With Asia*. Chomsky is wasted in half a page!

Edgar Z. Friedenberg, a professor of education at Dalhousie

1. Wrong had already shown his repulsion for *NYR* in a *Commentary* article (July 1969) on Christopher Lasch's *The Agony of the American Left*, which was excerpted in *NYR*, and stated in a letter to the editor of *Esquire* (July 1972) that, upon receiving his commission from Podhoretz, he "welcomed the opportunity to articulate my growing distaste for the *New York Review*'s fashionable radicalism."

University in Nova Scotia and a prolific all-around reviewer for
NYR, gets more space in Wrong's onslaught, but no more enlight-
enment. According to the Wrong–*Commentary* dope sheet, Friedenberg's problem is the same as Chomsky's. He is "given to such
extreme and absolute statements imputing evil designs to large
numbers of Americans that one is often inclined to dismiss him as
simply overwrought." The first citation of extravagance is Friedenberg's "As Kent State goes, so goes the nation" maxim and
"the honkies are killing us" remark (both uttered in response to
Jack Richardson's review of *Slaughterhouse Five*, which belittled
Vonnegut's political usefulness). Wrong claims he was shocked
"at the spectacle of a Jewish intellectual characterizing the bulk
of the citizenry by means of a derisive epithet originally applied
to Slavic immigrants and then adopted by Negroes to refer to
whites." Second, back in a 1965 piece on Erik Erikson, Friedenberg suggested that in "the age of the anti-hero" such public
figures as Adlai Stevenson, Nelson Rockefeller, Robert Kennedy,
Robert Wagner, and Leonard Bernstein might not fill the bill as
Erikson's "significant persons" deserving identification by youth.
Third, Friedenberg mentioned Abbie Hoffman and Dave Dellinger as contemporaries "of noble intent" possessing a "vision of
excellence." Fourth, in the same article (a review of Philip Slater's *The Pursuit of Loneliness* and George Grant's *Technology
and Empire*, June 4, 1970), Wrong is grateful that Friedenberg
stops short of justifying slavery after observing that "In pre-
industrial Southern towns and cities, there were no black ghettos
and no need for them—racial castes provided a more than adequate substitute for racial segregation, and the presence of black
residents was not perceived by whites as a threat to the neighborhood."

Surely, if Wrong wanted to defenestrate Friedenberg as an
NYR ikon, he could have done better than this. Friedenberg
seems to be more sensitive than most *Commentary* writers to the

evils our democracy permits, and he is the author of many hard sayings, but none of the positions Wrong ascribes to him is manifestly "overwrought." Even the Kent State quote doesn't look so hyperbolic in retrospect, what with the prosecution (albeit unsuccessful) of Kent State student and faculty demonstrators and former Attorney General John Mitchell's refusal to bring the murderous guardsmen to trial.

Fortunately for him, Wrong knows why the running dogs at the *New York Review* do as they do. While other critics have attributed their New Leftism to the desire to be with it, Wrong plunges into their collective unconscience for the answer. "The abandonment of past beliefs precipitated by the Vietnam war," the diagnosis goes, "has been *remissive* in its psychological impact on many of the *NYR* intellectuals. They have experienced a sense of liberation, of expanding horizons, of the rekindling of long-buried sentiments, of the exultant hanging of question marks on what were thought to be settled and thus boring issues. In the late Fifties, Daniel Bell rather smugly referred to his generation of intellectuals as a 'twice-born' generation; if so, then a fair number of them have been born for a third time in the Sixties." Who are these unnamed political Lazaruses chez *New York Review*, who have been raised from their dead anti-Red/pro-US ideology of the Fifties, only to return to their pro-Red/anti-US ideology of the Thirties? Stone? Chomsky? Steel? Lasch? Genovese? Kempton? Goodman? Sheldon Wolin and John Schar? Wilson? Rahv? Macdonald? McCarthy? The last three mentioned are the only ones who could possibly qualify in age and temperament. Irving Kristol gets specific where Wrong generalizes about this supposed ideological regression. "The typical case is Mary McCarthy, he says. "She was so sophisticated and tough-minded about contemporary ideologies and now she's so girlish. She was way beyond Marx. It was an example of a highly complex intelligence simplifying itself politically. This happened to Dwight Macdonald too. Lots of people who used to have complicated ideas in the Fifties hungered after simplicities in the Sixties." As Daniel Bell put it, McCarthy moved "from intellectual to moralizer" (*NYR*, February 29, 1968).

Regardless of the fit of Kristol's description, Rahv, Macdonald, and McCarthy have entered their politics in *New York Review* so spasmodically that Wrong cannot build his remission theory on them. He was seduced into this scenario by Susan Sontag's admission in *Styles of Radical Will* that "only within the last two years (and that very much because of the impact of the Vietnam war) have I been able to pronounce the words 'capitalism' and 'imperialism' again." Sontag's personal testament fitted so beautifully into Wrong's anti-thesis that he couldn't help stretching it to encompass a whole class—despite the fact that Sontag never wrote about politics in the *Review*.

All along, Wrong has been guilty of the same procedural error he linked to Chomsky—that of deducing harsh judgments from the premises of an intensive description of a highly particular and local situation, which can in no way logically support one's conclusion. If Chomsky was to be taken to task for manipulating evidence to suit preordained purposes, then so ought Wrong. For example, why was he so conveniently inattentive to the contributions of Arendt, Lichtheim, and Morgenthau? Why should Chomsky and Friedenberg be considered any more representative of the *Review*'s outlook than Goodman, Lasch, Robert Heilbroner, Kempton, or Stone, who barely rate better than passing mention? Why did he pick out John McDermott's special supplement "Technology: The Opiate of the Intellectuals" for synecdochic scrutiny and evade J. M. Cameron's "The Ethics of Violence" or Ronald Dworkin's "On Taking Rights Seriously"? Perhaps because "The Case" would have been more difficult to prove if the entire testimony were heard.

The *New York Review* had blundered egregiously in the past. And Wrong was often quite right when pointing out its past shortcomings. Still, he grants that the *Review* has recoiled from total and open identification with revolutionary romanticism, that Kopkind, Carmichael, and Hayden had disappeared from its pages, that it had been more disciplined and less defamatory than either the *Village Voice* or *Ramparts,* that strict standards had been maintained versus cultural swingers like Warhol and the Living Theater, and that *NYR* has "published valuable essays on American society and the university, critical of both contemporary radicalism and official liberals." What more could Wrong have asked from *New York Review?* That it flee naked from the New Left and become another *Commentary?* He seemed to leave no other alternative.

Like those that preceded him, Wrong ultimately condemns *New York Review* General Yamashita-style, not for what it has directly ordered, but for the crimes of its troops. Radicals, you see, are blithely pushing on to an apocalyptic climax, which they hope will result in a revolutionary millennium or, if need be, a fascist reaction stage preliminary to an even wider revolt of the masses. For encouraging, accommodating, and cloaking the apocalyptic tendencies of the New Left with intellectual respectability, the *Review* was judged by Wrong an accessory in the coming "confrontation on all fronts between the Movement at its arrogant, mindless worst and the demagogic, patrioteering Right."

* * *

Who is Dennis Wrong and why did he say those terrible things about *New York Review?* Dennis Wrong, forty-nine, is a sociologist by trade, a member of the faculty at New York University, and an expert in population studies and Max Weber. He's never had a hot book like Michael Harrington (*The Other America*) or Nathan Glazer (co-author of *The Lonely Crowd* and *Beyond the Melting Pot*) or a very large place in the intellectual sun like Howe or Hook, but he has been a steady performer in

Dissent and *Commentary*. As Podhoretz avowed, explaining his
choice for the assignment, "Wrong is detached enough to do this
sort of criticism. He has no special personal grievance."

Wrong was agreeable to a conference in an Eighth Street bar
around the corner from his office. He is frank and unassuming
about the article. He wrote it because Podhoretz asked him, and
because the pay was higher than usual. Did he regret anything
he said? Well, there were a couple mistakes about who does and
doesn't appear in the *Review* (C. Vann Woodward is back, and
Walter Laqueur is out), and I. F. Stone's hair-raising article on
Israel was *not NYR*'s only incursion into the thicket of Middle
East politics since the Six Day War. Also, the reproach, of "anti-
Americanism" which Wrong employed to define the basic political
stand of the *Review* stirred up an incommensurate amount of
controversy. "I'm sorry I used the word. But it was the most
descriptively accurate term. Better than New Left. Anti-Americanism is a proneness and readiness to find an anti-American angle
in anything the *Review* writers do. I meant it as a pejorative,
because finding an anti-American slant everywhere is just as negative and unproductive as finding an anti-communist slant everywhere. I also wanted to make the point that this was a fixed
position around which they operate." That is about the extent
of Wrong's retreat. His long triumphalist reply to a slew of negative letters in a later *Commentary* merely hardened his opposition. Privately, however, Wrong acknowledges he was caught up
in *Commentary*'s crusade against the counter-culture. "I wish I
had developed my own ideas more," he said. "Podhoretz wants
people to be more aggressive. I was afraid people would think
that I was an instrument of his revenge; but the money was so
good." To be sure, both author and editor were of like mind,
if not emotion, on *The New York Review of Books*. Whether
or not Wrong was susceptible to over-coaching, there is no doubt
it was his time (summer vacation) and trouble—not his soul—
that Podhoretz purchased with an extra-special stipend.

Funny, but Wrong doesn't look like one of Chomsky's "terrors of our age." He is, instead, Central Casting's idea of the tweedy professor, full of Chipsean charm and temper. Throughout the interview, he is refreshingly relaxed and unguarded about coping with mild-mannered questions from the Left. Why, for instance, have he and his colleagues been so alienated by the Movement's vehement reaction to Vietnam when all parties agree as to its evil, if not criminality? "We don't feel that rage. Is this the ultimate crime after Stalin and Hitler? I find the reaction excessive. Vietnam isn't important. It's a nasty little war. The Korean War wasn't all that different. The most morally shocking thing was the invasion of the Dominican Republic. It was what Chomsky wants to make out of Vietnam—a misapplication of cold-war concepts where they were once applied correctly."

But just as the young Wrong rallied against Hitler's crimes, can't he sympathize with the resistance of today's youth to an aggressive war waged not by a foreign madman, but by their own government? "Our own political pasts are an obstacle in opposing the war. A lot of us are tied in by cold-war assumptions." What, specifically, did he object to in the New Left position on Vietnam? "I don't believe that the war follows from the nature of American society or that vested interests are involved in its continuance." Whence, therefore, Wrong's stand on Vietnam? "If I thought that the arguments advanced for the war were true, then I would be for the war; if the domino theory worked, then I could see the war the way John Roche does."

This last attitude bears a family resemblance to the pragmatic school of warfare which many American intellectuals, Chomsky insists, faithfully attend. Pragmatism teaches that war is okay as long as you win, but unacceptable if you happen to lose. Thus, Arthur Schlesinger wrote in *The Bitter Heritage* that if the Vietcong had been defeated, we might "all be saluting the wisdom and the statesmanship of the American government."

The difference between Dennis Wrong and Noam Chomsky

can be illustrated by their respective postures on the Bundys. Wrong, the son of a Canadian diplomat, was reared in Washington. "I grew up with the Bundy boys. I can't regard them as war criminals." Chomsky, while the FBI was hunting down Daniel Ellsberg, picketed William Bundy's home in Cambridge to draw attention to the "real criminal" of Vietnam.

Norman Podhoretz, as is his custom when someone figures in a *Commentary* article, sent Murray Kempton a letter asking him if he cared to reply to Wrong. Kempton declined. "There's a lack of manners here," he would confide a few weeks after the deed. " 'You must be kidding,' I wrote back to Podhoretz. *Commentary* has reached a point in its circulation where there are no more witnesses to the act. Am I the best person to comment on what's said about me? What distresses me, underneath all this nastiness, is the impression that you're in nothing but a personal quarrel. What is moving Norman and Wrong is that they're not being taken seriously. They're continuously bleeding from scars where no one ever touched them. I feel that Silvers upstaged these guys." Kempton is a gifted conversationalist and does love to talk, especially over the telephone. He proceeds uninterrupted. "*Commentary* has a fake independence. The American Jewish Committee has no other function than to tell Jews to love the United States. Originally, the AJC was anti-Zionist. Podhoretz could play with the Left in the early Sixties, and then when young Jews ran away with heresies, he had to hold the line. I think he's representing the board, which is scared stiff of Protestant-baiting. Some of Podhoretz's best friends are Episcopalians."

The rumble of "The Case of the *New York Review*" was heard around the East and shook loose much leftish polemic. A leisurely *tour d'horizon* to survey the feeling about the *Review* uncovers no discernible shifts in loyalty. Wrong merely reconfirmed the suspicions of the *Review*'s enemies and appalled or bored its disciples.

b/The Right Faction

Irving Howe, fifty-three, ushers the visitor into his study high above the Hudson River on West Side Drive. He excuses himself in order to finish belting out a letter in progress. The "iron smile" Robert Lowell pasted on him in a derogatory poem entitled "The New York Intellectual"[2] is not immediately discerned. But Howe may reasonably be characterized as the "iron man," the Lou Gehrig of the Old Left, who is always there when you need him with a clutch position paper on the cold war, Vietnam, Eugene

2. From *Notebook 1967–68*, Revised and Expanded Edition:

> How often was this last salute recast?
> Did Irving really want three hundred words . . .
> How often one would choose the poorman's provincial
> out of town West Side intellectual
> for the great brazen rhetorician serpent,
> swimming the current with his iron smile!

McCarthy, confrontation, or sexual politics. In recent years, he has served as the Left's chief of protocol, correcting the manners of apocalypticians and calling for coalition always and everywhere.

He is now through mauling his typewriter. He swivels around, uneager but ready for another go in this marathon *mano a mano* between the Right and Left factions. So much happened since 1968 that one wonders whether Howe stands by his *Commentary* critique of the *Review*. Is *NYR* still guilty of handing out intellectual respectability to unworthy causes? "Yes, it's still true," he says, citing José Yglesias' lead article on the troubles of Cuban poet Herberto Padilla (June 3, 1971). Yglesias protested Castro's jailing of Padilla and the forced confession of the poet's counterrevolutionary sins. "It now falls to those of us," Yglesias wrote, "who are his friends as well as friends of the Cuban revolution to suffer the anguish—perhaps for more than whole hours— of the image that he and the revolution offer us of themselves."

"The Padilla piece is very interesting," according to Howe. "I'm very glad these guys signed the petition ["An Open Letter to Fidel Castro" signed by Sartre, de Beauvoir, Moravia, *et al.*, and published in the *Review*]. But people were in jail before Padilla. Yglesias kept quiet then. To say that Cuba was a model of socialism until the Padilla incident is grotesque. Yglesias wrote in sorrow more than anger and within the premises of Castroism. Before, the *Review* might have had someone else writing this kind of article saying, 'This is what happens in a one-party state.' My guess is, four or five years ago, they would have taken a different tack."

The presence of Hannah Arendt in the *Review* doesn't alter Howe's judgment a jot. "She's a big name and a distinguished person, and Silvers needs big names for his cover. It's also obvious that he's prepared to run things critical of the New Left. But he won't take people who make a sharp attack on the Left from the Left point of view. Arendt is out of this particular fight.

"There's a strong streak of authoritarianism in the New Left," Howe concludes, "and I feel that the *New York Review* has indulged in it or insufficiently attacked it. And the *Review* has, with one or two exceptions, glorified the third world revolutions. Silvers has printed a good deal of material which goes along with, plays into the hands of, and threatens, in my opinion, liberal institutions. Yglesias' piece, for example, was written within the orbit of acceptance of an authoritarian regime, that one should support Castroism minus the outrage of Padilla.

"The *Review* has no feeling of identification with those places in the world where significant social reforms have taken hold, and where democracy is preserved—Israel and Sweden, for instance. I think the crucial political lesson of the twentieth century is that socialism is impossible without democracy. This is the beginning and the end of wisdom on the Left. And I'm going to fight with anyone on the Left who says otherwise. I hate what's being done in Vietnam, but I won't let myself be driven into the grips of undemocratic politics."[3]

*   *   *

Michael Harrington is one of the few professed socialists who looks like he just might be a socialist—that is, if dungarees, wrinkled shirt, and general dishevelment are integral to the socialist *toilette*. Even the lower Broadway headquarters of the American Socialist Party, of which he was chairman until October 1972, appears to have been transported—paint chip by paint chip —from some Eastern European People's Republic. After only a minute of the interview, it is clear that note-taking won't do for

3. Howe reiterated his belief in the absolute primacy of political freedom at a University of Texas symposium early in 1972. Implicitly, his remark was directed toward *New York Review:* "The obligation to defend and extend freedom in its simplest and most fundamental aspects is the sacred task of the intellectual, the one task he must not compromise, even when his posture seems untractable, or unreasonable, or hopeless, or even when it means standing alone against fashionable shibboleths like revolution and the third world." (*The New York Times*, April 10, 1972.)

Harrington's rapid-fire speech. A tape recorder is introduced. The playback sounds incredibly like the clipped voice of Mort Sahl.

Harrington, forty-five, is a lesser evilist who could have voted in good conscience for regular Democrat Henry "Scoop" Jackson over both Nixon and a splinter peace candidate if the occasion had arisen. Though an ardent foe of the Vietnam war, he believes the peace movement may have been counterproductive and scorns the Berrigans for taking the easy way out. A working-class hero, Harrington gets his cues from the majority. Vietnam is a vivid example of where he and the *Review* parted company:

"At every point in the struggle to end the war, in addition to the ideal that the United States should get out of Vietnam, the major determinant of my position was where the American people were. My position in all things in the last ten years has been a next-step position. I try to define my ultimate aims as clearly as possible, but then dialectically to find where in American society is the next step toward peace. And I felt that the wing of the peace movement with which the *Review* was associated was self-righteous, gesture-oriented, would wave a Vietcong flag and not consider whether that might not prolong the war." This kind of thinking prompted one *NYR* regular to say, "The trouble with Howe and Harrington is that whenever they write on politics they begin to sound like Max Lerner."

"I was a conscientious objector during the Korean War. I was prepared to go to jail and fortunately did not have to. Insofar as that represents a giving of witness, I think there are times when one is obliged to do something, even though its political consequences are zero or even negative. There are transcendental obligations which are higher than pragmatic considerations. However, when you talk about ending the war, then I think you are required to look at the pragmatic dimension. It seems to me Chomsky, by putting such a great emphasis on essentially a middle-class mode of resistance that could appeal only to relatively few people on the morality question, did not ask the political question."

The political differences between the Right and Left factions in the New York intelligentsia are so at odds that the similarity of their moral aspirations is disregarded. Does Harrington believe his moral aspirations coincide with the *Review*'s? The query is important and posed too infrequently. "Yes and no," he answers. "If you take the formula of the pre-conservative Jacques Maritain, which I do, that 'means are the ends in the process of becoming,' then differences which appear at first to be differences over means often conceal differences over ends. The fact that a Stalinist will proclaim his fidelity to the end of the classless society, as I will, and that we simply differ whether we do so through totalitarianism and violence, that's not a matter of means but of ends. Obviously, the difference between myself and the *New York Review* is not analogous. No, I don't find an unbridgeable moral gulf. And I even hope that there will be a saner time in this country, particularly when the war is over, when it's possible to build a serious mass movement on domestic social change with some of these people." McGovern, at least, brought Harrington and *NYR* together in 1972; but so did McCarthy in 1968.

* * *

Despite the far distance rightward that Sidney Hook has moved in his old age—to the point of being inducted into Spiro Agnew's shadow cabinet—he is still admired in some Left quarters. Irving Howe, no ally of the later Hook, wrote in "The New York Intellectuals" that "it is a matter of decency to recall the liberating role he played in the Thirties as a spokesman for a democratic radicalism and a fierce opponent of all the rationalization of totalitarianism a good many intellectuals allowed themselves." Of all the old leftists Murray Kempton doesn't commune with any more, he misses Hook the most. "I always felt he was a man of integrity."

True to his more-than-one-beer polemical thirst, for which he has had forty years' practice, Hook, seventy-one, comes on strong against the "penthouse revolutionaries" of the *New York Review*. Did his listener know that I. F. Stone defended the Moscow Trials or that Dwight Macdonald and Paul Goodman opposed the war against Hitler, arguing that the working class had more to fear from Roosevelt than Hitler?

"I would regard the New Left as irresponsible," Hook says of current events. "America can do nothing right. Although they will be critical of the Soviet Union, they certainly aren't as critical of Cuba, whose totalitarianism is just as extreme from the point of view of one-party rule. But now maybe they'll turn against Castro, because it's fashionable. They kept quiet about the people in prison, the absence of elections, the very things we opposed in totalitarian cultures before Cuba. You can't be a Democrat and do that. The difference between the Old Left down on to Norman Thomas and the so-called New Left is that we're Democrats, and I think they have doubts about it. They are prepared to sacrifice democracy for what they regard as social welfare. "Vietnam has little to do with this disenchantment with democracy, because everyone's against the war."

According to Hook, the issue of political responsibility is at stake here. "Just as the extreme Left in the early Forties maintained that there was no difference between the United States and totalitarian countries, that the New Deal was moving toward totalitarianism, now the political gurus either draw an equation between totalitarian powers or they are prepared to abdicate and hope for the downfall of the United States to the Castros, the Che Guevaras, and the underground heroes of the Movement. This analysis I've given you doesn't lie on the surface. Of course, they would deny it."

Such is Hook's contempt for the *NYR* that one cannot help asking if he is more alienated from them or from Nixon. "I think I would have greater chances of survival under the Nixon administration than I would if the people at the *Review* ran the government. After all, they are the people who put a Molotov Cocktail and the instructions on how to make it on the front page."

*   *   *

Midge Decter was the yin half of a once thriving New York magazine dynasty. As executive editor of *Harper's* and Mrs. Norman Podhoretz in real life, she was the linchpin of the alliance—second only in power to the Epsteins at Random House and the *Review*. Nobody noticed the connection much until *Harper's* started publishing uncharacteristically harsh articles on the Panthers and the *Village Voice*. A pretty tough customer in her own right, Decter was a powerfully cohesive force at *Harper's* during the decline and fall of the Willie Morris regime. A run-through of her collected essays in *The Liberated Woman and Other Americans* suggests that husband and wife think and act alike. They are both critical hardliners, entirely at home with unpopular views. For example, Norman and Midge heartily endorsed the middle Mailer in the late Fifties and early Sixties, when Mailer was considered, in then prevailing Family opinion, damaged goods.[4]

The Podhoretzes have set up their redoubt on the corner of West End Avenue and 105th Street, one of the least fashionable spots (typically) on the Upper West Side. Decter, an attractive, sturdy woman of forty-six, receives her late-afternoon visitor dressed in slacks and a loose-fitting blouse. The apartment is cavernous and sparsely decorated. Norman is supposed not to care about money, and it shows. Decter was in voluntary retirement at

---

4. See Podhoretz's "Norman Mailer: The Embattled Vision," 1959; reprinted in *Doings and Undoings*.

the moment of our meeting (she would later become literary editor for *World*, Norman Cousins' remake of *Saturday Review*) and
feeling so fine.

The yang half just now enters after a hard day's day at the
Commentary office. She tells him that Arnold [*Nine Lies About
America*] Beichman called. No doubt the Podhoretzes' close-
ness goes beyond intellect. A good friend says, "It helps me every-
day when I read of the disintegration of the family and marriage
to think of those two." He nods and disappears into the back of
the apartment.

How did it all happen, the visitor asks once and for all? In
the early Sixties, it was Jason and Barbara and Norman and
Midge. Such good friends! "You could see the handwriting on the
wall with Berkeley," she said. "Nat Glazer's Berkeley piece was
rejected at the *Review*, and Jason said he finked out. Then it was
one issue after another—Cuba, Chomsky's 'The Responsibility of
Intellectuals.' Jason wrote an article on 'The CIA and the Intellectuals' after *Ramparts* broke the story. Jason of all people!
Jason, who was shoulder to shoulder with the rest of us, comes on
as the big judge of others. That piece was so ghastly to me,
because it was an ideological distortion of an experience we all
shared in common—such moral bullshit! There was a general
Left theory about intellectuals in the Fifties—Lasch's theory
that Bell and the rest were the grubby sons of immigrants who
were bought off by fat jobs, status, and money. Anyone who was
there knows this wasn't the truth—nobody was bought off.

"Every time we were together we would wind up having
fights. One was arguing with them that this was not Nazi Germany, this was not an imperialist war, and the country wasn't
going fascist. It got to be impossible to have a conversation.
Friendship can't survive politics. Politics is the religion of the
intellectuals, and remember, men have shed blood over the
Eucharist. These are really life and death matters."

David Halberstam, a former *Harper's* operative in Decter's time and a Random House fixture (*The Best and the Brightest*), wasn't anxious to go on the record about *NYR* lest he create more enemies. He has been blunt with Silvers in the past, he says, but has enough to worry about with the best and the brightest after his hide. (His caution would seem unnecessary after Mary McCarthy bit and scratched him in a subsequent *NYR* review of *The Best.*) However, Halberstam did urge sounding out Decter on the sociological underpinnings of the *Review.*

Her interpretation goes thus: "It's more than just radical chic. The American upper class WASP, the blueblood, has been radicalized for some time. He hates the country more than the Black Muslims. The literary community here has always been in love with the upper class, because they have a great common enemy—the bourgeoisie. So you get that and the kids and the blacks, and that's why they turned Left Wing."

Decter offers a unique variation on the theme of the *Review's* swing away from radicalism of the Kopkind sort. "It has shifted now from militancy to popular front. We have entered into that period where the New Left is finished—Panthers, bombers, etcetera. The first popular front statement is, 'I don't like their methods but . . .' This popular front is against the United States, not like the old one, which was organized in the interests of the Soviet Union."

*   *   *

Richard Rovere, fifty-eight, is a little stooped and slow of step as he leads a visitor down a long yellow corridor into his bare office at *The New Yorker.* "I generally agreed with the Wrong piece," he said, sinking deep into his chair. "I've been disappointed in the *Review's* politics, which I think kind of silly. I don't trust Izzy Stone, Malcolm Muggeridge, Conor Cruise O'Brien, not because of their political position, but because of their methods."

Is there some doubt about Stone's methodology? Rovere is asked to elaborate because, Stone, of all polemicists, rests his reputation on digging out the hidden facts.

"If Izzy says on page 537 of such and such a book you'll learn that so and so . . ., I won't believe it. I'll check myself. I don't think he's an honest controversialist. We had to check him every inch of the way when I was at *New Masses* in 1938–39, and just because of the Soviet-Nazi pact. He was more indignant about that pact than anyone I knew. His indignation didn't last long. He was a Stalinist—a loose and nasty term—but by my lights he was. It's not so much being a Stalinist as using their polemical techniques."

For instance? "He did a series in the *Review* on disarmament.[5] Stone said the Atom Treaty was a fake because there was more underground testing after the treaty than before, that the treaty was a fraud because it didn't lead to disarmament. But that wasn't the purpose, which was actually to depollute the atmosphere and get a treaty with Russia. The rise in underground testing was no special insight because it was expected to increase. But Izzy made the assumption that this was supposed to be the first great step toward disarmament. He made a very persuasive case, but based on a false premise.

"Another example. Stone wrote that the first day Johnson was President you knew he was lousy because he recognized the junta in the Dominican Republic. But the decision on the junta was made by Kennedy, and all poor old Johnson had to do was sign the papers. Izzy's scholarship is impeccable, but based on a load of crap.

"I don't like the people who give the *Review* its political tone—Stone, Chomsky, and in the earlier days Muggeridge, Stokely Carmichael, Staughton Lynd. I much prefer Genovese." Rovere also plays down the publication of Arendt and the like at the

5. *New York Review*, April 9, April 23, and May 7, 1970.

Review. "I don't think they're the stamp of the thing. Hannah Arendt gives off very abstract things on the nature of revolution. Lichtheim [now deceased] deals with European diplomacy. But I think their American politics are Stone's and Chomsky's."

* *

"On Being Deradicalized" (or "The Confessions of Nat Glazer"), published in *Commentary* in October 1970, is a Rosetta Stone of Old Left attitudes. It is the autobiography of a mild radical of the late Fifties gone mildly conservative by the Seventies. According to Glazer's ten-year-old guide, a radical used to mean people like Goodman, Macdonald, Howe, Harrington, and C. Wright Mills, who rallied against civil defense, urban renewal fiascos, large bureaucracies, outdated liberal reforms, the nuclear arms race, and the immovable US policy on Berlin. This brand of radicalism, with its emphasis on individual control and skepticism about grand liberal schemes at home and abroad, had connections with conservatism which, Glazer contends, the "freedom-denying" radicalism of today has severed. But it wasn't just the definition of radicalism that changed through the Sixties. Glazer himself changed after a year in Washington in the Housing and Home Finance Administration.

"I learned, to my surprise, that most of the radical ideas my friends and I were suggesting had already been thought of, considered, analyzed, and had problems in their implementation that we had never dreamed of. I learned to respect many of the men who worked in the huge bureaucracies, who limited their own freedom, and who made it possible occasionally for the radical ideas of others to be implemented. I learned that the difficulty with many radical ideas lay in the fact that so many varied interests played a role in government, and that most of them were legitimate interests. It was a big country, and it contained more kinds of people than were dreamed of on the shores of the Hudson. I learned, in quite strictly conservative fashion, to develop a certain respect for what was; in a world of infinite complexity, some things had emerged and survived, and if the country was in many ways better than it might be or had been (just as in many ways it was much worse than it might be or would be), then something was owed to its political institutions and organizational structures."

Berkeley was another deradicalizing experience for Glazer, fifty, and so were the civil rights movement and the anti-war movement. In each case, his initial radical sympathies were soured by the apparent absolutism of New Leftists. An animal faith in America prevented him from going all the way. Glazer remembered different times in the South, different wars in Europe and Korea. A stand had to be taken. "[I]t sometimes seemed," he writes, "that one of the key factors determining the division was a capacity for hatred. Did you hate Johnson enough—or Rusk, or Rostow, or the police, or the leaders of South Vietnam? Did you hate the Southerners enough, or the Northern white middle classes, or the Northern white workers, or the Jewish schoolteachers in New York?"

The student revolt won converts, but it estranged many intellectuals like Glazer, who saw the post-Berkeley radicalism as "a threat to the very existence of the University and to the values of which the university, with all its faults, was a unique and precious embodiment."

So, not surprisingly, Glazer thought highly of Wrong's article. "Wrong had to capsulize," he says during a brief phone interview from his office at Harvard's School of Education. "There are a number of different tendencies at the *Review*. There's no sense of a strict party line. They've always had an uneven hand—Heilbroner is good, but Chomsky seems to be working from newspaper clippings and an old Marxist handbook while living in Marseilles. Their editors are intelligent, but have an unsteady sense of social reality, accommodating violent people and highly intellectual people like Hannah Arendt. Both I. F. Stone and Murray Kempton are blighted in one way or another. The *Review* has a limited and distorted view of the government and how it works. It doesn't care about the interests or the range of the American people."

* * *

You have to get up pretty early in the morning and know exactly where to go to hear an encouraging word about the latter-day politics of Norman Podhoretz. Years before his counter-*Kulturkampf*, the publication of *Making It* sank his reputation like a rock in Family waters. As autobiography, *Making It* was judged bare; as success story, venal. It was difficult to get worked

up over Podhoretz's self-advertising, "frank, Mailer-like bid for
literary distinction, fame, and money all in one package." The
shadow of *Making It* has haunted him ever since. A prominent
Review personality who has felt the sting of Podhoretz's whip
speaks of him in a parable: "There are two kinds of ambition. The
first is to become President of the United States—which may not
be very beautiful, but it is understandable and part of the American landscape. The second is to want to be invited to the
White House for a cup of tea—which is neither beautiful nor
comprehensible."

Six years after the event, the book still smarts some people.
Hans Morgenthau got his latter-day licks in recently while reviewing W. W. Rostow's *The Diffusion of Power* for the *Times Book
Review* (December 10, 1972). "Yet while this is a bad book, it
is not lacking in a certain importance," he wrote. "It is important
in the sense in which Norman Podhoretz's *Making It* is important:
as the unintended self-revelation of a man's mind."

Parties *chez* Lillian Hellman and Philip Rahv, so the man
confessed, "always served as a barometer of the progress of my
career." Hannah Arendt was the unsuspecting hostess at one of
Podhoretz's Family-climbing soirées. She was doing an article for
Commentary during the Yuletide season and politely invited the
editor over for New Year's Eve. For the breathless editor, that
evening was raised to the private category of "landmarks." Invitations from Mary McCarthy, Louis Kronenberger, and the
socially prominent Askews became earthly signs of justification.
"And for the sake of these things, too"—Podhoretz bared his soul
—"I drove myself to write." Of course, Norman Podhoretz was
not the only family associate who ever felt pleased as Punch in
new-found social acceptance. But he was the only one to do triple
gainers about it in public. "The Establishment has properties, not
the first of which, we might suggest, is its absolute detestation of

any effort to classify or examine it," Norman Mailer observed in his own protective, yet less than glowing, *Partisan* report on *Making It*. Self-incrimination by association—that's why the Establishment banned the book. "So we may as well assume," Mailer concluded, "that the lightnings Podhoretz aroused came not because he was revealing the dirty little secret of others, but because he was exposing himself, and this act of self-exposure was received by The Family as a treason—one simply did not go around explaining any member of the clan. To do that was to weaken all" (Spring 1968).

The cold reception *Making It* occasioned supposedly plunged Podhoretz into gloom. At forty-three, he is no longer the picture of Bogart, posing gangster-style with a cigarette dangling from his mouth on the jacket of *Doings and Undoings*. Since *Making It*, his hair has turned completely gray, and the after-effects of tobacco deprivation have left him with a formidable pot. Yet the edge of toughness, the taste for the *outré* or, as Mark Krupnick put it pejoratively in *Modern Occasions* (Spring 1971), the "bush-league Nietzschean," remain. And so, apparently, does the "compound of Hugh Hefner, Melvin Laird, and Martha Raye" which *New York Times Book Review* editor John Leonard conjures up to describe Podhoretz's "monthly impersonations of Polonius in *Commentary*" (Introduction to Wilfrid Sheed's collection, *The Morning After*). "He's very much of a counter-puncher," observed Theodore Solotaroff, founding editor of *New American Review* and formerly an associate editor on *Commentary*. "He realized the mileage in an unfavorable position. He has a tropism for the unpopular stand, a risk-taker in 'My Negro Problem and Yours,' and his review of Hannah Arendt's Eichmann book. As the crowd in New York moved Left, he felt isolated."[6]

6. In "My Negro Problem and Yours," (*Commentary*, February 1963), Podhoretz admitted to a hatred for Negroes going back to his Brooklyn

Say what you will, Norman Podhoretz at least has got all his cards on the table—in contrast to Silvers and Epstein, who eschew showing their hands. The editor of *Commentary*, both in his monthly "Issues" column and in frequent interviews, lets it all hang out. New Left on his mind. In the spring of 1970, he took a three-month leave from the magazine and went up into the country to think and work on a new book. He emerged from this solitude with a clear sense of duty—to tell the truth, as he saw it. "We were living," he told the *Washington Post* in 1971, "a lot of us in the intellectual community were living, in a kind of reign of terror, which had no power behind it except the coercion of this intellectual community. The only way you can break through this terror is . . . break it—the Movement, the counter-culture, the radical ethos, that's the best way to describe it. Then you encourage others to come to the same conclusion. I knew that the first thing my critics would say was 'Agnew.' I was not disappointed. Most people are fearful of being called names. That is a very effective sanction."[7]

Nevertheless, allusions to Agnew come easily to the tongue.

---

childhood, when black kids regularly knocked his block off. He openly envied their physical grace and hoped a daughter of his wouldn't marry one. "How, then, do I know that this hatred has never entirely disappeared?" he wrote. "I know it from the insane rage that can stir in me at the thought of Negro anti-Semitism; I know it from the disgusting prurience that can stir in me at the sight of a mixed couple; I know it from the evidence that can stir in me whenever I encounter that special brand of paranoid touchiness to which many Negroes are prone." His Arendt review had the catchy title "Arendt on Eichmann: "A Study in the Perversity of Brilliance" (*Commentary*, September 1963). The perversity, of course, was Arendt's not Lieutenant-Colonel Eichmann's. Podhoretz dared to dress her down intemperately because her argument that Jews themselves were accomplices in the Holocaust and that Adolf Eichmann wasn't even an anti-Semite offended him greatly. Arendt had "a mind infatuated with its own agility and bent on generating dazzle." Her theory of totalitarianism, the a priori of her holocaust revisionism, could "go hang." Podhoretz went out on this limb while Stephen Spender was calling Arendt's book "brilliant" in *New York Review*.

7. Thomas Grubisich, "Norman Podhoretz: The New Left's Enemy From Within," The *Washington Post*, April 11, 1971.

For in his very first "Issues" (June 1970), Podhoretz ripped into the ",WASP patriciate" backers and Jewish intellectuals at the *New York Review*, "whose radicalism, such as it is, consists entirely in preserving and enlarging the heritage of hatred for America to which both groups, each for reasons of its own, have dedicated their lives and their fortunes and their sacred honor." Nixon's Nixon merely wondered if the *Review* made you "warm and snugly protected," but Podhoretz's Nixon, the new Podhoretz, seemed to be HUAC-ing away as he had in the early Fifties—cheering the Smith Act and blacklisting (see *Making It*, p. 292).

Then, in the second column (July), he would tell a homely tale with a moral even Agnew wouldn't touch in his wildest imaginings. One day, the story proceeded, Podhoretz and *Harper's* then editor-in-chief, Willie Morris, were touring a Confederate graveyard in Vicksburg, Mississippi, with Morris' aged grandmother in tow. Morris read the Gettysburg legend—"that these men shall not have died in vain"—from a plaque posted at the entrance. Podhoretz asked him if he thought the 22,000 Southern boys planted under their feet a century ago did die in vain. Morris deferred to his grandmother, who replied, "I don't know. [Pause.] I reckon they all would have been dead and buried by now anyway." And thereupon Podhoretz finished with a Sevareid flourish: "That astonishing remark—which says, among all the other things it says, that to die young in a war is one of the possible ways for mortal beings to die, and not necessarily the worst—has been much on my mind today, Memorial Day of 1970, as the wanton American involvement in Vietnam comes closer and closer to an end."

However wanton the involvement, Podhoretz could not rouse himself to a condemnation of the Cambodian invasion, which was the cataclysm of the month that May. "Despite the invasion of Cambodia," he wrote neutrally in the opening sentence, "the

end of the Vietnam war is clearly in sight . . ." Podhoretz had
bought Vietnamization over immediate withdrawal and the con-
sequent shame of an American defeat—and Cambodia wasn't
going to louse up his game plan. "Why make so much out of it?"
he asked an incredulous friend. "Nixon is ending the war, and
Vietnam isn't much of an issue anyway."

That's about where Podhoretz was at when the author interviewed him shortly after the Dennis Wrong article hit the streets.
To penetrate the American Jewish Committee building on East
56th Street, where *Commentary* is housed and fed, you must give
your name to a man in the lobby, who phones the party you
wish to see for corroboration. The office of the magazine is off
the main foyer on the eighth floor behind a steel door you would
swear was leading into a john. Instead, it opens on a long rec-
tangular room with a series of glass and steel-walled cubicles
along the left side. Secretaries on the outside, bosses on the
inside. The only office graffitti in sight are some framed *Commentary* Chanukah cards. (There is a definite interior decoration
gap between this place and the headquarters of the *Review*,
which is a funhouse of funky memorabilia. By their furnishings
you shall know them.)

Podhoretz presides in the first cubicle, which is as neatly
arranged as the rest. Although he is practically the sole proprietor
of a 100-page or so monthly, there is not a stray paper clip on
his desk. A revolving set of framed *Commentary* covers hanging
in Podhoretz's direct line of vision is the only hint of flamboyance
in the whole operation.

He warns his guest to watch his head as he sits down opposite him in a plush black leather couch. But it's too late. The
visitor cracks his skull on a low-slung bookshelf. Then Podhoretz
comes out swinging—at the questions as well as the people he is
asked to discuss. Having just done a story on Philip Berrigan for
the *Review*, the visitor guesses that his objectivity is tainted.

The session begins with Wrong's "Case." "Almost exactly the sort of article I had in mind. I wouldn't have written the piece myself, because I'm not a disinterested critic like Wrong." A curious coincidence though, isn't it, that Wrong would punish Friedenberg more than any other *NYR* offender, when it was Friedenberg who lampooned *Making It* in the *Review?* "Friedenberg represents as well as anyone their prevailing point of view," rebuts Podhoretz. "Wrong chose Friedenberg himself. As for the review of *Making It*, I had just rejected two of Friedenberg's pieces.[8] But if he didn't do it, someone would have. If they were loyal to their ideology, they would have had to criticize it for its heresies." What heresies? "Heresies like the favorable attitude the book takes toward the possibilities of intellectual and political

8. Friedenberg takes issue with this interpretation of the events preceding his review of *Making It:* "Podhoretz's statement is wholly inaccurate. Aside from one superficial travel piece on Bulgaria, which I offered *Commentary* over a year before *Making It* was published, mostly to see whether they would publish anything favorable about a communist country, I had written nothing for *Commentary*, despite several requests for reviews, since late 1964, when they rejected a piece on the work of Erik Erikson that I set aside until Bob Silvers, whom I told of it, asked to see it; *NYR* published it in May 1965. At that time, the last previous piece I had submitted to them [*Commentary*] was an article written, at their request, on Charles Osgood's program of "graduated initiatives toward peace"; the topic itself shows how long ago that must have been: Christmas 1962, I think. There may have been one article in between, but I don't think so. Podhoretz's response to the Osgood piece did, however, adversely affect my review of *Making It*, though not for the reasons he suggests. He rather irritably rejected the second draft, saying that he hated to do so on political grounds, because I referred to American policy in Indochina as more intransigent than that of the Soviet Union. This not only deprived me of a chance to get on record as one of the earlist opponents of the Indochina war but, more to the point I think, clearly contradicts the position on that war Podhoretz attributes to himself and to *Commentary* in *Making It*, which of course shook my confidence in the honesty of the book. My impression of Silvers' reasons for giving me *Making It* to review is that he thought me one of the few available reviewers familiar with the New York literary hassle who had no political ambitions with respect to it, one way or the other; I have never been attracted to the life of 'the Family.' It is quite true, however, that I am an ideologically biased reviewer in that I despise the patriotism of self-made men. President Nixon must surely, by now, have aroused some sympathy for this position."

life in the United States and toward its frank and open avowal
of the ambition for worldly success."

If Podhoretz were to make a hate-list, kids Elizabeth Hardwick, Nasser and Edgar Z. Friedenberg would be numbers one
and two. From the conversation, though, it would seem that Noam
Chomsky has emerged as a contender for the second spot. "Chomsky's reputation is pretty much in decline," he says, adding that
he was startled professionally to see "The Responsibility of
Intellectuals" in the *Review*, since it had been published previously in the Harvard journal *Mosaic*.

"America is not as bad as it seems, and it is much better
than it seems to many people in the academic world," says Podhoretz. "They've been helping to encourage a view of the United
States that is evil, and I violently repudiate that view. Chomsky
makes you think from the way he writes that he was a Kant
wakened from his dogmatic slumber to do his moral duty. Actually, he had these views all his life. Chomsky isn't responding
concretely to the war. He's a radical ideologue and always was.
And true ideologues don't need external confirmation for their
own beliefs, only confirmation to persuade others.

"I always opposed the war since the Taylor Mission in 1961.
I haven't been consistent about many things, but I've been consistent on Vietnam. Still, I never used Vietnam to turn the cold
war on its head. Vietnam was an immense misuse of the contain-
ment theory. Others see it as an exposure of evil tendencies hidden
in American politics. The whole revisionist view of the cold war is
not only wrong academically but morally, and consequently serves
bad politics. It matters enormously how we interpret the mistakes
of Vietnam. It makes a big difference whether you think it's a
mistake or a crime."

Chomsky would agree to the last sentence, all right, but his
conclusion is opposite to Podhoretz's. Mistakes, like the poor,
we always have with us. Mistakes are why we put erasers on
pencils. Thus, Chomsky prefers the category of crime to describe

what the United States has perpetrated in Vietnam. The semantics lose Podhoretz at this point. "Why should that be essential? If it's a mistake or a crime, what's the difference?"

The editor of *Commentary* contents himself too much with being Right From the Start. He may have quarrelled with his country's Indochina policy earlier than his intellectual compatriots, but during the escalation years 1965–68, he had a war record only his mother could have loved. During LBJ's *deluge*, *Commentary* read like a collaborationist's journal, and Podhoretz seemed practically Pétainist in his sympathies for the occupying power. While *Commentary* could scarcely avoid the subject of the war, its voice was lowered and without passion. In the pages of *Commentary*, Vietnam was (is) a diplomatic blunder and no big moral deal. Instead of the constant rage and surveillance the conduct of the war received in *New York Review*, *Commentary* went AWOL most of the time. And even when Podhoretz sent in reinforcements, it was usually in the form of a diplomatic note from Lichtheim or Theodore Draper, or a diversionary *feuilleton* from David Halberstam on Vietnam reportage, or Edward Hoagland on the small troubles of an average draft-card burner. Podhoretz published only three war-related articles in 1965, only one in 1966, three again in 1967, and a grand total of four in 1968 (including Mailer's "The Battle of the Pentagon"). Podhoretz took a four-year walk away from the human ravages of Vietnam and the moral guilt of America. He countenanced no serious condemnations of his former White House tea partner, Lyndon Johnson, until March of 1968, when it was too late to make any difference. If you were looking for information on refugees, the Thieu-Ky dictatorship, dirty weaponry, the air war, peace initiatives, and domestic resistance, you didn't find it in *Commentary* 1965–68. Proportion not being his strongest suit, Podhoretz would get madder at Philip Rahv for his politicized *NYR* review of Leon Edel's *Henry James: The Master* (February 10, 1972) than he ever got at those responsible for Vietnam ("Issues," April 1972).

,   What made Podhoretz a closet resister when he knew in his
bones the war stank to high heaven? Late in 1967, Gerald
Walker, an editor at *The New York Times Magazine*, asked him
if he could use his name on a letterhead for the Writers and
Editors War Tax Protest. Walker was then gearing up for a mass
solicitation and wanted Podhoretz for a draw. The signators had
to pledge that they would either not voluntarily pay the proposed
10 per cent income tax surcharge and/or not pay the 23 per cent
of their current income tax shipped overseas to finance the war.
Podhoretz was hip. According to Walker, he gave the okay without hesitation on the phone. A couple of weeks later, says Walker,
he called back to say he had thought the matter over and
couldn't give up on the system yet.[9] Apparently neither could any
Commentary regulars. Walker managed to round up a score of
Review writers (no editors, though), but not a single identifiable
hand at *Commentary* (see the Writers and Editors War Tax Protest ad in *NYR*, February 15, 1968). Walker supposed Podhoretz's first instinct dictated the scrubbing of Vietnam, but his
second reflection held him back. Even after LBJ retired to the
Pedernales, and the coast was clear to knock Nixon's war, Podhoretz kept his peace. The fact that his mentor Daniel Moynihan
was a presidential counselor with cabinet rank and the sort who
would call the man who dropped more bombs on Vietnam than
LBJ "a president of singular courage and compassion" may have
slowed his response.[10]

> 9. Podhoretz has a somewhat different recollection: "My memory of the
> episode is very dim, but I believe I told Gerald Walker when he first called
> me about the Writers and Editors War Tax Protest not that I would sign but
> that I would think the matter over. Having then thought it over, I decided
> that I did not wish to resort to civil disobedience as a means of opposing
> American military participation in the Vietnam war. It's possible that
> Walker's memory of our first conversation is more accurate than mine, but I
> doubt it (and so does my wife)."
> 10. See excerpts from Moynihan's valedictory speech in *The New York
> Times*, December 23, 1970; his worshipful interview with candidate Nixon,
> "How the President Sees His Second Term" (*Life*, September 1, 1972) should
> also be noted.

Finally, in May 1971, a year after he had given Nixon a vote of confidence "despite the invasion of Cambodia," Podhoretz was ready to pull out or—depending on your point of view—shut the barn door after the horse was gone. He let Nathan Glazer do the official honors in *Commentary* with "The Case for Immediate Withdrawal," but reserved an "Issues" column for his own explanation.

For those who wondered about Podhoretz's lockjaw on the war, he had the most disingenuous answer. "I have refrained out of certain diffidence toward the experts from writing about Vietnam." A startling statement from a man who made general critical intelligence his intellectual calling card. His whole life Podhoretz never knew from diffidence, and he had to pick *Vietnam* to be diffident about!

Is that why he is "embarrassed" to speak up now? No. He is "embarrassed" because, "as one who never believed that anything good would ever come for us or for the world from an unambiguous American defeat," he finds himself advocating immediate withdrawal, "unhappily moving to the side of those who would prefer just such an American defeat to a 'Vietnamization' of the war . . ." Like Chief Executives Johnson and Nixon, Podhoretz did not want to be the first editor of *Commentary* to lose a war—even though he was opposed to it from the beginning. His domestic attitudes follow the same my-system-right-or-wrong route. When the Movement overreacted, he blamed the Movement itself instead of what they were overreacting against. When intellectuals grew despairing, he called them anti-American. When the odor of repression was all around, he and his *Commentary* Gridleys said we never smelled so good.

An unreconstructed Right factionist, Podhoretz went fishing during the 1972 presidential campaign. Although Howe and Harrington, more or less enthusiasts of the new *Commentary*, endorsed McGovern (in a letter to *The New York Times*), Pod-

horetz did Nixon a favor by writing off the Democratic nominee
as a tool of the "New Class and New Politics" (*Commentary*,
September 1972). After the election, he and Mrs. Podhoretz
would rally to Ben Wattenberg's "Come Home, Democrats"
Coalition for a Democratic majority, sponsored by such Vietnam
Veterans for the War as John Roche, Eugene Rostow, and James
Roosevelt. A friend says Podhoretz was delighted with McGov-
ern's defeat. But what price defeat?

Podhoretz is revisited in the spring. The deadly bookshelf has
been removed, and the interview unrolls without a ruffle. That
earlier crack about the *Review*'s backers' and editors' radicalism
consisting "entirely" of hatred for America seemed unfairly sweep-
ing. How does Podhoretz know? Patron Gianis, for one, is aghast
at the anti-American label. "If I thought it were true, I'd withdraw from the *Review* immediately. I don't even know what their
politics are, but I think the charge is a lot of horseshit."

"It's strong, and I believe it," Podhoretz insists in defense
of his labelling.

"But 'entirely'?"

"Would you be satisfied if I said 'almost entirely'?" Not
really, because who can say what goes on inside another's mind.
"Barbara Epstein is about as radical as my grandmother," Podhoretz continues, laughing now at the incongruity of leaguing Barbara Epstein and radical in the same concept. "And Jason I don't
even want to talk about."

If he had, he might have referred to Jason's *New York
Review* piece entitled "Living in New York" (January 6, 1966),
in which Epstein remarked that it took $50,000 a year to keep a
family "in reasonable comfort and safety" in Manhattan.

Epstein dropped the following counterrevolutionary statements along the way:

Without it [money] one might as well as be dead, or return to the provinces or the surrounding boroughs.

To be without money in New York is usually to be without honor.

They [the very rich] are the true bishops and judges of the city, and for all its triviality their style is often exhilarating.

"Living in New York" was what Epstein had instead of *Making It*. He may not have gone on about the success ethic as much as Podhoretz, but his delectation in the good life is certainly much greater than his former friend's.

Podheretz is not shy about taking credit for an alleged *apertura a dextra* at the *Review*. For while the body of Wrong's piece was still warm, *NYR* published an issue (January 7, 1971) with an unusual list to their Right.

An accident or calculated move to blunt Wrong's attack? "I think they're changing," Podhoretz says, "partly in response to *Commentary* and some of the things I've written [a Che Guevara poster falls at the *NYR* office]. I get a general sense that in the last few months there's an effort to dissociate the pages from certain of the positions for which it has been criticized." Anti-Americanism, however, is not one of them. "I'm not sure how principled the paper is here. I can't imagine it setting itself against the prevailing cultural fashion."

When Podhoretz returned from the wilderness, convinced of his mandate to rid the United States of crisis-mongering, nation-hating, and soft-on-violence *clercs*, he phoned at least one old *Commentary* hand to enlist him in the struggle. "I've been thinking about our condition, and I have my own thoughts," he said. "I hope you'll write something to further our common purpose."

The person on the other end of the line, a Jew and an academic who moved Left after Kent State, while Podhoretz was passing him in the other direction, decided there was no convergence possible. He explained with sadness how he saw the situation in New York:

"From the summer of 1970 *Commentary* has been operating on *la grande peur juive*, that is, the Jewish fear of the blacks, of their reputation for being associated with radicals, and for the state of Israel—unless the Jews stopped beating upon Vietnam there would be no US support for Israel. These are perfectly understandable reasons, but I find a hardness of heart and an insensitivity to other problems like racism and criminal war. The moral burden is still being carried by the young, and for Norman to turn on them in the unremitting way he has I find unacceptable.

"Norman's purpose is to try to organize Jewish opinion. He wants tolerant liberal Jews to cease being tolerant of attitudes that will destroy the Jews if they are tolerated . . . And he doesn't want Jewish opinion to become overly sympathetic to radicalism. In short, he wants to save Jews from their own generosity."

The *grande peur juive* theory is reasonable to Podhoretz. "There is a Jewish consideration in the campaign I've been trying to wage. Indeed, there is a threat to the Jewish position in the United States from radicals. And the fact that I believe this is a factor, but not the only one.

"The radical Left and the counter-culture seem to me to pose a present threat to intellectual values, democratic values, and Jewish values. Of course, people say, 'Podhoretz was traumatized by the school strike.' Yes, that was a turning point for me." (See Podhoretz's "Issues," August 1971, for his analysis of the 1968 New York City teachers' strike and its anti-Semitic effects.)

Transcending earthly politics, Podhoretz believes in a higher wisdom to which the intelligentsia owes obedience. "My belief is that intellectuals have a spiritual role to play not based on any systematic ideological preconception. Their role is to be critical of the culture. *New York Review* is not even an ally, for it is politicizing the culture. I think that the potential readership of

Commentary and the *Review* is so overwhelmingly Left in its sentiments that our job is to be critical of that ethos—not to whip the troops into line. I'm saying something similar to Trilling in *The Liberal Imagination.* I consider it much the job of the intellectual periodical to play the adversary role of that community. This is what I try to do."

If only he didn't try so hard.

c/The Middle Faction

Vital centrist Arthur Schlesinger, fifty-six, is related to the *New York Review* strictly by marriage. His second wife, the

young and absolutely gorgeous Alexandra Emmet, was once Bob
Silvers' assistant and, unto this day, she sublets her East Seventies
apartment to her old boss. Schlesinger wrote two pieces for the
Review during his hitch in the Kennedy White House and one
after the assassination in 1965. He did not write for them again
until his Autumn 1971 assault on Daniel Ellsberg's criticism of
the "quagmire myth," whereby American leaders are thought not
to have known the morass they were getting into in Indochina.
Schlesinger sent his piece in to Silvers over the transom and was
surprised to have it accepted. Why the split between him and
NYR? "Not on great matters of principle," comments Schlesinger.
"I had disagreements. I find their political stuff distasteful, but not
un-American. The *Review* seems to me based largely on stereo-
types in international politics, although it's not fair to say they have
a partisan line. I think Silvers is a very gifted editor. He reminds
me a bit of Kingsley Martin at the *New Statesman*. Between *Commentary* and *New York Review*, I prefer the latter. I don't agree
with Podhoretz on anything."

d/The Left Faction

Andrew Kopkind, thirty-eight, then holed up in a Vermont
commune, was incommunicado on the subject of *NYR*. "I'm pretty
turned off by articles about the *New York Review*, and I'm getting
tired of the mindless attacks on the same two or three phrases of
mine that seem to crop up in every liberal critique I've seen."
A pity—because the rise and fall of Kopkind are regarded as
milestones in the *Review*'s cyclical political life.

*   *   *

I. F. Stone was a prepubescent radical. "The first book
which began (about twelve) to open my eyes to the modern

world was Jack London's *Martin Eden*," he wrote in the farewell issue of the *Bi-Weekly* (December 1971). "By the time I was *bar mizvah*, I had read Herbert Spencer's *First Principles* and became an atheist. My idol a few years later was Kropotkin.

Engels' *Socialism Scientific and Utopian* was enthralling, and I
joined the Socialist Party, becoming a member of the New Jersey
State Executive Committee before I was old enough to vote. But
Kropotkin's communist anarchism, his vision of a voluntary society without police or oppression of any kind, seemed to me then,
and still seems to me now, the noblest human ideal."

Enticed by the excitement of the newsroom, Stone cut himself free from the mast of the University of Pennsylvania in his
junior year (an escape he would always regret) and dropped into
daily journalism full time. For the better part of thirty years
(1923–52), he toiled as a reporter, columnist, and editorial writer
for a succession of New Jersey, Philadelphia, and New York
City newspapers. When the New York *Daily Compass* folded in
1952, and his old (1940–46) spot as Washington editor of *The
Nation* didn't open up, he seized upon the newsletter "as a last
resort." There were more propitious times to launch a Left-Wing
paper than the fabulous Fifties, when Senator Joseph McCarthy
and his pack were bound to be among your most avid readers.
Stone was a pariah in Washington, a one-man Red Menace. The
straight and narrow press ignored him, and his appearances in
print were restricted to obscure leftish journals like *The Monthly
Review*. "The early years were lonely," Stone recalls. "I am
naturally gregarious, but found myself ostracized." His *Hidden
History of the Korean War* really finished him. While Judge
Irving Kaufman was blaming Julius and Ethel Rosenberg for
igniting the Korean conflict in his famous death sentence
speech,[11] Stone's *Hidden History* advanced the then unappetizing
view that an imperialistic United States precipitated the war all by
itself for the secret purpose of controlling Southeast Asia. Lots of
luck. The *[Bi-]Weekly*'s circulation cruised at extremely low

11. [. . .] I believe your conduct [. . .] has already caused the communist
aggression in Korea with the resultant casualties exceeding 50,000, and who
knows but that millions more of innocent people may pay the price of your
treason" (April 5, 1951).

altitudes during Eisenhower's double shift in the control tower—
only 10,000 people subscribed in the first three years. By 1963,
however, Stone could count on twice that number. Johnson's Great
Society was quite good for the [*Bi-*]*Weekly*, as circulation soared
to 40,000 by 1968. And Nixon brought things together to the
tune of 10,000 new subscribers per annum in his first three years
in office. When the sixty-four-year-old Stone decided to cash in
the *Bi-Weekly* chips at the end of 1971, he quit well ahead of the
game. In addition to the *New York Review*, *The Progressive* and
The Monthly Review were interested in buying up the subscription list of 70,000. But Stone sold out to his home away from
home since 1964.

I. F. Stone is garrulously profane over the telephone in
response to Wrong's "Case," but doesn't wish to be quoted except
for the malediction: "Never kick a dead skunk." Since no one,
including Rovere, is sufficiently prepared to mount a sustained
challenge to Stone's long-distance running, the only way to defense
him is with innuendo. Thus Wrong dug up Stone's 1967 review
of Sartre's *Les Temps Modernes* symposium to pin an anti-
Israeli rap on him. No exegesis of Stone's text cluttered Wrong's
argument. We are told merely that Stone was "sharply critical of
the Israeli position" after the Six-Day War and that this alleged
about-face was repudiated by "those who remembered that Stone
had once held quite different views of Israel back in 1948, when
the state was established with strong Russian support, and when
Stone was a fellow-traveler (though it's considered dirty pool to
recall such things today)."

The imputation of fellow-traveling bothers Stone much less
than being painted as an enemy of Israel (which is precisely what
Podhoretz calls him). Although the statute of limitations should
have run out several years ago on the charge, Stone *was* a fellow-
traveler. He doesn't deny it. He couldn't even if he wanted to,
which he emphatically doesn't. In 1956, the Senate Internal

Security Subcommittee identified him as one of the eighty-two most active and typical sponsors of communist-front organizations. Sure enough, Stone was an energetic popular-fronter. He believed in the correctness of joining front groups against fascism and still adheres to the *pas d'ennemis à gauche* philosophy. This historical Left-Wing favoritism, he insists, leads to distortions of his record. His deviationism, he feels, has been carelessly blurred. "First they blame you for things you never said," he complained to Nat Hentoff on educational TV in New York. "The damnedest lies are told about you. Like, for example, that I had spread the germ warfare thing in the Korean war. I never did. I opposed it. It's not in my book. Some idiot said recently that I had applauded the Russian purge trials. I never did. I never believed in them."

Nevertheless, there's no disputing that Stone was in love with Stalin's socialist paradise in the Thirties. A few days before the Russo-German Non-Aggression Pact became public in 1939, he and several other prominent Soviet sympathizers (including Granville Hicks, Max Lerner, Clifford Odets, James Thurber, and William Carlos Williams) had the ill luck to sign an uncritical open letter of all-out support for the USSR (*The Nation*, August 26, 1939). Stone *et al.* were responding to a manifesto of the newly organized Committee of Cultural Freedom (including Sidney Hook, Max Eastman, John Dos Passos, Edna Ferber, and the ubiquitous William Carlos Williams), which had earlier declared against "the rising tide of totalitarianism" (*The Nation*, May 27, 1939). Hook *et al.* were calling a dictatorial spade a spade without regard to place of national origin. "Under varying labels and colors, but still with an unvarying hatred for the free mind," they protested, "the totalitarian idea is already enthroned in Germany, Italy, Russia, Japan, and Spain." Stone's group objected to the linking of Russia with the four rightist dictatorships and in ten uplifting points tried "to make it clear that the Soviet and fascist policies are diametrically opposed." Their closing sentence would turn out to be the killer almost overnight. "But Soviet aims and achievements," they so wrongly guessed, "make it clear that there exists a sound and permanent basis in mutual ideals for cooperation between the USA and the USSR in behalf of world peace and the security and freedom of all nations." Stone did not formally break with the Russkies until 1956—after a six-day sojourn in Mother Russia. On the way back from Moscow he agonized over the good he had anticipated and the evil he experienced firsthand. What was to be done? Should he make common cause with John Foster Dulles by revealing his distaste for Russian communism or keep expediently quiet? Dulles never had such an improbable ally. "I feel like a swimmer under water who must rise to the surface or his lungs will burst," he finally wrote in the *Weekly*, (May 28, 1956). "Whatever the consequences, I have to say what I really feel after seeing the Soviet Union and carefully studying the statements of its leading officials. This is not a good society, and it is not led by honest men . . . Nothing has yet happened in Russia to justify cooperation abroad between the independent Left and the communists."

This belated confession cost him more subscriptions than any other stand he took in nineteen years of the *Weekly/Bi-Weekly*.

But the Israel business—that's another kettle altogether, especially for a born Jew. Stone bristles at the suggestion that he has pulled a Benedict Arnold on Zion. He is still proud of his *Temps Modernes* article which, he claims, is in the best Jewish tradition. His Jewish credentials are in perfect order, and you could quote him on that, too, that is, until he called back a few minutes after the interview, saying he'd thought it over and would rather not come to his own aid in this manner.

Stone is profoundly emotional about his own Jewishness and his relationship with Israel. Perhaps this has something to do with changing his name from Isadore Feinstein to I. F. Stone in the

Thirties, or the fact that he risked his hide on three separate trips to Israel in the tempestuous days of its foundation. He was there in 1945, dodging the Haganah's dirty work before statehood. He was the first journalist in the world to come aboard a Haganah ship filled with casualties of the Holocaust and bound— despite the British blockade—for the Promised Land. He covered the Arab-Israeli war in 1948 and was the first foreign correspondent to enter Jerusalem when the siege was lifted.

In 1959, Stone happened into an East Berlin theater which was showing a Bulgarian-East German film about the love of a Jewish concentration camp girl and a Wehrmacht officer. "In that darkened movie house, amid all those Germans," he wrote in his newsletter, "I cried, remembering those survivors with whom I travelled as a reporter from Poland to Palestine in the spring of 1946, and the stories they told me." Naturally, Stone feels he is mistakenly condemned for trying to lay some old time magnanimity on Israel. In the last number of the *Bi-Weekly*, he resurrected a passage from a controversial piece, "The Harder Battle and the Nobler Victory," published in the *Bi-Weekly* in July 1967. The passage read in part:

Abba Eban exultantly called the sweep of Israel's armies "the finest day in Israel's modern history." The finest day will be the day it achieves reconciliation with the Arabs. To achieve it will require an act of sympathy worthy of the best in Jewry's Biblical heritage. It is to understand and forgive an enemy, and thus convert him into a friend. A certain obtuseness was unfortunately evident in Eban's brilliant presentation to the Security Council. To rest a case on Jewish homelessness and refuse at the same time to see the Arabs who have been made homeless is only another illustration of the tribal blindness which plagues the human race and plunges it constantly into bloodshed. The first step toward reconciliation is to see that Arab bitterness has real and deep roots. [. . .] Israel cannot live very long in a hostile Arab sea. [. . .]

No quickie military victories should blind it to the inescapable
—in the long run it cannot defeat the Arabs. It must join
them. The Jews played a great role in Arabic civilization in
the Middle Ages. A Jewish state can play a similar role in a
new Semitic renaissance. This is the perspective of safety, of
honor, and of fraternity.

And Stone's headline ran: "From My Article on The Six-Day
War, Which Has Been So Unfairly Distorted."

* * *

"It's really a war on Chomsky," remarks Murray Kempton of
the anti-*New York Review* ethos. "I don't understand why they
hate him so much." Elementary, my dear Kempton. It's Mr.
Chomsky's needle's-eye ethics. Either you are with him on Vietnam,
it seems, or you are a war criminal or soft on war crimes.
"Chomsky actually believes that anyone who disagrees with him is
under evil influence," says Martin Mayer. "Not even stupidity is
allowed."

Chomsky threw down the gauntlet for his peers in 1967 with
the publication of "The Responsibility of Intellectuals," wherein
he insisted the task of the *clercs* was "to speak the truth and to
expose lies," especially in life and death matters like Vietnam. But,
all around him, Chomsky saw intellectuals doing their thing for the
war—planning it (William and McGeorge Bundy, Walt and
Eugene Rostow), analyzing it (Roger Hillsman, Ithiel de Sola
Pool, Samuel Huntington), and apologizing for it at various stages
(Arthur Schlesinger, Richard Goodwin, Henry Kissinger, Irving
Kristol—normally strange bedfellows but linked, to Chomsky's
way of thinking, in this regard).

Vietnam is such an unspeakable event to Chomsky that he
comes to the polemic repressing a feeling of absurdity. "By entering
into the arena of argument and counter-argument," he wrote in
the introduction to *American Power and the New Mandarins*,

"of technical feasibility and tactics, of footnotes and citations, by accepting the presumption of legitimacy of debate on certain issues, one has already lost one's humanity." Further on, he described the Vietnam war as "simply an obscenity, a depraved act by weak and miserable men, *including all of us*, who have allowed it to go on and on with endless fury and destruction—all of us *who would have remained silent had stability and order been secured.*" [Emphasis added.] You notice that Chomsky does not absolve himself from blame. He admits in the same introduction that his 1965 enlistment in the anti-war forces was fifteen years too late. Notice also the dislike for the pragmatic viewpoint. If the war had been dispatched with speedier results, he implies, disenchantment with Vietnam policy would not be as great as it is. Of course. But even opposition based on the casualty reports, a more moral sort of pragmatism, does not pass Chomsky's test for purity of resistance. "The principle that we retract our claws when the victim bleeds too much is hardly an elevated one." The only untainted position against the Vietnam war, the only stance that satisfies Chomsky's imperative, transcends good and evil intentions. "What about opposition to the war on the grounds that we have no right to stabilize or restructure Vietnamese society, or to carry out the experiments with 'material and resources control' that delight the 'pacification theorist? Such opposition is slight, and in the political arena virtually nonexistent. The pragmatic and responsible student of contemporary affairs does not descend to such emotionalism."

It is pronouncements like these that have made Chomsky a burr under the saddle of the liberal Left. Nobody, least of all an intellectual, suffers gladly the mark of ethical obtuseness. In a hard-fought *Commentary* exchange (June 1970), Schlesinger shot to kill Chomsky: "[. . .] it has long been impossible to believe anything he says, and now it becomes increasingly difficult to believe that he exists. His most recent communiqué obligingly offers us a fresh example of his intellectual crookedness."

Noam Chomsky is truly Lincolnesque—long, gangly, and un-handsome, devoted to plain talk and plain dress. Home is a white, split-level ranch on a recently developed country site of land in Lexington, Massachusetts. Chomsky, forty-five, may be radical, even anarchist, but chic he isn't.

A house call on him during Christmas vacation begins in the kitchen over morning juice and an exchange of notes on Sesame Street. An effigy of Big Bird clings to the refrigerator, and one thing led to another in a discussion of staggering nonsequiturs. Sesame Street was losing its glow for Chomsky's five-year-old boy, but the program was still boffo for his visitor's two-year-old girl. Where do you go from there? Very quickly to Chomsky's upstairs study for more serious business.

Chomsky's contempt for the *Commentary* axis is typically undisguised in the conversation. "Would they have been opposed to the war," he asks rhetorically, "if we could have won? There's a sense now that cold-war ideology can be rehabilitated while criticizing the war. Glazer talks about being deradicalized, but I don't ever recall his being an activist. And why should the actions of radicals have anything to do with his politics?"

Liberal incantations on the necessity of nonviolence at home also nettle him. As one of the heavies of the New Left and, inci-dentally, an early advocate of the tactics of nonviolent resistance, he is constantly having the specter of Movement fire and pillage thrown in his face. His retort: "The Weathermen are only a drop in the bucket in proportion to Podhoretz's passive position. Is it important to publicly expose the wrongdoing of those engaged in good acts [the burning of an ROTC installation]? Is Irving Howe a pacifist? Then why oppose debate? It [the pro-violence position] *is* arguable."

Chomsky doesn't stump for violence himself, but he doesn't censure its uses outright either. "Suppose, for example," he writes in *Modern Occasions* (Spring 1970), "that students burn down an ROTC building, as has happened in many places. It can easily be demonstrated that this act does not persuade people to oppose the war, violates the right of some, and so on. These are all relevant considerations. They are not the only considerations, however. Presumably, the act is not intended to persuade people that the war is wrong or to extend academic freedom, but rather to hinder aggression by increasing domestic disorder and, in the case of ROTC, hampering the recruitment of officers. If one agrees that opposition to aggression is a legitimate goal, then one must weigh these considerations in the balance."

An attempt is made to pin Chomsky down. Where in the balance would he place the 1970 Marin County courthouse incident in which Judge Harold J. Haley became the most innocent victim of Jonathan Jackson's gun-toting rescue attempt of two black brothers? "I find it hard to criticize that. There was only a slight chance of winning. Under those conditions, it's difficult to say they should be condemned for escaping from a system which never gave them half a chance." (At this point, one can almost hear Podhoretz saying, "I told you so. I told you Chomsky was an ideologue who didn't let events interfere with his beliefs.")

Chomsky was apparently unhappy with this end of the interview. "I might have been a bit inaccurate in referring to my own criticisms of the student movement, violence, and so on," he wrote a few days later. Citing several places where he had taken moderate to conservative stands on just such issues, he then elaborated on some of the unfinished themes of our previous session.

"It would be cheap and rather silly to criticize excesses of the student movement merely to 'protect one's flanks' against critics from the right. It is worth criticizing what is irrational and wrong in ways that may lead to change. (It is for this reason that I was glad to publish on the subject in the *Activist*, or to speak at Columbia, for example.) Furthermore, it must be remembered that the sum total of all violence, fanaticism, or whatever, on the part of students, Weatherman, and so on, does not even weigh in the balance when compared to the silence of those who permit the war to continue, or who take the line that 'Sure, it's bad, but let's not do anything about it' [. . .] such attitudes are surely worse morally than those of Sidney Hook or McGeorge Bundy, who approve of the war. One has to keep a sense of proportion, and one also has to realize that the attacks on the students, the Weathermen, and so on, are surely motivated in part by an effort to rebuild support for the war and American militarism in general, or at least to rebuild the eroding cold-war consensus, the quiescence that permits the executive to operate with impunity. Glazer says that he is deradicalized by the excesses of the Left. Apart from the absurdity (why should someone else's actions change his political convictions?), I would be interested to know what he did before he was deradicalized: What was his involvement in the civil rights movement, or the peace movement, before the Weathermen scared him away? More than anything else, it is important to continue to combat the primary violence, the violence of the state. When a criticism of student violence comes from Dan Berrigan or Dave Dellinger, I take it seriously. When it comes from Sidney Hook, Norman Podhoretz, or Nathan Glazer . . . that's a different story.

"Well, just wanted to get this off my chest."

Chomsky had wind of Wrong's article, but really hadn't seen it. He is handed a copy and asked to comment on what Wrong has to say about him. He reads the two paragraphs and objects immediately to Wrong's methodology, that is, associating him *with*, and attempting to make him look ridiculous *for*, ideas expressed in *At War With Asia*, which are not only the property of others, but whose proper attribution—in quotes yet—could not have been clearer in the text. In light of the to-do which Arthur Schlesinger started when he gleefully pointed out a serious Chomsky misquotation of President Truman's cold-war views in a review of *American Power and the New Mandarins* (an oversight Chomsky admitted, pleading no malice aforethought), it is extremely interesting to witness the Wrong-Chomsky clash. It tells much of the pitfalls of partisan polemic.

Specifically, Wrong judges Chomsky ill for (1) mentioning Japan as a factor in the Vietnam war and (2) for the implied exaggeration of the title—*At War With Asia.*

Chomsky replies, once again in post-interview correspondence:

"I was mulling over our conversation after you left, and a couple of things came to mind. If I remember correctly, one of Wrong's criticisms had to do with my regarding American concern for Japanese neo-colonialism as a 'controlling assumption' in Vietnam policy. Again, if my memory is correct, the phrase was in quotes, attributed to me. I checked to see what I said about the matter, and it is this (*At War with Asia.* pp. 33–8). In a discussion of the Dulles-Eisenhower policy of the mid-Fifties, I referred to several articles by Walter LaFeber, who was the first (to my knowledge) to bring out the fact that they constantly referred to the potential effects on Japan of the 'loss of Indochina.' In an article called 'Our Illusory Affair with Japan,' LaFeber says: 'This thesis became a controlling assumption: The loss of Vietnam would mean the economic undermining and probable loss of Japan to communist markets and ultimately to communist influence, if not control.' I quoted this statement and pointed out that LaFeber regards this as 'now wholly irrational,' though reasonable (if cynical) in an earlier period. (He describes the Dulles-Eisenhower statements as 'intelligent and persuasive.') I then added some other evidence that supports the same conclusions as LaFeber's, rather convincingly, I believe. My evidence, incidentally, was from impeccably conservative sources, as you can see by checking, if you have the book. Later, I wrote that 'although the Indochina war in part develops through its own dynamics—the President, as noted earlier, is hardly likely to be willing to face the domestic political consequences of an American defeat, even if the alternative is a possible global war—it may be that the 'controlling assumption' that LaFeber persuasively identified remains an important factor in accounting for the persistence of the American effort to control Southeast Asia.' Notice that my only use of the phrase 'controlling assumption' is in quoting LaFeber, who is identified as the source of the phrase. Notice further that the primary reference is to the early and mid-Fifties. Finally, notice that the suggestion that this 'controlling assumption' of LaFeber's theory may still operate is highly qualified. In fact, the statement could be strengthened. In an interview in *The New Yorker*, July 4, 1970, Eugene Rostow returns to this thesis and endorses it, as I pointed out in a later article that appeared in the first issue of *Modern Occasions*. Rostow was selected by *The New Yorker* for the interview because of his association with policy planning, of course. If one compares all of this to Wrong's account, I think it reveals a serious irresponsibility in his handling of evidence.

"I also recall (I think) that he objected to the title of the book as an 'exaggeration.' Of course, the title is an adaptation of a prediction by John Fairbank given in full in the lead quotation, pp. 3–4. I point out that, as he predicted, we are being drawn step by step into an extended war with the people of Asia—Cambodia being the most recent step—and quote such radical rags as the *Far Eastern Economic Review* and *France-Soir* to indicate the dangers of spreading war. (In fact, the *FEER*, in an editorial that I didn't quote, suggested that the US might find itself engaged from West Bengal to the China Sea.) I also point out that we have many possibilities to escape from this trap and that it is by no means inevitable. Thus the chapter (Chapter 1) ends. Again, I think he has, shall we say, missed the point?"

When Wrong was familiarized with Chomsky's self-defense, he said he would have to check the text. At the close of his interrogation, his interviewer recommended stopping by Brentano's,

a few steps away on Eighth Street, in order to settle the quarrel
there and then. Wrong obligingly agreed. After reading the passage in question, Wrong stubbornly refused to budge from his
original judgment. Of the LaFeber business, he would say "quib-
ble"; of Fairbank, he mumbled "Stalinoid."[12]

12. Dennis Wrong's memory of this episode differs from the author's.
He explained his recollection in the following exchange which occurred in
Esquire (July 1972):
While appearing to disavow the implication, Nobile manages to suggest that
I wrote my article as a willing accomplice or "tool" of Norman Podhoretz in
his alleged personal vendetta against the *New York Review* in return for a
fat fee, and that at least some of its content was dictated, if not actually
written, by Podhoretz himself.
        [. . .] I told him that I knew and regretted that some people believed I
had written it as Podhoretz's "agent," that such a view was entirely false and
did a grave injustice to both Podhoretz and myself, that Podhoretz had asked
me to write the article—as he had asked me to write others in the past—just
before a summer vacation, and that I had agreed to do so since I had the free
time, would be paid adequately for my efforts, and welcomed the opportunity
to articulate my growing distaste for the *New York Review*'s fashionable
radicalism. I also told Nobile that Podhoretz obviously knew in general what
my views were on these matters because I had expressed them before in *Commentary* itself as well as elsewhere, but that he had made no editorial suggestions, let alone alterations in my article, beyond advising a few cuts. [. . .]
        One reported "quote" referring to an individual ought to be corrected:
I never "mumbled," nor declared in any other tone of voice, that John K.
Fairbank was a "Stalinoid." I *did* use the term, prefixed with an "ex," to
describe I. F. Stone, both in the interview and in the article.
                                                                        Dennis H. Wrong
                                                                        Princeton, N.J.
                Author's Reply:
[. . .] Indeed, I did suggest Wrong was in league with Norman Podhoretz's and
Commentary's campaign against the likes of *New York Review*. And Wrong
himself supplied the evidence in a quotation he declines to challenge: "I
wish I had developed my own ideas more fully. Podhoretz wants people to
be more aggressive. I was afraid people would think I was an instrument of
his revenge; but the money was so good."
        I did not *appear* to disavow the money motive (another of Wrong's
admissions) in the acceptance of the *Commentary* commission. I *did* disavow
when I wrote ". . . I have no doubt it was his time (summer vacation) and
trouble—not his soul—that Podhoretz purchased with an extra special
stipend."
        As for the origin of the article's contents, nowhere, absolutely nowhere,
did I hint either the dictatorship or the borrowed prose of *Commentary*'s
editor. I simply mentioned that Wrong "may have been susceptible to over-
coaching." In view of Wrong's testimony about the underdevelopment of his

Chomsky also figures in the dodgy question of the *Review*'s Middle East relations, which Wrong rightfully exposes as rock bottom. While *Commentary* opened up an all-night concession stand dispensing assorted Arab-Israeli items after the Six Day War, *NYR* became a veritable Mecca of evasion. There was I. F. Stone on the *Temps Modernes* symposium in the summer of 1967 and Amos Elon's review of two books on the diplomatic background to the war[13] in 1968. In other words, that is, right up until the fall of 1971, the pages of the *Review* were as unwelcoming to Middle East material as the *Christian Science Monitor* is to cancer features. Why? Wrong's assessment is almost as good as any. "Since New Left student groups and the black militants are fervidly pro-Arab, while a larger segment of the liberal Left academic world still supports Israel, one suspects that the *NYR* editors find it politic to avoid the subject." He would have been more exact if he had substituted radical intellectuals for "student groups and black militants," who, after all, do not loom that large in the *Review*'s operational scheme. Neither faction is checking the *Review* to see which way the wind blows and never did. But Silvers does have to answer to Zionist-leaning contributors and compatriots.

Wrong also notes—and here's where things get ticklish—that Chomsky publishes his Middle East material beyond the fringe of the *Review*, peddling "an anti-Zionist point of view sympathetic to the claims of Al Fatah and the Palestinian Arab nationalists."

own ideas and Podhoretz's aggression imperative, my remark would seem the mildest of possible interpretations. One could ask, If Wrong didn't develop his own ideas fully, just whose ideas did he develop?

Despite Wrong's correction on the "Stalinoid" appellation, I stand by my text. I could not have invented the term since I had never heard it before, nor could I have confused Fairbank with Stone because we discussed the Fairbank matter in a bookstore after our formal interview was finished. Incidentally, Wrong's label for Stone in *Commentary* was "Stalinist fellow-traveler," not "ex-Stalinoid." If he can't even remember what he wrote, I should scarcely expect him to have total recall of our conversation!

13. Walter Laqueur's *The Road to Jerusalem* and Theodore Draper's *Israel and World Politics*.

There is indeed talk that Bob Silvers rejected an article Chomsky wrote in 1969 entitled "Nationalism and Conflict in Palestine." The article was originally commissioned for a collection[14] put out by Mouton in The Hague, and it eventually surfaced stateside in *Liberation*. But would Silvers, one of the Western hemisphere's keenest editorial heads, really send a star correspondent away like that, returning a perfectly decent manuscript on a rather newsworthy subject of likely interest to the *Review*'s readership and thereby leave Chomsky's Middle East views out in the relative cold of the Holy Cross College alumni magazine? Well, Chomsky did pass the article on to Silvers, a custom he observes with a lot of his material even when it is not necessarily intended for the *Review*. Chomsky prefers not to elaborate and suggests the author pick up the thread with Silvers. "Chomsky's article was not submitted here," Silvers states, cutting off the larger question. Gathered evidence suggests a fuller version of this incident: Silvers read Chomsky, but turned him down because, among other reasons, he considered Chomsky's call for a binational Palestinian State "sentimental." "Silvers knew," says one Zionist elder of the *Review*, "that certain people would be unhappy with Chomsky's piece on Israel." According to the same Elder, Isaiah Berlin, Silvers' traveling companion on a trip to Israel, was shown the manuscript and made his displeasure apparent to Silvers. Chomsky himself believes constraints obtain at *NYR* on the Israel-Arab problem that do not exist in other domains. Nathan Glazer thinks the *Review* chickened out of the Arab-Israeli issue by excluding Chomsky. "I saw it as a test, and they withdrew. It has affected them ever since." In any case, this three-year moratorium on the Middle East was not *New York Review*'s finest hour.

The *Review* broke its three-year Middle Eastern silence with

14. *Reflections on the Middle East Crisis,* edited by Herbert Mason, 1970.

mystery guest Atallah Mansour. His "Palestine: The Search for a New Golden Age" (October 7, 1971), a lengthy, historical, and moderately toned survey of Arab-Israeli stand-off gave little to Zionists like Podhoretz. Mansour scotched Chomsky's bi-nationalism:

> If we take into consideration the long history of the Jewish people, a history full of persecution and humiliation, we reach the certain conclusion that there is not even a slight hope at this time of convincing a significant percentage of Israeli Jews to cooperate with the Palestinian Arabs in a mutual homeland and state.

and Stone's bring-them-together pluralism:

> They [the Israelis] prefer a small state dominated by Jews to an empire governed mutually by Arabs and Jews.
> And what of the Palestinian Arabs? I have no doubt that the vast majority would refuse to live in a bi-national state with the Jews, for the same reason.

However, he did revive the idea of a Palestinian State, anathema to right-thinking Zionists and Golda Meir, but not to the independent Left and liberal opinion in Israel, as well as to certain influential Egyptian commentators and Stone himself, as the solution to conflicting claims for the common homeland.

> I should add, however, that two such states, Palestine and Israel, in the land of Palestine might be the first step toward a federal union which would reunite Palestine and inspire a Middle Eastern unity open to all peoples striving for liberation and social, political, and economic progress.

Mansour was partly Stone in sheep's clothing, yet the Zionist wolves didn't howl. A couple of months went by, and Midge Decter still hadn't read the article. Irving Howe was unmoved,

because he felt he had no fight with the author: No, Mansour
never called him an Old Left stick-in-the-mud. The *Review* came
out of the shower, and it came out clean this time. For Atallah
Mansour, as described in his contributor's page bio, is an Israeli
Christian-Arab novelist and member of the editorial board of the
Hebrew-language daily *Haaretz*. If Mansour didn't exist, Silvers
couldn't have invented such a germ-free carrier of the *NYR*'s
anti-Zionist line. Eleven months later, the *Review* published two
Middle East pieces in the same issue yet (August 31, 1972)—
"The Price Israel Is Paying" by Yehoshua Arieli and "Where
Nixon Was When Sadat Gave the Russians the Boot" by I. F.
Stone. But the more things changed, the more they remained the
same. Arieli, an Israeli professor at the Hebrew University in
Jerusalem, criticized the military and political status quo that
grips his homeland. "For the sake of annexation of the territories
we occupy," he wrote, "we are sacrificing, unintentionally, our
true security, the quality of our society, our free progressive spirit,
our internal integrity and unity, and economic, social, and spiritual
well-being." Better Arieli should say this than an American leftist
Jew. Even I. F. Stone wasn't going to open up the Zionist can of
worms again in his diplomatic dispatch. He allowed Israeli politi-
cian Arie L. Eliar do the talking by quoting his statement to the
effect that the Palestinians, not Egypt, should be Israel's central
concern. "Any American writer who dares say as much," Stone
realistically observed, "exposes himself to the charge of anti-
Semitism." Thus an all-Israeli team of Middle East Commentators
keeps *NYR* off the hook stateside.

J. L. Talmon is one Israeli dove that got away. Talmon, a
professor of modern history at the Hebrew University of Jerusalem, gave a speech in 1970 to a conference organized by the
Israeli leftist group *New Outlook*. Silvers read a transcript of the
speech which hit Israel's occupation policy rather hard and asked
Talmon if he could publish it. Talmon, according to associates,
said no. His speech was unfinished and would have to be put in

political context before it would be fit for foreign consumption. Otherwise Talmon, an ardent Jewish nationalist, feared the nature of his dovishness would be misunderstood in the United States and that his differences with the Israeli government could be blown up tendentiously. Silvers agreed. Talmon sent his revised version to *NYR* but heard nothing. Talmon finally cabled Silvers about the piece and Silvers replied with a renewed request to publish the original text. Talmon, of course, refused. *Dissent* wound up accepting what *NYR* rejected.[15]

Talmon was left to suppose that Silvers wanted a less complicated or less ambiguous critique of Israel. Not only do you have to be an Israeli dove to represent *NYR* in the Middle East, you have to fly their route. "I am struck by the narrowness of opinion on Israel in *New York Review*," comments Harvard's Martin Peretz. "Isn't it odd that someone so eminent as Isaiah Berlin, who has written positively on Jewish nationalism elsewhere, has never appeared on this subject in the pages of *New York Review?*"

* * *

Bob Silvers advises a pow-wow with Ronald Steel. Steel's name crops up a couple of times in the context of required research. After an interview with him one clammy summer noontime in his walk-up on upper Madison Avenue, Silvers' counsel is understandable. For Steel, a trim, boyish forty-two-year-old bachelor, is a level-headed fellow of sound Left instincts and an unideological sense of the past. You don't get asked to do Walter Lippmann's authorized biography (as Steel has been) if you can't hack it.

Just who is the *Review*'s one-man State Department and its most traveled diplomatic correspondent? Ronald Steel gained a Master's in political economy from Harvard and dropped out of both Yale Law School and the Foreign Service. (He was very

15. See "The Impotence of Victory," in *Dissent* (November-December 1970). Talmon's article is also reprinted in his book *Israel Among the Nations* (pp. 167–90).

briefly our vice-consul in Cyprus.) After settling in London in the early Sixties, Steel began to contribute skillful pieces regularly to *Commonweal*, *The New Leader*, and *Commentary*. Silvers apparently noticed him in *Commentary*, a perfectly suitable talent pool for the *Review* in those days, and sent him Raymond Aron's *The Great Debate: Theories of Nuclear Strategy* (February 25, 1965). ("I have nothing against writing for *Commentary* again— there's certainly no moral principle involved—but they haven't asked me in years.") Frequent appearances in *NYR* therefore assured him of instant recognition.

Steel has a double major at the Review—in statesmenlike personalities (Ball, Kennan, Eisenhower, De Gaulle) and in troublespot pieces (Havana, Greece, Prague, Oakland), but his pace slowed down in 1969 when he started working on the Lippmann biography. "I take time off to review books," he remarks, "only when I find the subject irresistible, as in the case of Dean Acheson's *Present at the Creation* and Graham Allison's *The Essence of Decision*."

Steel is asked about Irving Howe's critique of the politics underlying Yglesias' *Review* article in defense of Cuban poet Herberto Padilla and reminded of the sore ideological points rubbed by Wrong in his "Case." Steel speaks with unforked tongue:

"Yglesias knows and loves Cuba. He feels the philosophy is good but the practice is bad. Do these awful things happen because of Fidel or because of the structure? Maybe if things like Padilla's imprisonment hadn't occurred, we would put the Cuban situation in a different perspective.

"When I went to Cuba, I may have been romanticizing.[16]

16. The conclusion of Steel's 'Letter From Havana" (April 11, 1968) reads: "It is a perplexing society: exhilarating and repressive, experimental and puritanical, idealistic and expedient. It is a country, an experiment, a state of mind, quite unlike any other; a seductive place that it is perhaps dangerous to take at face value, but impossible not to admire for the courage of its people and the daring of its vision."

When you go to a place like that you see the oppression, but you are aware of many of the good things. When I look back on that Panther piece, too, I think I probably gave them the benefit of the doubt on some issues.[17]

"It's hard to judge in retrospect. There was a climate of crisis in the late Sixties—the war was escalating, and Johnson was going to run again. Perhaps we were overly pessimistic. But all kinds of people, including Walter Lippmann, thought China was coming in. This was the time of Watts and Detroit, and extreme situations elicit extreme attitudes. I don't think those attitudes were necessarily inappropriate at the time. I felt much more alarmist then and had a sense of doom.

"It's difficult to express, but I feel differently about things now than I did before. Certainly, the political climate has changed, and it's obvious that violence did not bring about the kind of results that its practitioners desired. Maybe the *Review* was more receptive then to those who believe in direct action. I know I was. In this sense, the riots were a good thing because they forced people to recognize discontent."

In his heart, Silvers knows Steel is right about the attitudinal revisions at the *Review*.

* * *

Hannah Arendt is a gray eminence's *éminence grise* and therefore just the person an editor would love to have among his contributors, especially if his magazine is defamed for being

17. Steel wrote in his "Letter from Oakland: The Panthers" (September 11, 1969) that: "It takes courage to join the party, to submit to its discipline, and to face the likely prospect of imprisonment or death. But for some there is no other way. As Eldridge Cleaver has written, 'A slave who dies of natural causes will not balance two dead flies on the scale of eternity.' [. . .] Beneath an inflammatory vocabulary of ghetto hyperbole and a good deal of facile Marxist sloganizing, the Panthers seemed to me serious, hard-working, disciplined, and essentially humanistic in their work within the black community and in their vision of a more just society. For the Panthers, weapons are an instrument of self-protection and ultimately the means to achieve the revolution that, in the absence of a peaceful alternative, will make liberation possible."

squishy soft toward the Left. Any paper that publishes Hannah
Arendt can't be all bad is an apology often tendered for *New
York Review*. How so? J. M. Cameron said it in *NYR* in a review
of two of her books:[18] "But there she is, blocking the road,
stubborn, Gothic, simple where we look to find the complexity,
complex where we expect platitudes, an admirer of many styles of
thought and life and yet, surely, in the end a pessimist, a defender
of reaction, one who aches with nostalgia for a dead political
order."

Even Irving Kristol, the almost-was "domestic Kissinger,"
digs her in his fashion. "I admire her tremendously," he says, "but
her politics often puzzle me. I'd just as soon that she not be in
New York Review, because I think she's so superior to them. I
assume she's there because she's a good friend of Mary Mc-
Carthy's." (The two women have dedicated books to each other—
Arendt's *Crises of the Republic* and McCarthy's *Medina*.)

Skeptical of many Left tendencies, yet lofty enough to escape
the flak of ordinary ground level partisanship (*q.v.* Kristol's remarks), Arendt, according to conspiracy buffs, has an uncommonly long leash at the *Review*. Actually, her appearances have
been few. They would be more numerous if she would only accept
commissions (e.g., Silvers' offer to review Albert Speer's *Inside the
Third Reich*). But Arendt writes strictly for herself and not at the
behest of editors.

Arendt receives her visitor in her plainly furnished Riverside
Drive apartment, where neither rust nor moth could consume very
much. She is a pleasant, grandmotherly sort of woman with pro-
truding teeth and a thickly settled German accent. One would not
say she must have been beautiful when young but one could well
say she has attained, at sixty-five, a serenity of face that makes her

18. *Between Past and Future* and *Men in Dark Times*, November 6,
1969.

beautiful now. A dish of cashews and a plate of crackers have been set out on the corner of a coffee table.

The Jewish Mother in Arendt graciously offers to fix some supper. No, says her guest and, fortunately, she doesn't force the matter, which saves him from not a little embarrassment. Perhaps the free meal wouldn't have been as gauche a move as kicking over a full glass of cider, which he manages to do next by clumsily crossing his legs under the coffee table. ("See, that wouldn't have happened if you had sat at her feet," Murray Kempton quipped, attesting to Arendt's status as salon-keeper.) Arendt politely allows the spill to sink into her oriental rug without a fuss and fills her visitor's glass a second time.

"And what do you do?" she inquires before allowing her guest to proceed with the interview. She is well aware of his intentions —to discuss *New York Review* with her—so she can only be feeling him out by such direct inquiry. Gray eminences don't talk, at least not freely, with perfect strangers. The visitor quickly recites his vita—M.A. in philosophy from Boston University; a Ph.L. from the Higher Institute of Philosophy in Louvain, where his doctoral thesis on the problem of evil has been in abeyance for the past four years; a former editor at *Commonweal* and currently freelancing. Had she seen his reportage in the *Review* on Philip Berrigan? He evidently passes his orals, because she nods her head, and the talk pushes on.

When the author asked Harvard professor John Fairbank, an old China hand who is far right of *NYR* in his politics, what he was doing writing for Silvers, he replied, "Maybe I'm a fig leaf." Has Arendt ever wondered whether the *Review* was using her to hide its political *partes inhonestas*? No. Her acquaintance with Silvers and the Epsteins assures her of their issue orientation. They would never be so crass as to use her solely to cover their radical pudenda. Snobbism, however, is a motive Arendt does not rule out.

In the battle of the New York intelligentsia, Arendt has thrown in with the *Review* group rather than on the side of *Commentary*. Like many former *Commentary* contributors, she cannot abide the magazine's new direction.

Despite differences with *Commentary* and some of the *Review*'s leftish fancies, Arendt is remarkably even-keeled in her criticism of both. Although she describes Wrong's "Case" as criminal, she was not greatly perturbed by its presence. For that's the way things happen to be. Intellectuals do get vicious, even *New York Review* intellectuals (although the latter seem to Arendt to behave better). And what of those times when the *Review*'s viciousness appeared to veer out of control, when the *Review* allegedly crossed state lines with the intent to incite riot? Arendt admits that the *Review* may have lost its cool on occasions past, but she attributes this to Silvers' broad-mindedness (since narrowed, of course).

On the Arendt scale of intellectual irresponsibility, Wrong's charging the *Review* with anti-Americanism weighs heavier than Kopkind's "Morality, like politics, starts at the barrel of a gun." She sees a certain amount of inconsequential humor in Kopkind's slogan, but hears a note of smear in Wrong's testimony.

Before taking leave of the Left press, Arendt urges her visitor to read *The New Yorker* (yes, *The New Yorker*). She insists William Shawn's *New Yorker* is more radical on Vietnam and the Presidency in its "Talk of the Town" columns than Bob Silvers' *New York Review*.

On the way out Arendt is asked why she consented to be interviewed when her custom is to refuse such incursions. She tells her visitor that she thought the *Review* could benefit from a friendly word.

Hannah Arendt, a Jewish mother indeed.

5

The Care and Feeding of Talent

a/The Young

If you are young, gifted, and white, don't call the *New York Review*.[1] And they probably won't call you, either. *NYR* just isn't in the talent developing business. There is no on-the-job training. A Random House contract may help, e.g., contributor Emma Rothschild (*Paradise Lost*) is twenty-four. A good word from F. W. Dupee or Alfred Kazin might get you a look, but even their recommendations are passed over.

[1]. "And if you're black," sings Leadbelly, "get back, get back, get back." As far as this author can reckon, the *Review* has published fewer than ten Blacks in ten years. Among those who have broken *NYR*'s color line are Ralph Ellison, James Baldwin, Stokely Carmichael, George Jackson, Harold Cruse, and an anonymous Ghanaian. No doubt other Blacks have been assigned books and, for one reason or another, their reviews were either never completed or rejected. Kenneth Clark is an example of the former, Roger Wilkins of the latter.

Women are not in the same boat as the Blacks, but the frequency of their appearances at the *Review* is scant. Not counting Elizabeth Hardwick, Mary McCarthy, Ellen Willis, and Francine Gray, the *Review* publishes no female writers with any regularity—that is, more than twice a year. Books by feminists or about women also tend to be reviewed by men—e.g., Gore Vidal on *Patriarchal Attitudes* by Eva Figes, Richard Sennett on *Dialectic of Sex* by Shulamith Firestone and *Woman's Estate* by Juliet Mitchell, and Erwin Singer on *The Female Orgasm* by Seymour Fischer. Adrienne Rich's essay taking off from Midge Decter's *The New Chastity* is the only feminist "statement" the *Review* has ever printed (April 20, 1972).

189

If you want to break into the *Review*, your best bet is to establish yourself elsewhere and hope somebody over there loves you. But even if you are fortunate enough to plant your foot in the door before forty, you're not home yet. For, in general, the *Review* has a wretched reputation when it comes to dealing with young and/or "unimportant" writers. The magazine put the new generation of critics on notice in a 1967 advertisement which flaunted the reigning merito-gerontocracy: "The *New York Review* has been accused of being the house organ of the intellectual establishment . . . Yes, it's only too true, we must agree with our detractors; our roster of critics does sound as though there were a conspiracy among the most articulate and influential men and women writing today. It's a conspiracy against bad writers . . . *against the wet-behind-the-ears young punks that don't know what to bite next.*" [Emphasis added.]

The *Review* prefers great page-consuming baobabs in its landscape—the better the older. "Every two weeks, *The New York Review of Books* publishes the world's best writers and scholars," blared a 1972 ad, "—Edmund Wilson, Isaiah Berlin, Robert Lowell, Erik Erikson, Lewis Mumford, W. H. Auden, Alfred

Kazin, Mary McCarthy, Hannah Arendt, and many others." The average age of this peer group was sixty-five. The seniority system counts for more in the society of letters than it does in most societies. The literary establishment tends not to look with very much favor upon the young, and the *Review* is establishmentarian to a fault.

Take the strange case of Charles Thomas Samuels, thirty-seven, professor of English at Williams College, frequent contributor to the *Times Book Review*, movie critic at the quasi-scholarly quarterly *American Scholar*, and author of four books.[2] Samuels was a mere boy in the fall of 1965, when the contact was initially made. One day he received in the mail a packet of five books including Updike's *The Music School*. There was no accompanying letter. Samuels couldn't figure it out. Three days later, a note from Bob Silvers arrived asking him to review the books. Who me? Write for *New York Review*? Samuels was transfigured. "In my first year of reviewing, it seemed like the laying on of hands." Samuels had to refuse Silvers, however, because he had already done *The Music School* for *The Nation*. Nevertheless, Samuels wrote Silvers what he himself calls an "ingenuous reply," expressing appreciation for having been noticed and offering alternative suggestions for fiction reviews. Then a second packet came, containing Christina Stead's *Dark Places of the Heart, The Collected Works of Jane Bowles*, and Hortense Calisher's *Journal from Ellipsia* (none of which Samuels had in mind). Although the combination of these ladies threw him off, Samuels went ahead with the tripartite review. "I disliked it," he says. "But Silvers thought it was excellent and published it, ignoring my corrections of the galleys. I cravenly accepted this." A month later, another unannounced packet appeared, followed by yet another letter. The request was for a piece on Jewish fiction spinning off from recent

2. *Encountering Directors, The Ambiguity of Henry James, John Updike,* and *A Casebook on Film.*

books by Arthur Cohen, Meyer Liben, and Isaac Rosenfeld. This
was a very yawn-producing subject for Samuels, and the fiction
wasn't too impressive to boot. He told Silvers the books were unworthy, proposing once again other possibilities. "Silvers responded with praise of my candor. How delighted he was to find
a young critic who didn't . . ." But history repeated itself a fourth
time—packet, letter, expectation of joint review of disjointed
books. Reluctantly, Samuels proceeded to review Robert Shaw's
Man in a Glass Booth, Alfred Chester's *The Exquisite Corpse*,
and Burt Blechman's *Maybe*. "They didn't go together at all, but
I did my best." Suddenly, all correspondence from the *Review*
ceased. Samuels says his piece was well aged before Silvers returned it, criticizing the Chester segment as incomprehensible and
paying him off at a price considerably less than they had agreed
upon. Samuels was surprised by the non-negotiable aspect of the
rejection and the smaller fee but, after publishing the Chester in
The Nation and the Shaw in *The New Leader* (both unrevised),
he let his anger ride. There was no percentage in forcing a row
with the *Review*, and an ambitious young writer wisely plays the
percentages. Months passed without a packet in the mail. Samuels
should have known he was all washed up at the *Review*. Lust for
recognition does funny things to young minds, however. To wit:
Samuels wrote Silvers, inquiring whether he might possibly review
three movie books. Complete silence. Not even a "Thanks, but no
thanks." Months later, Samuels was in New York chatting with
his friend film (not movie) critic John Simon. Upon hearing
Samuels' predicament, Simon urged him to phone Silvers before
quitting town. Samuels did. "In the coldest imaginable voice, Silvers
told me that the books I was interested in had already been
assigned." Samuels got the picture.

It is now several years later, and Samuel's annoyance, however quiescent, still lingers. "The *New York Review* is the best
intellectual generalist's magazine in the country," he gladly affirms,

"but I hold two things against them. They haven't fulfilled one of the primary obligations of a new journal that seeks greatness— they haven't sought out enough new native talent, particularly in *belles lettres*, another sign of their relative indifference to this area, and they have neither nurtured nor even treated decently the few new voices they've discovered. Why haven't they published young critics like Morris Dickstein, Leo Bersani, Robert Garis, Elizabeth Dalton, Samuel McCracken, Peter Shaw, Alvin Kibel, Cynthia Ozick, William Pritchard?"

Samuels' obiter dicta are more personal, but still admissible evidence. "Furthermore," he says, "they destroyed in me a sense of distinction conferred by utterly ignoring my own sense of what I was best for. What were they hiring? Surely, not a name, since I had none. Presumably a talent, but they knew less about the nature of my talent than any publication I've ever written for. Would Silvers dictate to his big names, let alone anyone writing about current affairs, the way he dictated to me? Or so thoroughly ignore my preferences? I think not. So, despite his considerable virtues as an editor, he is also top-lofty."

Although the Charles Thomas Samuels story is one of dashed hopes and glory denied, too many like-sounding complaints are heard in literary circles to suspect him purely of sour grapes. Silvers has the bad habit of waxing enthusiastic over a new face and then waning inaccessibly when his anticipation is unrealized. Richard Gilman, who has recently graduated from "young critic" to "younger critic" (a designation bestowed when you cross over into your forties to distinguish you from older critics who are not as young as you are), was also wiped out by the *Review* in precisely this manner.

A few years ago Silvers and Gilman met at a party. Gilman happened to mention he was resigning as literary editor of *The New Republic* and going up to the Yale School of Drama. Well, then, he would be free to do something for the *Review*. Yes, he would. Gilman thereupon reviewed the posthumous *Mystery and Manners* by Flannery O'Connor (August 21, 1969). Silvers praised the author all the way to the Century Club where, over lunch, he asked him to become a regular contributor on films. Gilman accepted and opened with a piece on *Easy Rider* and *Coming Apart*.

Then the ordeal began. Gilman waited for weeks without a hint. Here he was the *NYR*'s new film critic, and he couldn't even get a screening of his first review. Eventually, judge and supplicant came together quite by accident at Robert Brustein's summer place on the Vineyard. "We had trouble with it," Silvers sheepishly informed Gilman. "Too aesthetic," were his exact words. Perhaps Gilman would do a major rewrite? Not a chance. Gilman published the *Easy Rider* part in *Partisan* without changing a line, and *NYR* fell back on Ellen Willis for a less aesthetic treatment.[3] Willis seemed a strange choice to back up Gilman. Although an exceptionally fine writer, she is also a radical feminist, a counter-culture star, and a former communard in her callow youth—just the kind of kid the *Review* warned itself never to play with. But Willis was also *The New Yorker*'s rock columnist. Serving youth as he never had before, Silvers subsequently asked Willis to cover the Manson trial. Willis, down on Los Angeles, nixed the invite, but surfaced again to review *Deep Throat* (October 3, 1972).

3. Her lead paragraph reads: "In 1969, the Year of the Pig, participants in what is known as (descriptively) youth culture or (smugly) hip culture or (incompletely) pop culture or (longingly) the cultural revolution are going through big changes. For choices have to be made now; they can no longer be left to a dubious mañana. After hearing Nixon's speech—'North Vietnam cannot defeat us; we can only defeat ourselves'—who can doubt that America as we have known it could completely disappear between one day and the next? Or maybe it already has, and what we are feeling now is phantom pain from an amputated limb. In this crisis our confusions and ambivalences about this country, *our* country, no matter how securely they seem to have occupied it, become more than intellectual gossip. Our lives may literally depend on how we resolve them" (January 1, 1970).

b/Missing Persons

Dennis Wrong made hay over the fact that certain writers no longer appear in the *Review*. He listed Lionel Abel, David T. Bazelon, Lewis Coser, Midge Decter, Oscar Gass, Nathan Glazer, Irving Howe, Benjamin De Mott, Richard Hofstadter (now deceased), David Riesman, Richard Rovere, C. Vann Woodward, and Dennis Wrong. Wrong would have us believe that the aforesaid were declared unpersons by the *Review* for having criticized the New Left or positions favored by the editors. Strictly circumstantial evidence. With the single exception of Irving Howe, none of the supposed dropouts was ever a regular reviewer, and most of them departed long before family quarrels heated up the atmosphere. For example: Abel—two appearances, both in

1963; Coser—three appearances, last time in 1964; Decter—three appearances, last time in 1964; Gass—three appearances, last time in 1965; De Mott—four appearances, last time in 1964; Hofstadter—five appearances, last time in 1967; Riesman—a lone appearance in the special 1963 Kennedy memorial issue (which Wrong had already said wouldn't be counted if the only occasion a writer published in the *Review*); Richard Rovere—three appearances, last time in 1965. The precariousness of Wrong's accounting became painfully obvious after C. Vann Woodward's eulogy of Hofstadter ran in a December 1970 issue of the *Review*.

Now it is perfectly possible, even probable, that the *Review* applies a political test to some of its contributors some of the time. What magazine doesn't? And why isolate *NYR*'s ideological discrimination? But in this instance Wrong's evidence failed to support his point. He should have known better than argue *post hoc, ergo propter hoc* unless he could demonstrate the connection. If he had cared to check David Riesman about his ties with the *Review*, he would have learned that Silvers has repeatedly tried to get him in the magazine, but that Riesman simply doesn't enjoy doing reviews. Richard Rovere says there has been "no overt political break" between him and the *Review*. Benjamin De Mott admits an estrangement, which has nothing to do with politics. Midge Decter's separation from the *Review* was literary in origin. And even after some unpleasantness over the rejection of her review of Mailer's *The Presidential Papers*, she was asked to contribute again (and turned down the particular assignments). When the Podhoretz-Epstein friendship began to fall apart, it was only natural that Decter would also fade away from the *Review*. If people no longer speak to each other, they should not be expected to function well together professionally, should they?

Editorial relations are not so different from human relations. They can flounder for an enormous variety of reasons on the editors' *as well as* the writers' part—pique, revenge, loss of interest or confidence, hurt, meanness, misunderstanding, jealousy, lethargy, writers' block, and, of course, politics (including the office kind). A bad review of a contributor's last book, especially if written by an avowed enemy or someone thought to be such, leads to strain (e.g., Eric Foner's review of Theodore Draper's *The Rediscovery of Black Nationalism*). Conversely, if a contributor attacks the *Review* in another publication, his welcome may be rescinded (e.g. Irving Howe, but not Alfred Kazin). No matter how it's sliced, then, Wrong's reductionism does not convince.

*   *   *

Consider the banishment of Benjamin De Mott. Politically motivated? Hardly. Any student of New York literary diplomacy with half a memory would direct you to his *NYR* review of Podhoretz's essay collection *Doings and Undoings* (April 30, 1964). Instead of confining his comments to the book, which was treated to a chapter-by-chapter acupuncture, piercing Podhoretz's style and stance, De Mott went after bigger game—the New York intellectual ecology. "That the reminders [of incontrovertible truths] are dully phrased," he wrote like a drugged kamikaze, "that their source is a writer whose literary taste and manner are undistinguished, that the soundness of this writer's public intelligence is poor justification for extending privileged status to his ventures at criticism, that the crowd which extends the privilege is still too arrogant and coarse to grasp the nature of its mistake—all these matters warrant regret and attention." Both Jason Epstein and William Phillips responded angrily in letters to the editor. And De Mott has not been seen in the vicinity of the *Review* since. On paper, it's an open and shut case. De Mott screwed a friend of the *Review* and, as night follows day, he was screwed in return. But as day follows night, the story is not as simple as that.

Ben De Mott is a large, loping lumberjack of a fellow with formidable extremities. He talks with the New England backwoodsy twang of Orson Bean and dresses like him, too—in natty blazer and slacks rather than in the furry tweeds and fading corduroys which dominate East Coast faculty wardrobes. He shows his visitor to a corner in Amherst's small, pour-your-own faculty bar and describes what happened between the lines at the *Review*.

"I didn't write for them any more, partly because I still owed them a piece. They wanted me to do an omnibus review of several books on drug addiction and drug culture, and I really didn't know what to make of it—I was no expert. It was too embarrassing for us all to renegotiate the thing. Then, just at the time I took that review on, I accepted a regular reviewing job at *Harper's* and started writing for *The New York Times Magazine*. Maybe they thought this bucket was going to the well a little too often. We were interested in De Mott when he was ours."

Strange, isn't it, that De Mott would be handed another review *after* his demolition of *Doings* was sent in, but *before* it was published? "There was no communication before publication," he says. "I don't think Bob and Barbara realized what the reaction would be. I think I came by the office with a reply to some letters about the piece. I talked just for a minute. But Barbara seemed upset about the review. What made the situation difficult is that it was the kind of discussion you would have about a manuscript. But it wasn't a manuscript. It was already published."

Only an innocence fed by twenty years of Pioneer Valley isolation and a firm faith in the indefectibility of man could have allowed De Mott to say what he said without full knowledge of the consequences. You don't mess with branches of the Family the way he did and land without a scratch. "It's one of the things that happens," explains De Mott, "when you're away from the city and don't know the map of relationships. The principal problem was that this review might hurt the magazine, and I worried about it because I cared for the *New York Review*. I liked writing there. The *Review* was becoming a cultural force. For God's sake, I didn't mean to make an assault of any kind on Podhoretz. You know, I was offered more advance money than I have ever been offered to write a muckraking book on the literary establishment. People who see the literary life as a conspiracy saw me as their spokesman. This made me feel quite understanding that the *Review* wasn't hounding me for my drug piece."

Speak the name De Mott, and Podhoretz winces. "There are some people who can't stand to have other people do them favors," he says, meaning that he introduced De Mott to New York in *Commentary*, and De Mott felt obliged to slay him accordingly. Podhoretz cut out the largesse, though, as he closed *Commentary*'s temple doors on the cursed infidel from Amherst. (N.B., Dennis Wrong.)

*   *   *

Over the years there have been conspicuous absences from the pages of *New York Review*. While some of the vanishing acts are larded with significance, others are not. There is little to be said about Saul Bellow's work stoppage, which came after V. S. Pritchett's review of *Herzog*—"In his new book, *Herzog*, we find him once more scattering the high-class corn" (October 22, 1964). The notoriously thin-skinned Bellow still refers to "that terrible Bob Silvers." But give Bellow the benefit of the grudge, for how would you like to be caricatured by David Levine hanging naked from a cross with your typewriter perched on the transverse?

Bellow corresponds from Chicago:

The review of *Herzog* was not responsible for the "break"* between me and the *NYR*. I never quarrel with reviews or with reviewers. It was the politics of the paper I objected to.

---

* "I didn't 'break'; I never joined."

Or rather, the social policy of the *NYR*, its view of American life and institutions.

My main criticism of the *NYR* is that it never seriously and comprehensively attempted to review books. It was rather a paper which gratified the needs of militant profs. Kazin's review of my book [*Mr. Sammler's Planet*] was part of the thing. It was not, properly speaking, a review at all, but rather a policy statement, entirely tendentious, and having nothing at all to do with literary criticism.

*   *   *

Truman Capote, like Bellow, appeared only once in the *Review*. How come? The reason seemed obvious from a bitchy remark attributed to him in an *Atlantic* profile of Gore Vidal (March 1972): "He has built his career very carefully. He wants to be in the *Saturday Review* and at the same time he wants to be in a snot-rag like the *New York Review*." "Snot-rag?" That's a new one. Whatever does Capote mean? When faced with his quote for the first time, Capote denies he ever made the equation attributed to him. "I know what I did say. I remember I said Gore tries to play the game all different ways—movies, plays, and at the same time he's on the editorial board of *Partisan Review*. I've had nothing but very pleasant associations with *New York Review*. I just don't like book reviewing. I wrote a review [of Michel Butor's *Mobile*, September 12, 1963]. It's the only book review I ever did, and it wasn't very good. I said snot-rags like *Partisan Review*. There are magazines that bore me to death. To be perfectly frank, *New York Review* is rather dull. I don't think it should be called *The New York Review of Books*. Most of their articles are on politics. It's extraordinary that they never give space to creative writing. [. . .] There's one writer at *New York Review* that I think is marvelous. Whenever he writes for them I pick up the issue. But I can't remember his name. [The author suggests the name of Robert Mazzocco.] Yes, I think he's really bright. I called up Silvers and asked to meet him. He's an extremely good-looking boy. He looks like a movie star. I don't know why he lives like a recluse. He considers himself a poet, but he doesn't publish."

*   *   *

Norman Mailer's eight-year stomp-out is, as you would expect, part of the public record. A letter to Bob Silvers, published in *Cannibals and Christians,* because Silvers would not print it in the *Review,* recounts the circumstances behind the split. Mailer's note is in answer to a request for 1,800 words on the new Hubert Humphrey.

> . . . A year and a half ago, you asked me to review *The Group.* Said you had offered the novel to seven people—all seven were afraid to review it. You appealed to my manhood, my fierce eschatological sword. St. Mary's wrath (according to you) was limned with brimfire. Would I do it, you begged, as a most special favor to you? Perhaps, you suggested, I was the only man in New York who had the guts to do it. A shrewd appeal. I did it. Two months later, my book (*The Presidential Papers*) came out. You had given the book to Midge Decter for review. Her submitted piece was, in your opinion—I quote your label—'overinflated.' That is to say, it was favorable. Changes were requested. The reviewer refused to make them. The review was not printed. No review of *The Presidential Papers* appeared in *The New York Review of Books.* Only a parody. By a mystery guest. Now we have my new book, *An American Dream.* I hear you have picked Philip Rahv to review it, Philip Rahv, whose detestation of my work has been thundering these last two years into the gravy stains of every literary table on the Eastern seaboard.
>
> In the name, therefore, of the sweet gracious Jesus, why expect me to do eight words on your subject?

Was Decter's review actually "overinflated"? Overinflated? It was a veritable dirigible (see it aloft in *Commentary,* October 1964). The *Review* wasn't buying the then-minority notion that "no one is currently telling us more about the United States of America [than Norman Mailer]." What the *Review* really

thought of *The Presidential Papers* was expressed in a parody
entitled "The Sixth Vice Presidential Note" by Xavier Prynne, a
play-on Xavier Rynne, the pseudonym for the writer of *The New
Yorker*'s "Letter From the Vatican" column. An excerpt:

> This 6th note was ignored by LBJ, but attacked by the Black
> Negroes and the FBI. One admits that a lot of it is lousy—I
> was having personal troubles at the time—but I still think it
> is lousy but good. The Bitch Goddess didn't quite get into
> bed with me this round, but at least she didn't get into bed
> with Bill Styron either, up in his plush Connecticut retreat.
> All the Bitch did was blow into my ear—one of those mys-
> terious pre-psychotic Jackie Kennedy whispers. My answer to
> the FBI would run this way: *The existential orgasm would
> make atomic war and even atomic testing impossible . . .*

The scarlet parodist was Elizabeth Hardwick.

Did Mailer suppose the *Review* turned down the Decter
piece which, while hyperduliac, was not unlike many others *NYR*
had deigned to print, in deference to Hardwick? His reply from
South Londonderry, Vermont: "I would guess that Silvers was
unduly respectful to Lizzie Hardwick [whom Mailer calls "boss-
lady"] in those days and much more disposed to keep in her
good favor than in mine. I can hardly blame him. Lizzie was
much more use then than she is now." This was in 1971.

In 1973, however, Mailer seemed to be launching a grand
comeback in *NYR* with a piece on *Last Tango* and an excerpt
from *Marilyn*. What gives? Mailer writes from Stockbridge, Massachusetts:

> Silvers works, I believe, on the premise that feuds, or at any
> rate literary feuds, dissolve in time and so without making a
> great deal of it, he had invited me every now and then to do
> something for the *New York Review*, once specifically I re-
> member he wanted me to do a review of *El Topo*. Finally,
> with *Last Tango in Paris*, I agreed after seeing the film. Silvers
> and I have been perfectly ready to talk with one another over

the past several years at cocktail parties and besides I've come to the grudged conclusion that willy-nilly the *New York Review* was the best literary magazine around, or at least the most interesting for someone like myself so I don't think Bob had to twist my arm very hard. Since they also do a fine job editorially, full of cooperation without ever leaning . . . I did not hesitate to offer them a part of *Marilyn*. As for being "together again," my name is not likely to appear in the *Review* that often. Not from animus however, so much as that I simply can't afford to get sidetracked much longer from the novel I hope to pick up again and criticism can often catch me up for a surprising amount of time.

Ironically, before the 1964 nasty business transpired, Mailer and Hardwick were the villains in another *interruptus* at the *Review*. Mailer's uncharitable review of *The Group*, which followed immediately upon Prynne-Hardwick's unforgivable parody of "The Gang" was more than sufficient for Mary McCarthy to throw in her pencil. Was this her reward for helping out in the early days? How could her friend Hardwick do this to her? A tearful scene ensued, and McCarthy walked out on Silvers and the *Review*, not to return until four years later, when Silvers offered her, at Hardwick's insistence, a trip to Hanoi.

* * *

Whatever happened to Malcolm Muggeridge? Once a prolific contributor (seven appearances between 1963 and 1965), he bit the dust rather suddenly, an insider discloses, after suggesting Max Beerbohm was a closet queen and secret Jew in a review of David Cecil's biography, *Max*. Asked about the Beerbohm affair and how he presently regards the *Review*, Muggeridge responds from Park Cottage, Robertsbridge, Sussex:

> I started off writing quite a lot for *The New York Review of Books* and very pleased with the whole venture. I liked Bob Silvers, too. However, the same thing always happens with such magazines; they drift into taking what to me is a com-

pletely untenable and fatuous leftist position. This culminated in the diagram they gave for making a Molotov Cocktail, which struck me as completely infantile.

Yes, there was a row about my review on Max Beerbohm, which again annoyed me, because I realized from it that the magazine had fallen into another trap—of devising its own orthodoxy. [. . .]

In short, I consider the magazine a casualty to radical chic. I was more surprised than annoyed when they published a very scarifying review of a collection of articles of mine, which included quite a number that had, in fact, appeared in the *Review* and had been wildly praised by the editor. [*The Most of Malcolm Muggeridge*, reviewed by D. A. N. Jones, December 29, 1966.] However, that's life.

Muggeridge adds a handwritten postscript in thick blue-ink strokes:

About Max B, Yes, I challenged David Cecil's, as I think, very feeble biography, pointing out that Max was an [the word "ashamed" is crossed out] Jew and homosexual and an insensate snob, tho I liked and admired him. This caused a furore at the *Review* office. First they said they lost the copy, then, when I sent my black [i.e., carbon copy] Bob telephoned from N. Y. in a state, saying, as I recall, F———— David Cecil. Finally, they used the piece, but it was my last.

* * *

For eight years Susan Sontag was the *Review*'s most missed missing person, and there isn't a textual clue for her long disqualification. She came through for the premiere number and was featured on the cover of the third issue with a review of Camus' *Notebooks 1935–42*. In the succeeding ten months she did four pieces—and then not a trace until her obituary of Paul Goodman in September of 1972. Her swan song happened to be a broadside against Ionesco's *Notes and Counter Notes*, but this was scarcely the sort of thing one was excommunicated for.

Sontag's distress was well veiled in a passage from her long essay "Trip to Hanoi." She went to North Vietnam in the spring of 1968 with Robert Greenblatt of the People's Peace Treaty and Andrew Kopkind. Having considered her own ambivalence toward an "ethical society" like North Vietnam, where she could not live without sacrificing the "astonishing array of intellectual and aesthetic pleasures" of her own "unethical society," she wrote:

> What came to mind this afternoon was the sentence of Talley-rand that Bertolucci used as the motto of his sad, beautiful film: "He who has not lived before the revolution has never known the sweetness of life." I told Andy, who knows the film, what I'd been thinking, and he confessed to similar feelings. We were walking alone in a quarter of Hanoi, far from the hotel and, like truants, began talking—nostalgically?— about San Francisco rock groups and *The New York Review of Books.*

Sontag told the story at one of William Phillips' *nostalgie du temps perdu* dinners in the spring of 1971. For a while now, Phillips has been inviting Right and Left representatives in for the express purpose of airing out some of the "bad humor" that has contaminated the intellectual environment of the city. Lionel Trilling, Irving Howe, Richard Gilman, Peter Brooks, Hannah Arendt, Harold Rosenberg, Jack Newfield, and the like have broken bread under Phillips' roof. Sontag related that one day toward the end of 1964 she got a call from Bob Silvers, a friend of twenty years. We don't want you to write for us any more, she said he told her.

What Sontag did not mention was the fact that she had been rehabilitated in the eyes of the *Review* after her Hanoi article appeared in *Esquire* in 1968. Silvers recommended she do something for the *Review* on film directing, and she was asked to cover the first moonshot as well. But neither article turned up. Silvers

then gave her some feminist books to review. Why, then, didn't
she mention she was back with the *Review*? "Oh, that's just
Susan," a friend says. "She likes to be mysterious." Another friend,
who is an *NYR* regular, showed less equanimity. "If they ever
treated me that way, I'd never write for them again." After repeated denials, someone privy to the *Review*'s decision-making
finally came out with it. "I know what the reason is," the person
suggested. "One of the two editors didn't like her writing very
well." What writing? Probably Sontag's excursions into the "new
sensibility"—for example, her homage to homosexual taste in
"Notes on Camp," which exploded in *Partisan Review* in 1964,
not long before her *NYR* exit. Which editor? According to someone close to Sontag, Silvers was outvoted.

A *Partisan Review* associate of Sontag's brings up the matter of literary politics. "Susan has always been such a figure that
if you publish her, it seems you're committing yourself to something. It's almost the same thing with Mailer—some writers'
accents are so strong that you look like creatures of them." Perhaps that's what has happened with Robert Brustein, previously a
frequent contributor to the *Review*. Ever since he moved to Yale
as Dean of the Drama School, Brustein has been sounding off
like David Susskind on radical students, Black Panthers, the
counter-culture, and the decline of professionalism. Since 1968, his
liberal-minded lovers' quarrel sanities have been published by
the *New Republic*, the *New York Times Magazine*, and *Modern
Occasions*, but never by the *New York Review*. Although Brustein has been displeased with *NYR*'s "tendency to turn life into a
melodrama," he says his relations with Bob Silvers have always
been cordial. He had recently called him up offering coverage of
the Theater of Ideas' Mailer-Greer-Trilling symposium on women.
Sorry, Susan Sontag was already doing a feminist piece for the
Review, and she might want to include the evening in her report.
A colleague believes Brustein may be blocking here. The *Review*

doesn't seem to be the natural habitat for the writer of the following:

Thus, we find New York hostesses transferring their charitable impulses from the Junior League and the hospital fund to the Black Panthers and other radical groups—raising money, over cocktails and canapés, to help such movements achieve their objectives. (Obviously, I am not criticizing the sincere efforts of serious civil liberties groups to protect the physical safety and civil rights of radicals threatened with police violence and legal harassment.) There is something profoundly disturbing about the moral spectacle of these affairs, when guests file past private guards or through these intricate safety systems that have become so common in Manhattan today to be exhorted by those whose announced aims include the abolition of private property and the extermination of the "pigs."[4]

Especially when Silvers attended Leonard Bernstein's mythic party and Jason Epstein criticized Tom Wolfe for his "lack of compassion" in *Radical Chic*.

* * *

To what can we attribute the loss of William Styron? "It's probably political," hypothesized a New York magazine editor. "He probably doesn't like the *Review*'s politics." Is that so? Ask the man who knows:

There were no hard feelings or differences of opinion involved in the fact that I have more or less stopped writing for the *New York Review*. It is simply because, although I am not adverse to writing an occasional critical piece, criticism really doesn't interest me too much, and that is why my work has not recently appeared there. Although I find the *Review* often

4. "Revolution as Theatre," *New Republic*, March 14, 1970, reprinted in *Revolution as Theatre: Notes on the New Radical Style*.

long-winded and boring, I think it is an invaluable publication and wouldn't do without it.

While a bad review often erodes affection, a good notice makes the heart grow fonder. As Styron's conclusion shows, *NYR* is a two-edged sword:

> On purely personal grounds, I am especially appreciative of the fact that the *Review* published the historian Eugene Genovese's defense of *The Confessions of Nat Turner* against the black writers who attacked it, exposing their hysteric foolishness and paranoia for what it was. It was a bang-up job, and I don't know of many other publications which would have given the piece so much space, or in whose pages the essay would have received such serious and valuable attention.

*   *   *

Theodore Draper, high-level debunker of official versions of Vietnam negotiations, the Dominican invasion, black nationalism, and the Cuban revolution, won't put his foot inside the *Review* again. A friend points to the long-winded letters of dissent which Silvers published in response to his article on black nationalist Martin Delaney, "The Father of American Black Nationalism" (March 12, 1970). But that wasn't it, says Draper, who is now at Princeton's Institute for Advanced Study. "The trouble came subsequently with a review of my own book *The Rediscovery of Black Nationalism* [October 22, 1970]. Silvers gave it to a man [Professor Eric Foner of Columbia] who went around for weeks saying that he would get the book. I think the phrase was 'fry him on toast.' I felt if Bob was going to give my book to someone who was going to treat it that way, I saw no reason to collaborate on his paper. [. . .] It just made me feel queasy. When I saw he was continuing to push Foner, I decided I wasn't welcome. I just didn't want to publish in a magazine that treated me that way. Foner, in my opinion, had written the kind of review that would convince me not to give him another book. It was a quiet withdrawal." Did Draper know that Silvers knew of Foner's alleged premeditation? "I don't know. Maybe he didn't."

Foner calls Draper's story "ridiculous." He says the phrase "fry him on toast" is not in his repertoire. "In fact, I don't think more than three or four people knew I was reviewing Draper's book before the review appeared."

* * *

At least two expulsions from the *Review*'s garden had blatant political overtones—Irving Howe on the Right and Andrew Kopkind on the Left. Off the record, Silvers offered to explain the real reason Howe was let go, but the author refused to listen to Silvers' secret if it could not be quoted. Howe's version is on the record. "I would guess I did as much for them as anybody else [fourteen pieces from the first issue to mid-1968]. But once I published my critique in *Commentary*, they never asked me again. There was no quarrel, however. Instead, there was an amusing incident. They had a strictly literary piece—a review of Renato Poggioli's book on modernism. Suddenly, they had objections. The review was too abstract, and they wanted changes.

"I was surprised by their reaction. I thought this was a petty response. I attacked *Partisan Review* in *The Age of Conformity* and in a piece on the *PR Reader* in *New York Review*, and they kept asking me. That's part of mature relationships, unless there's a knock-down, drag-out fight, which I don't think the *Commentary* article was."

* * *

Andrew Kopkind has a history of moving on. He began at *Time* and then went to the *New Republic* and then the *New York Review* and then, with James Ridgeway and Robert Sherrill, he founded his own independent newsletter, *Hard Times*, which eventually was stapled into *Ramparts* before it petered out in 1972. He wrote six pieces for the *Review* in 1967 and three in 1968. Not once has he darkened their doorstep in the meantime.

How come? Two citations: (1) Bob Silvers reads one of Kopkind's left-of-Left articles in *Hard Times* and says, "I can't print that stuff." Of course, he couldn't. In 1969, the *Review* was in full retreat from its scorch-the-earth radicalism, and no way was it going to march with the forward brigades of the movement which were seeking therapy in action. "*Hard Times* was something of an anomaly in that critical activity: at once traditional in form and style and radical in content and action," Kopkind and Ridgeway observe in their *HT* anthology *Decade of Crisis*. "Increasingly, the writers and editors abandoned much of their roles as detached critics and observers and became part of the process they were describing. It could hardly have been otherwise; in one sense, detachment, privatism, and professionalism were underpinning values which had to come under attack." Colleagues of Kopkind differ on who alienated whom. Jeff Shero says Kopkind shed the *Review* just as he had shed *Time* and the *New Republic*. "It was a way station on his journey" (which recently stopped off in the weekly Boston *Phoenix*, where he is writing pretty tame stuff compared to *Review* days, and on Boston's WBCN-FM, where he co-hosts the gay *Lavender Hour*). Another friend hints he would still like to contribute to *NYR*.

(2) "Kopkind turned out to be a pain in the ass," Merle Miller quotes Epstein in the *Times*. In response to one query as to the cause of his separation from the *Review*, Kopkind answered:

> I never did write anything about my relationship with the *New York Review*. I didn't notice that I came and went very quickly; I did several long pieces of reportage and criticism for the paper over the space of two years. During all of that time, my contacts with the editors were (at least in my view) excellent. I thought then, and still do, that Bob Silvers was

the best editor I had ever worked with; I didn't work much with Barbara Epstein (who handled literary criticism more than political writing), but on the few occasions we did work together, I found her equally good. After many years of doing that kind of journalism, I felt I needed some change of writing perspective and began grinding (or winding) down; *Hard Times*, which was a paper Jim Ridgeway and I put out weekly in Washington for two years, merged into *Ramparts* as a monthly supplement to that magazine; I do occasional pieces for *Ramparts* now, but that's about the lot of it. I didn't "leave" the *NY Review*, or quit, or anything like that, although I heard, second hand, that some people there were rather put off by a more activist, personally-involved political writing I began doing in *Hard Times*. But that is all second hand, and I believe my relationship with the paper is still viable. But Bob would have to confirm that.

c/Daumier Lives!

There is a good David Levine and a bad David Levine. The good David Levine paints tender chauvinist portraits of garment workers and bathers at Coney Island beach. The bad David Levine draws Saul Bellow on the cross and Richard Nixon with dripping fangs.

This awfully split personality resides in the flesh of a dark-complexioned, forty-four-year-old man of medium height and

Jewish face-in-the-crowd looks. If you were going to caricature
Levine, you might seize upon his slightly beaked nose and
straight-back haircomb. Other than that, he is physically nondescript, especially when dressed in khakis and polo shirt as he
was one fine summer day in his clean, well-lighted Brooklyn
brownstone, located a chip shot from Prospect Park.

Whatever evil lurks in the heart of his caricatures, David
Levine is not by nature a ghoul. The motives behind the political
drawings are purely political. "They are men with extraordinary
power to affect everybody," Levine explains in a steady mono-
tone. "It's not as if these politicians come into an issue without
bias. I know what these guys stand for, but I don't have a novel
to describe their complexity. By distorting Johnson's ears or
Nixon's nose, I help people to think of them critically. Caricatures should be used against power. I'm a radical-socialist, and if
a socialist came to power, I'd have to use the caricature against
him, too."

Levine's hardness on geopolitics coexists with a deft, knowing vision of literary figures. How can he be so consistently right?
When does he have time to read up on the ten caricatures he
does for the *Review* every month? It turns out Levine doesn't
read much at all. "I call myself an illiterate literary caricaturist."
Would you believe he wings his drawings with a little help from
the accompanying article, an engraving or photograph, and common recall? When he's really stuck, though, he phones Barbara Epstein to learn more about the subject. Improvisatory as
this technique appears, a skilled draftsman has no problem gen-
eralizing body features and projecting historical characteristics.
Levine is safe as long as his art imitates life.

He remembers only one instance when his instinct failed him.
Without reading the text of the review, he assumed Bernard
Malamud's *The Fixer* was just another Jewish novel. Poor Mala-
mud was mistakenly identified as a tefilin-toting Orthodox. Levine

had a run-in with Norman Mailer over another Semite matter. It seems that Mailer strained his eyes to see satanic designs in a series of nine Podhoretz caricatures which illustrated Rust Hills' review of *Making It* in *Esquire* (April 1968). In his *Partisan Review* essay on *Making It* (Spring 1968), Mailer hauled off on the caricatures, which were allegedly "so connotative of old nightmares in the pages of *Der Stürmer* that one was finally obliged to wonder what occult species was Levine and how ammonia-odored was the hand which held the drawing pen of such a crotch—did the fingers stink of crap or bat or pigeon piss?" Scatology got Mailer nowhere though; Levine was perplexed rather than perturbed.

On rare occasions, the *Review* will reject a Levine. "I once did a drawing of Dylan Thomas with a tail coming out of his rear. The reference was to *Portrait of the Artist as a Young Dog.* They thought it obscene. I did a very grotesque caricature of Sidney Hook, which they never published. Recently, I drew Nixon as a fetus for a Philip Roth piece, which they never used either." Sometimes, the objection is political rather than aesthetic. "Bob was critical of a drawing of a militant Buddhist leader, and I guess he was right. I had him standing with a match on his shoulder which suggested the waste and silliness of self-immolation. But Bob insisted that you had to respect the feelings that led to this extreme gesture."

The only person Levine has been instructed to leave alone is Hannah Arendt. ("She was not happy with the prospect.") Otherwise, he is without restriction. The *Review* simply sends him the articles from the upcoming issue, which are then read and underlined. When he has decided which ones he wants to illustrate, he pretty much goes right to work and completes four or five caricatures in the space of a day and a half. Each one takes him about two and a half hours, crosshatching the hair being maybe an hour's job in itself. Levine is so clearheaded about where he's going on his pad that he recalls starting over just three caricatures in his entire career: the *Time* cover of William Buckley and Ingres and Dora Carrington for the *Review*.

Some drawings, however, he couldn't start at all. Blacks used to give him trouble. ("You hand them over to a loaded audience.") He was extremely dissatisfied with a caricature of Eldridge Cleaver. For Malcolm X, he could do nothing more than an X angled to appear like a cross. Levine was also blocked on the Kennedys for a year and a half after JFK's assassination. The family was not pleased with a later and unflattering caricature of Bobby rendered exquisitely as half-hawk, half-dove, and web-footed.[5]

* * *

Dialogue from a literary party. Time: Winter of 1968, shortly after David Levine caricature of Norman Podhoretz appears in the New York Review. *Place: a Manhattan salon.*

PODHORETZ (*disappointed*): Oh boy, did you miss me! You didn't get me at all. I'm not that heavy. I've been on a diet. You missed my nose . . .

DWIGHT MACDONALD (*interrupting*): Hey, Levine, you missed my nose.

* * *

Ex-*NYR* typographer Sam Antupit suggests asking his friend Levine whether he ranks painting higher on the scale of art than caricature. In other words, does Levine the painter consider himself slumming in the *Review*? "Oh no, it's really a joy," he replies, unoffended by the obvious question. "I'm a very conservative and tradition-bound artist, and there's a long tradition of caricature in art going back to Greek wall paintings. I don't see it as separate

5. This particular drawing accompanied Andrew Kopkind's equally unflattering comments on the Senator in the course of reviewing Ralph de Toledano's *RFK: The Man Who Would Be President* (June 1, 1967).

from Da Vinci. Quite a few great artists had caricatures in their sketch books."

The fact that his caricatures have made him relatively rich and famous while his paintings are almost unknown doesn't seem to bother Levine a whole lot. But he is baffled by the shifting criteria applied to his dual talent. "Critically, the paintings are put down for the very things the caricatures are up. When the critics see Daumier, Doré, and Tenniel in my caricatures, they think it's great. But the traditionalisms in my painting are negative features. Canaday called me a 'legitimate anachronism.' If you don't follow a certain course, if you don't admit Cézanne changed the world, or Picasso or Warhol, they don't think you're with it." Levine is less ruffled by a host of imitators who have not only appropriated elements of his style, but have actually stolen some of his ideas. It humors him to keep a file on these trespassers. He pulls out a rather shocking instance involving a noted editorial cartoonist, whose drawing of Nixon and Kosygin is a direct conceptual lift from an especially clever Levine caricature of Nixon and Humphrey (*circa* 1968).

"Isn't this unethical?" the visitor asks. "You should have seen what caricaturists did to each other in the eighteenth century," says Levine. Instead of resenting copyists, he gets a kick out of seeing his influence on the field. Levine, the visitor learns later, is a very popular fellow around town, equanimity being one of his cardinal virtues.

You can buy a David Levine—the price ranges from $300 for a 4 x 4 inch *Esquire* column accompaniment to $500 for an 11 x 14 inch *Review* caricature—but you can't buy David Levine. He turns down twenty to thirty calls a year from money-waving advertising agencies. If he chose to go the way of Peter Max, psychedelia's gift to capitalism, he would be a wealthy man today. As it is, he is content to diversify in low-return ventures like buttons, crossword puzzles, and calendars.

Before the visitor departs, Levine shows him his studios upstairs. There is a sparsely furnished front room on the third floor, where he does the caricatures sitting down at a plain wooden desk. The painting studio is directly above in a long sky-lighted attic stretching the length of the house. Two beach can-vases lean unfinished against their easels. The place is like an empty church. "I have a great problem doing anything major in painting now," Levine admits. "I'm having a terrible time. Pecu-liar things happen in different media. I can get right back to water color, but not oil." Why doesn't he slow down then, perhaps cancel the *Esquire* account, where his work is always dwarfed. "I don't know why I'd have to. I'm used to living the good middle-class life. Unless I went into advertising, I couldn't live this way. Besides, there is a peculiar pride in staying with *Esquire*. It's exciting to keep the thing going."

So it is with David Levine—both of them.

d/The Un-Corsican Brothers

While the editors of *New York Review* haven't killed them-selves setting up a *Jugend* section, it is not entirely kosher to charge them, as Dennis Wrong does, with launching "no promis-ing young writer or critic." Faithful readers of the *Review* should recognize the name of Robert Mazzocco, alias William Mazzocco in the Manhattan Directory, and known to friends as Bill Maz-zocco. He was an *NYR* regular in his early thirties, eight publishers have tried in vain to collect his *NYR* articles, and he seldom consorts with other magazines. Granted, playwright Jack Richard-son, thirty-five, had turned various literary tricks prior to *NYR*, but he was "launched" there as a book critic in 1969.

Mazzocco and Richardson are rule-proving exceptions to the *Review*'s preference for critics of a certain vintage. They are

both employed selectively, often going up against big or pivotal books, where the *Review* needs to acquit itself well. Mazzocco tends to handle heavier material (Sontag's *Against Interpretation*, Trilling's *Beyond Culture*, and Raitt's *Prosper Mérimée*, although he handles light stuff too. Richardson, likewise, gets the nod for both classics (Marquez's *Hundred Years of Solitude*) and commercials (Vonnegut's *Slaughterhouse Five*). What is most queer about the pair is that, apart from their youth and the *Review*, they have absolutely nothing in common. Unlike the Corsican Brothers, when Richardson overindulges, Mazzocco doesn't reach for the Alka-Seltzer.

Actually, Dennis Wrong can be forgiven for slighting Mazzocco in his negative universal. For there has always been speculation as to whether Mazzocco truly existed. The constant credit line—". . . is a regular contributor to *New York Review*"—seems purposely cryptic to the conspiracy-minded. The refusal to spread oneself around in a town where everybody is supposed to belong to everybody else is judged an unnatural act. Richard Poirier, a *Partisan Review* editor, chairman of the Rutgers English Department and author of *The Performing Self* and *Norman Mailer*, once doubted there was any such person. For a while he suspected Philip Rahv was using the name. Steven Marcus, Poirier's associate at *Partisan*, held the bizarre theory that Mazzocco was a pseudonym for W. H. Auden. Charles Thomas Samuels guessed he represented a syndicate. And Elizabeth Hardwick, of all people, never laid eyes on her fellow West-Sider (at least until the spring of 1971).

Who is this masked man? Robert Mazzocco isn't anxious to tell. This author feels like a Polaroid-bearing anthropologist standing before some lost Amazon tribe as he attempts to convince him he will not steal away his soul in an interview. He is gradually persuaded in the course of a long telephone chat, and a meeting is arranged. Astonishingly, the interview goes on for four hours.

(Recalling how freely he spoke, Mazzocco would later lament he'd been had, insisting that the only reason he showed was because the author had been a Catholic seminarian.)

How did such an unassuming, unpublished, and utterly unconnected writer attach himself to the *Review* at the tender critical age of thirty-two? You can be sure the first move was not his. Rather, he was literally *discovered* while writing brief anonymous reviews for the Kirkus Service. Toward the end of 1964, two Kirkus items on Robert Lowell's *For The Union Dead* and Stephen Spender's *Selected Poems* struck Barbara Epstein as exceptional. She called Kirkus to learn the name of the author, and thereupon Mazzocco became a regular contributor, writing nine pieces in 1965 alone and a grand total of twenty-three in the next six years.

Access to the *Review* has not changed Mazzocco's literary habits much, however. He still lived off three Kirkus reviews a week. An intensely serious man with the dark, brooding good looks of a mature Rex Reed, he is just not interested in parlaying his *NYR* situation into other, less demanding gains. Mazzocco doesn't revel in his poverty. He'd like to increase gross earnings, but the terms must be his own. He and Auden once collaborated on an anthology of modern poetry for Holt, Rinehart & Winston which might well provide a modest yearly income if it catches on as a text. Besides criticism, he writes plays, poetry, and fiction—all unpublished except for two poems in *NYR*. He has put thirty poems together and may attempt something with them. Auden, whom he called by his Christian name, Wystan, read them and approved. The novel is apparently secret, and he won't divulge the plot. "It's too special, and I don't want to give it away," he says grinning. Perhaps he's constructing a putative best-selling entertainment Graham Greene-style, a conscious plan to make a lot of money without betraying sensibility. And what would he do if he had a million dollars? "I'd direct movies."

Like his friend Susan Sontag, Mazzocco ranges far and wide as a critic, uncorking a self-taught eclecticism on films, plays, fiction, biography, and other critics. F. W. Dupee says *NYR* ought not to have assigned him Trilling's *Beyond Culture*, the review of which caused something of a stir when unranked Mazzocco laced into the still-champion Trilling (December 9, 1965). First, a few quick jabs—"the usual impression is that of trudging uphill, scanning hazy vistas, martyred with abstractions, pestered with fuddy-duddy phrases"—followed by some solid body work, and Trilling is set up for the big punch: "whatever the case, in the end, I'm afraid, Professor Trilling's book is really beyond criticism and, in that sense, 'beyond culture' as well."

Dupee defended his Columbia colleague in a brief letter to the editor. Agreeing with Mazzocco that Trilling was hard going in some of his theoretical essays, Dupee insisted that the book as a whole was done "a monstrous injustice." Letter-writer Martin Greenberg was not so polite. "I object," he wrote, "to the sneering, contemptuous tone in which his [Mazzocco's] ignorance expresses itself, to the brutality of his callowness." Undisturbed, young Mazzocco replied, calling Dupee's letter "gentlemanly gibberish" and Greenberg's "a mess." "Of course," he closed without pity, "it's possible I've missed the point of *Beyond Culture*. It's also possible to find a needle in a haystack."

As long as Mazzocco hangs on steadfastly to his uncollected status, his promise will remain inchoate. Critical essays tend to be highly dispensable products, unless they are gathered together and forged into a view of one's own. Mazzocco doesn't think he's ready just yet for that sort of pinning down. This hesitation leaves other critics unprepared to venture an opinion on him. "Mazzocco, hmm . . ." is the standard reaction. A friend of Trilling's faulted Mazzocco's overripe prose and weakness for puffery, mentioning reviews of Susan Sontag and Elizabeth Bishop. Actually, he is as swift with the dagger as he is with myrrh. As a wordsmith, though,

he could benefit from a long talk with E. B. White. For Mazzocco
is comma-crazy and parenthesis-possessed. Once he starts riding a
sentence, he doesn't know where to get off. Of Chester Kallman,
W. H. Auden's companion in this life, he writes:

> And yet, for all that, no other poet, I think, seems, here and
> there, so quaint, so much the poor proverbial drunk endlessly
> searching for his wallet under the streetlamp although he lost
> it up the alley.[6]

Of Paul Goodman:

> It is an earnestness that pervades not only the shameless data
> (homosexual, but heterosexual as well, *pari passu*) in the
> poems, some of the fiction, and *Five Years* (revelations, in-
> cidentally, that tend to strike terror in the hearts of his critics,
> partly, no doubt, because they seem so incongruous when set
> side by side with his civic-minded concerns), but, more im-
> portant, a quality that circumscribes his whole demeanor, his
> vocabulary of moral supplication, urgency, and cantanker-
> ousness.[7]

If we know too little about Robert Mazzocco, we know
practically all there is to about Jack Richardson, who has been
exposing himself body and soul in such public accommodations as
Esquire and *Harper's* since 1967. "It was not the universe that
was failing me," he wrote in the April 1967 *Esquire*, "I was failing
it. In my scramble for indulgence, I was leaving behind me the
usual refuse of the community of which I'm a part: a divorce, a
half-dozen or so squalid affairs, some unmemorable literary jot-
tings, one or two dedicated enemies, and a sense of possibility
that had got me started in the first place." This passage describes
his state following the crack-up of his playwriting career. Once
leagued with Edward Albee and Jack Gelber in the early Sixties

6. *New York Review*, June 15, 1972.
7. *New York Review*, May 21, 1970.

for two off-Broadway successes—*The Prodigal* and *Gallows Humor*
—Richardson had just undergone the Golgotha of not one, but
two, consecutive Broadway flops. A couple of putative dogs by
the name of *Lorenzo* and *Christmas in Las Vegas* ruined him, and
so he took to gambling. Always willing to exploit a voice, *Esquire*
put Richardson up to an involved journalistic tour of the world's
great casinos (with Farrar, Straus staking him to the chips against
book royalties). Richardson beat houses in Las Vegas, Japan, and
Europe before falling apart in Baden-Baden. This bit of ill luck
gradually moved the study out of the travelogue category into the
slow-going region of memoir and philosophy. "Whores That I
Have Known," a splendid chapter on the classy call girls he rang
up along the route, surfaced in *Harper's* (August 1970) to the
tune of 3,000 pre-*Prisoner of Sex* cancellations. Bob Silvers admired the piece sufficiently to ask for an excerpt. See "Jack Richardson in Las Vegas" (August 1971) in the *New York Review*.
Yes, the *New York Review*.

Jack Richardson is most likely the only *NYR* writer who has
ever done cheesecake. (A regular female contributor once
modeled in the nude for E. E. Cummings, but the session was
aborted when Cummings approached the pretty young thing instead of the canvas. Maybe that's why they called him E. E.) The
Jack Richardson starred in the *Esquire* spread "Europe for the
Debauched Swinger" (February 1968)—naked, pink, and grab-
bing all the gusto he can—is not the Jack Richardson this reporter interviews. Tall, thin, and grievously adenoidal, he appears
to be temporarily overcome by some subtropical deficiency dis-
ease. Richardson wears a clinging white shirt, open, Alain Delon-
style, at the top, and even the hairs on his upper chest seem
singularly unaroused. Despite the listlessness of the moment, he
leans back on a long white couch in his mildly elegant East
Side apartment and speaks of his short life.

Richardson's early years, were streaked with precocity: Army intelligence in Germany as a teenager, B.A., M.A., and Phi Beta Kappa from Columbia in three years, philosophy teacher in the American Institute at the University of Munich, off-Broadway awards. His thirties have not been as kind, coming as they did so soon after *Lorenzo* (with Alfred Drake, mind you!) and *Christmas*. But Richardson is still in full possession of his considerable powers, writing, one can argue, some of the steeliest prose around. That gambling volume, whenever he cashes it in, will put his name back in lights.

As a regular at both *Commentary* (where he has been drama critic since 1968) and the *Review*, Richardson is in a most peculiar situation. Although the crossfire affects him only indirectly, he'd rather see peace in his time. "I feel somewhat sad that this split occurred between two magazines which emerged from the same sensibility. America doesn't have that many places where opinion is stated well. But I don't feel any deep ambiguity about it." Where is Richardson politically that he can work comfortably on either side of the trenches? "I take bits from both of them, depending on the issue. I think the *Review* is right in attacking our foreign policy as asinine, but wrong sometimes in seeking domestic alliances." He doesn't recall the specifics of Dennis Wrong's case, but he readily admits the *Review* has printed some "hysterical" pieces.

Inadvertently, Richardson got mixed up in a little politics himself after giving *Slaughterhouse Five* a scathing review (July 2, 1970). Despising the literary ground Vonnegut walks on, he laid it on and on:

> For if there is one hard irony issuing out of all the novels and stories of Kurt Vonnegut, it is that should those drab, mindless worlds he conjures up so easily ever come to pass, his work would fit in perfectly with their values. After reading *Player Piano*, for example, that novel of what life will be like when man lives in a society based totally on technological

efficiency, one can imagine those infantile executives of the state reading and enjoying the very work that created them. After all, what else could their minds grasp but a book which deals with the broadest simplicities of a technocratic world, which is written in a prose that appears to have been designed by a computer programmed for slang and a "natural style," and which ends with the incendiary insight that the common man should take preference over the most intricate of his tools?

Of *Slaughterhouse*, in particular, he observed: "[. . .] not one attitude in all of Vonnegut's darkly humorous anecdotes of life and death stays in the mind except the infantile stoicism exemplified by the recurrent and infuriatingly Olympian phrase 'and so it goes.' "

In the next issue, the ubiquitous Edgar Z. Friedenberg accused Richardson of bad faith for choosing not to mention the fact that *Slaughterhouse* was published in 1952 and therefore could not be treated as, in Friedenberg's words, "a piece of modish trash written to exploit the spirit of the times." Incensed by Richardson's apolitical stance, Friedenberg wouldn't let up. "Far from being Olympian," he said in peroration,

"so it goes" to me conveys the author's grim awareness that the honkies are killing us and that, given the structure and values of our society, we probably can't stop them on any occasion. As Kent State goes, so goes the nation, and many other nations as well. There would be no harm in being Olympian, if a stable mountain were available; but this phrase is just the contrary—it is the written expression of a shit-eating grin. And it makes things clearer.

There was no response from Richardson.

Elizabeth Hardwick says that Richardson's unenthusiasm was upsetting inside the house, Vonnegut being one of her personal favorites.[8] The editors probably would have been more distressed if Richardson had followed through on some Brautigan books that were to have been reviewed jointly along with Vonnegut. ("I thought Brautigan so beyond civilized judgment that I didn't want to do it.") Curiously, or not so curiously, Brautigan got a rave in a subsequent *Review*.[9] "I would have felt my life more cohesive," Richardson comments dryly, "had that review not appeared, but . . ."

Richardson was just about to start research on a review of Leavis' *Dickens the Novelist*. He would have to go back to Dickens and then read a dozen or so critical biographies. He doesn't need this sort of aggravation for a measly $300. Why bother? "Discipline, if I can say that without being pompous, honoring that area of the world you respect. It's nice to have all that time and space in the *Review* and not be pressured by any other considerations. You can use all your intellectual cylinders there. And you like to think you can be as good a critic as anybody else."

e/Craft Ebbing

Reducing inflated reputations and calling attention to frauds were among the founding principles of *The New York Review of Books*. So to give credit where credit is due, the *Review* was the first journal to put the Indian sign on the dubious, best-selling *Memoirs of Chief Red Fox*.[10] And credit was taken in a full page *Times Book Review* ad (June 4, 1972). Irony of ironies, then, that *NYR* should have gotten itself into one of the most bizarre publishing imbroglios of the day.

8. See Hardwick's comments in "The Editor Interviews Elizabeth Hardwick," *Modern Occasions*, Spring 1972.

9. UCLA English professor Robert Adams dug Brautigan's *Trout Fishing in America* and *The Abortion, inter alia* (April 22, 1971).

10. *The Memoirs of Chief Red Fox* was reviewed by Peter Farb, December of 1971.

Robert Craft is, in W. C. Fields' pre-Movement language, the alleged Ethiopian in the *Review*'s fuel supply. For years his literary collaboration with the late, great Igor Stravinsky has been viewed with benevolent skepticism. In current dispute is the authenticity of the entire Stravinsky-Craft *oeuvre*, which consists of six books and several magazine articles, interviews, and reviews. What nobody knows and what Craft has only begun to tell is who really said what in these joint enterprises. In other words, how joint were the joint enterprises?

The sky fell on Craft with embarrassing suddenness after the death of Stravinsky in 1971. *Times* music critic, Donal Henahan and *Times Book Review* editor John Leonard scissored him hard in their paper. *Book World* reviewer Richard Freedman theorized, at his own peril, whether Craft was "the thinking man's Clifford Irving" (a speculation that brought a million-dollar suit against *Book World*'s publisher, the *Washington Post*).[11]

Freedman's earlier review of *Retrospectives and Conclusions*, the last Stravinscraft book, had been ignored, despite the harshness of its challenge to the integrity of the authors and the *New York Review*, where some of the material had originated. "I wonder, in short, just what the real proportion is in these heady martinis," pressed Freedman. "The only time I ever heard Stravinsky speak was on a TV documentary and I could not make out the thickly accented English words he mumbled. By what necromancy does the *New York Review* elicit these fluent idiomatic pearls of English prose from the same man? I think that the magazine ought to clarify for us the morality of publishing these interviews as pure Stravinsky. He is too important a man to be tampered with in this manner" (February 15, 1970).

11. Henahan in *The New York Times*, May 4, 1972; Leonard in *The New York Times Book Review*, December 3, 1972; Freedman in *Book World*, June 18, 1972.

A March 3, 1972 front page *New York Times* story on
Lillian Libman's memoir *And Music at the Close: Stravinsky's
Last Years* (timed more to beat the reviews of Craft's own
memoir due that June than to coincide with her September publication date) finally moved Craft into the open. Libman, the
Maestro's personal manager and press representative, was
quoted as saying that Stravinsky "did not write as much as he is
supposed to have written—other than music," and she suggested
that by 1964 her former boss was a tired old man uninterested in
maintaining his previous journalistic pace with Craft. "I loved
Stravinsky very much," she said, "but Bob loved him more deeply
in a different way. He came to live Stravinsky's life for him."

Impossibly up against the wall, Craft now admitted all was
not as it seemed (or better—was precisely as it seemed) in the
Stravinsky-Craft bibliography. "He had opinions, and I would take
them down," Craft told the *Times* (March 3). "Not the words, of
course. Stravinsky spoke, and I put the words together. I don't
say they were his words. But it's this or nothing, just as it was
with Aristotle's *Poetics*, which were not written by Aristotle but
by a grade-B student." He added to his *Times* confession the next
day (March 4), remarking that, "The earlier books in the series
were practically all autobiographical. Toward the end, the words
were mine more than his, but he approved." We must also presume that Stravinsky "approved" of the four "Performing Arts"
concert review columns that ran under his name in *Harper's* in
1970 when, at the age of eighty-seven, he was exceedingly infirm
and a year from death.

When Craft gets around to clearing up the misunderstandings
that cloud his association with Igor Stravinsky, he should not
neglect a passage from the last interview, published in unfinished
form, in the *New York Review* (July 1, 1971). The passage
reads:

NYR: What are your thoughts about the new euthanasia movement, Mr. Stravinsky?

I.S.: First of all, I noticed on their appeals that the two leading promoter organizations share the same building as the *New York Review*; which, I hope, affords you a little cold comfort now and then. I hope, too, that they are merely passing the hat around, and that the contribution they want is not *me*.

Just who is that "you" at *New York Review* that I.S. is speaking to? Are we to believe that Robert Silvers or Barbara Epstein conducted this deathbed interview? Or, following custom, was Craft the person behind the questions?

What has the *Review* to say about its role in the Stravinsky-Craft affair? Nothing direct. Elizabeth Hardwick worked a nice word for Craft into a *Times Book Review* review of *The Coming of Age*. "In our own time," she wrote gratuitously and against her own no-nonsense critical grain, "the magical collaboration of Robert Craft and Stravinsky is valuable in itself. Furthermore, the record of the great old master living out his life among us, in the American scene, is a rare contribution to a literature and cultural history like our own, that is rather empty of such treasures" (May 14, 1972).

Robert Kotlowitz was managing editor of *Harper's* when Stravinsky was purportedly dashing off those concert reviews. Kotlowitz, now Vice President, Director of Programming at New York's public television station WNET, does comment on what the *Review* maintains no-comment. "I never had any sense that Stravinsky was getting up and going to the typewriter every morning. I accepted the situation and did not question what I would have with another person. I made adjustments for Stravinsky's genius." Kotlowitz was not alone.

f/Concupiscent Classifieds

Mother *NYR* worries about its readers, too.

Are you tired of randy dating games, singles bars, and joyless one-night stands with boorish company? Has your sex life atrophied because you never meet the right people? Is your fetish hard to match? Then let *The New York Review of Books'* classified help light the fire in your loins. For forty cents a word (fifteen-word minimum), you can be in touch with its vast clientele of discreet, worldly readers.

Although the personals go back as far as 1968, when a "quiet, attractive, faithful woman" advertised for an "intelligent, kind, with adequate income" husband, they seemed to have picked up volume and flair only recently. According to Whitney Ellsworth, who would like the *Review* to emulate the revered London *Times'* classifieds page, each entry is judged on its own merits, and few have had to be rejected. Consider the following from a variety of issues:

WIDOWER CRIMINAL LAWYER, 42, own teeth, 5'11", 210 pounds, has hair, 4 teenagers, and an insane hope that a really shapely young thing will be foolish enough to answer this ad. Photo only please and must sew. I cook pretty well now and make about twenty grand a year. NYR, Box —.

WANTED: An incurably romantic feminine female who thinks life should be like a Ruby Keeler picture, but who can cope with those times when it isn't. SF area, 36 yrs. old. NYR, Box —.

WITCH-WOMAN—intelligent, attractive, long-legged (5'11"), old-fashioned, highly romantic, but crazy with literary, musical and philosophical penchants, age 25, seeks mature, sincere, witty, not necessarily Rock Hudsonish, hopefully professional man of varied intellectual interests—age 30 to 60. Located Midwest—will travel. NYR, Box —.

COLLEGE PROFESSOR, writer, tall, attractive, easygoing sense of humor, personable, affectionate, seeks intelligent interesting lady, preferably married, in 20s or 30s for occasional dates and whatever in NYC. Must have husband's approval. Please enclose phone number. NYR, Box —.

WOMAN, 30, attractive, sometimes stunning; intelligent, sometimes brilliant; socially acceptable, sometimes charming. In short, not a bad egg; wants to meet a man stable enough and mad enough to like her. NYR, Box —.

BRITISH ACADEMIC, US resident, quietly disorganized, cheerful, affectionate, cultured (Mozart-lover), humanist—43, divorced; loathes "Feminine Mystique"; seeks brainy, tomboy fellow-loner, 24-34; small, slim figure, urchin features, expert cook and fuse-fixer; joyful outlook on love, sex, life. Real risk of marriage. NYR, Box —.

SWINGING, AFFECTIONATE GAL in early thirties with features and body of a Hollywood starlet and matching brains and imagination seeks steady relationship with business or professional man in late thirties or early forties who is both cultured and athletic. NYC area only. If married, give details. NYR, Box —.

MALE, 22, seeks feisty correspondence with females who think Podhoretz is a yenta but admire Krassner, Barthelme, and the Collyer Brothers. NYR, Box —.

GAY MALE, 28, literary drudge, simpatico, likes Szell, Solti, hiking, seeks adjusted, tallish, hirsute, Bostonian comrade. Sense of humor and the absurd essential. NYR, Box —.

IS THERE A 6'2", high IQ, and single man who is a Christian Scientist over 35 who likes rock dancing? B. B., Palo Alto, California 94303.

LOVE DROPS. Sensational for massage and sex. Erotic bottle. (In velvet pouch worth $1.50 FREE with this ad!) Rush $6. Exotica, Box —, Grand Central, NYC 10017.

INDIVIDUALISTIC GENTLEMAN, tall, personable, forty-plus, Protestant-origina, nonreligious, liberal. Broad, diversified, untypical interests and background. Wish to establish communications with an independent, unneurotic, relaxed lady. Probably career, outdoors, or artistically oriented, rather than a housewife. Objective: Social and recreational synergy. Write: NYR, Box —.

I WOULD LIKE TO HEAR from women who love the ocean. L. C., Santa Barbara, California 93111.

LOVABLE, GOOD-LOOKING, BRIGHT, funny, healthy, relaxed female, late thirties, seeks male equal or better. Some interests: Music, skiing, movies, travel, and tennis. Detroit area. (313) NYR, Box —.

SUCCESSFUL WRITER IN LATE FIFTIES, tall, attractive, amusing, seeks quasi-Platonic relationship with mature, sensitive woman interested in wearing rubber. Montreal area. NYR, Box —.

It is salutary to learn that Mr. Rubber was completely shut out. No *NYR* females, adventuresome as they may be, were about to don a diving suit for sex thrills. Perhaps some would have been forthcoming if they knew the request was made for art's sake. "This ad was inserted," admits Mr. Rubber, "in the hope of contacting women interested in the subject of rubber fetishism, who might help one discover its popularity and thus contribute to the verisimilitude of the novel I was writing at the time." A likely story, but apparently true, for our kinky correspondent is a published novelist.

Mary Baker Eddy helps those who help themselves. For choosy Christian Scientist "B. B." may have found Mr. Right through her wholesome solicitation. "Last week, I met a man from Calif.," she confides in a letter. "His personality was compatible with mine, and we enjoyed each other's society—strange, isn't it? We had Chinese food together, visited a nearby zoo, a library, and then came back to my apartment to play 'Revelation,' a new Bible game I received for Christmas. He explained his church to me, and I explained some basics of Christian Science (the Science, Principle, and Truth of Christ's healings and teachings and how we believe in the Bible and the Holy Word). He said he would come back to go to church with me one day.

"Also, I received a letter from [More] saying they saw my ad and asking me to place the ad again with them."

"LOVABLE, GOOD-LOOKING, BRIGHT" from Detroit threw herself at *NYR* readers by publishing her phone number. Her aggression paid off, however.

"There happened to be a kind of desert period in my life at the time I decided to write. I wasn't seeing anyone, and nothing was happening, and it didn't look like I was going to any great scenes where I would be meeting new people. I hate to say it was an act of desperation, but it was sort of . . . What have you got to lose?

"I've never done anything like this before. In fact, I answered a single ad and before I even received an answer . . . I suppose it started when I fantasized about the kind of person I was responding to, and that encouraged me to conjure up a little fantasy of my own.

"I dashed it off in about five minutes. I was sort of surprised when it appeared. I wrote it, but there it was.

"I wasn't advertising for fancies. I was advertising for, you know, it was a very honest ad, which described me quite well, except that I exaggerated about my age. I'm not in my late thirties. I'm in my early forties. But I took into account the kind of prejudice that prevails about over forties and that kind of stuff.

"My ad was exceptional, because it gave my phone number. I wasn't interested in any correspondence course. What I really wanted to do was flush out all the local yokels who were hiding behind their books. I wanted someone geographically convenient so I would not be involved in some kind of fantasy which, of course, I am involved with now. It was faster and more direct. I also thought that people really appreciate an immediate feedback in the voice and that kind of thing.

"My God, I didn't even think about obscene phone calls. I've never gotten one. After all, anyone who reads *NYR* just wouldn't be obscene. They were all marvelous and very tender respondents.

"I got three letters and twenty-five phone calls from places like New Jersey, Pennsylvania, Ohio, Indiana, Georgia, Illinois.

Most of my callers sounded isolated, a little low, lonely, special circumstances like recently moved to college campus—you'd think he would meet gals, but hasn't. I got a few East Indians, who were difficult to understand and seemed very, very lonely. I got maybe a couple of eccentrics—theater, and ballet fanatics who were more interested in corresponding and making contact than in a flesh-and-blood exchange.

"They were, I'd say, mostly about my age, in the late thirties. Couple in mid-twenties that I tried to discourage for age reasons. I wasn't interested in those who had never married. I have my set of prejudices and felt I could be selective in this situation. There were quite a number of callers who had never married, and I thought it was in keeping with my idea that they're really looking for something that doesn't exist—a kind of perfectionism they don't find in their immediate surroundings, and some think somebody out there is going to be different.

"I didn't expect to meet Mr. Wonderful. I thought it would be adventurous. Who knows? I was presenting myself as available and I wanted to find out what was out there. I thought that *NYR* would be selective enough. I would never put an ad in the *Village Voice* or the *L.A. Free Press*. I'm very selective locally, which is probably why I don't have as much available to me.

"I had one short-term affair without emotional bumps. I really knew exactly who I was dealing with. And I felt sort of privileged to be in the company of a brilliant, fascinating guy. I knew exactly what his hang-ups were. In some ways, it was difficult for him, because I wanted a mature male-female relationship, and he was a boy [. . .] I've begun to realize that some of the people who answer those ads are not typically *NYR* people, if there is such a creature. There were several men who didn't sound that literate, that someone had told them, 'Hey man, you better read *NYR*, they got some nice broads in there.'

"After all, if any woman's kind of making it and has things going for her, she certainly doesn't have to advertise unless she's covering up some aspect of herself she wants to withhold. That's not fair.

"I'm much better than my ad. My friends were worried that the kind of people I would be sniffing out wouldn't be at all suitable, because I'm not at all in the category of a loser, which they thought would be the kind of people advertising. Otherwise, why advertise? Why can't they make it in the flesh? I was satisfied, because I didn't expect anything. I was curious. I was bored. I hadn't done anything like that. I had nothing to lose. It was just a sheer lark."

"INDIVIDUALISTIC GENTLEMAN" from New York had it with the creeps who answered his *Village Voice* solicitations, and the "sonavabitch" who runs a local East Side paper insisted on opening all responses before forwarding. For him, the *Review*'s classifieds are manna. "It's a sad social situation, and there's no apparatus to solve it except pathetic little efforts on the part of some church groups or Parents Without Partners type of thing. What *New York Review* does should be financed by the Ford Foundation as a means of overcoming some of the social awkwardness of people getting acquainted." He received fifty letters, answered twenty-five (turning down a Ph.D. in physics, who sent him a picture of herself in a bikini, and a professor who emphasized her perfect pitch), corresponded with fifteen and met ten. "I'm delighted," he attests. "I got more than my money's worth, even if it weren't for J——. She was exactly what I was looking for—an above-average, intelligent person who was at least average or better in appearance, who was relatively free of her motherhood, who was looking forward to developing something for the next twenty-five years that was different from the last twenty-five years."

Take one guess who J—— is? She's "LOVABLE, GOOD-LOOKING, BRIGHT," and "INDIVIDUALISTIC GENTLE-MAN" is her fantasy. The last one heard from *NYR*'s fun couple, he was flying out to Detroit to consummate the correspondence.

How Good Is Katherine Anne Porter?
or: Off with Toothless Old Reviewers

In December of 1967, Bob Silvers wrote a letter to Lewis Coser. According to Coser, Silvers accused his former contributor of making a "defamatory attack" on the *Review* in *Time* that was alleged to be "both false and extremely damaging to us." Since Coser refused to back away from his *Time* statement, Silvers told him the *Review* was considering "what public steps to take" in order to rectify the situation.

The *Time* story Silvers referred to was a two-column Press section report (December 8, 1967), in which *NYR* was pasted for its new illiberal tone and New Left partisanship. Apparently, *Time* thought it bad form to substitute Paul Goodman, Conor Cruise O'Brien, Andrew Kopkind, and Noam Chomsky for Nathan Glazer, Oscar Gass, and Coser. "I wanted to write critical reviews," Coser casually volunteered to a *Time* reporter, "not the kind of demolition jobs they asked for. They kept telling me to sharpen the knife more." In light of the *Review*'s professed combativeness, Silvers' reaction to Coser does appear a bit excessive. For didn't *NYR*'s maiden editorial announce its intention to reduce temporarily inflated reputations and call attention to

239

frauds? Hadn't Silvers criticized the *Times* and *Tribune* to a *Newsweek* reporter in 1963 for their "lack of character, lack of any real involvement with a subject, a kind of cautious faint praise and timidity"? Wasn't the *Review* advertising itself in 1967, in the very season of Coser's remarks, as a "conspiracy . . . against toothless old reviewers that never seem to draw blood"? No matter. Silvers demanded proof from Coser. Where and when had he ever suggested anything so foreign to the *Review* as knife-sharpening? Coser replied by enclosing a letter Silvers had written him in October 1963, criticizing his treatment of Oscar Handlin's *The Americans: A New History of the People of the United States* and asking for revisions. (The letter was missing from Silvers' files and so escaped his attention.) Coser no longer has a copy of that letter, but claims to remember it as a request to sharpen the knife more. Silvers declined to take the "public steps" he had contemplated against Coser.

Despite official denials, one cannot readily swallow the notion that the *Review*'s notorious punch-ups have always gone off entirely independent of editorial complicity. "We have been very naïve in looking upon signed pieces as an expression of the talents and ideas of gifted, experienced, and vain persons," Hardwick comments ironically about the tendency to read between the reviews at *NYR*. "Apparently, writers are only flour-sacking, mute stuffings moved about by the howling puppeteers in the editorial offices" (*Modern Occasions*, Spring 1972). Well, *NYR* writers are and they aren't. For example, *NYR* has published a number of things inimical to their personal (though not political) interests—Frederick Crews on Wilson's *The Bit Between My Teeth*, Murray Kempton on Roth's *Our Gang* (which was edited by Jason Epstein and excerpted in its pages), and so on. But it has also rejected reviews for, in the reviewers' opinion, not being inimical enough—Hilton Kramer on John Simon's *Private Screenings*, Roger Wilkins on Seale's *Seize the Time*.

PR's Steven Marcus became disenchanted with the *Review* when he detected a gratuitous hostility toward big reputations there. He postulates this negativism the following way: "We're going to put you down, because we're going to show you that you're not as important as you think you are, and the way we do it is with a bad review." If Marcus' thesis is correct, it might help to explain why Trilling's *Beyond Culture*, Hellman's *Little Foxes*, McCarthy's *The Group*, David Halberstam's *The Best and the Brightest*, and Mailer's *An American Dream* were drawn, quartered, and paraded around on the tips of spears in *NYR*. Perhaps it explains the attitude behind the cover headline "How Good Is Katherine Anne Porter?" that heralded a review of her *Collected Stories.*

The real question apropos of demolition jobs and reputation-snatching is not whether they have a right to life (of course they have) or whether they should be cooked to order (of course they may), but who the perpetrator is and under what circumstances he is writing. When is a hatchet job truly a hatchet job? When does literary feuding become literary gangsterism? The dividing line is not instantly visible, so let us examine the three most common motives behind hacheting in order to appreciate the situational ethic. The three motives often overlap, but in general they break down in the following manner:

The ideological (in the broad sense) motive: Should a writer be asked or permitted to review the book of his ideological foe? No, if it means *NYR* board member Jason Epstein is going to review Tom Wolfe's *Radical Chic and Mau-mauing the Flak Catchers*, which badmouths *NYR* and pokes fun at Murray Kempton and the Panthers (when Kempton was doing a book on the Panther 21 for Epstein at the time). No, if it means Stravinsky's stand-in Robert Craft is going to claw up Broadway Lenny Bernstein's masscult *Mass*. But what about the less self-serving examples of ideological polemic: rationalist Noam Chomsky on

B. F. Skinner's behaviorist manifesto *Beyond Freedom and Dignity*, bisexualism evangelist Gore Vidal on Dr. David Reuben's uptight bestseller *Everything You Always Wanted to Know About Sex*, and orthodox Marxist historian Eugene Genovese on unorthodox revisionist historian Staughton Lynd's *The Intellectual Origins of American Radicalism?* On the one hand, the bias of Epstein and Craft would seem to have been too predictable to sustain interest, not to mention the unwritten canons of fair literary comment. Chomsky, Vidal, and Genovese, on the other hand, advance the dialectic with their antitheses. Their bias, although predictable, is instructive and therefore legitimate.

The suspicion of personal motive: Should a writer review the book of someone who has—or who he may feel has—wronged him or his friends either directly or indirectly? Not if it means Edgar Friedenberg may be licensed to shoot at Podhoretz's *Making It* after the pair had been at odds, according to the latter, over manuscripts Friedenberg submitted to *Commentary* (let alone the complication of how Epstein is characterized in the book under review). Not if grudge-bearer Gore Vidal will be free to equate Norman Mailer with Charles Manson. ("There has been from Henry Miller to Norman Mailer to Charles Manson a logical progression. The Miller-Mailer-Manson man [or M3 for short] has been conditioned to think of women as, at best, breeders of sons; or worst, objects to be poked, humiliated, killed."[1]) But perhaps yes, if it means Dwight Macdonald will be able to explore his misgivings about "parajournalism" in a two-part review of Wolfe's *The Kandy-Kolored Tangerine-Flake Streamlined Baby*, with its "anti-parody" of *The New Yorker*, even though Macdonald has been a staff writer there since 1951. That Wolfe portrayed *New Yorker* editor William Shawn as a retiring neurotic whom, he said, Leopold and Loeb just missed killing in

1. Quoted from review of *Patriarchal Attitudes* by Eva Figes (July 22, 1971).

1924 and that Shawn was Macdonald's friend does not necessarily rule out an objective abhorrence for Wolfe's modus operandi, which blended fact and parody without making clear when the funning stopped and God's honest truth began. Macdonald's bibliography (see *Against the American Grain*) is too full of literary muckraking to accuse him of *merely* carrying water for his employer. And besides, Shawn wasn't looking for a public defense. Macdonald's point-by-point exposé of Wolfe's mis-facts, to which Wolfe offered no serious rebuttal, transcended the ordinary bounds of subjective hatchetwork. Friedenberg and Vidal, however, whether or not writing out of premeditation, would seem to have flunked the transcendence test in these cases, especially when the *Review*'s antipathy for Podhoretz and Mailer (of that period) is figured in. The historical circumstances weighed Friedenberg and Vidal down, while Macdonald wriggled free from out-and-out conflict of interest with the aid of careful and irrefutable research.

Actually, *New York Review* could have done without Macdonald's demolition of Wolfe. Despite the good copy (worth a page in *Newsweek*) and the slaughter of the new boy in town, it probably seemed more trouble than it was worth. For after the part-one *Streamlined Baby* review appeared (August 26, 1965), Clay Felker, Wolfe's editor at the *Herald Tribune*'s *New York* magazine, where the piece originally appeared, put *NYR* on legal notice, charging that Macdonald was "maliciously inspired" by a "desire to injure." Where did Felker get that idea? As Felker tells the story, Macdonald came up to him in the Algonquin bar one afternoon just before his first part debuted and taunted him about the sharpness of his upcoming second-wave assault on Wolfe. "You better get a lawyer to defend yourself," Felker remembers Macdonald's recommending. Macdonald doesn't recall inviting a libel suit so directly, but he does admit saying to Felker that if the *Streamlined Baby* business was rough, wait till he sees the next piece. In either case, Felker scared the *Review* into holding up part two until it was rechecked by *Review* staffers, including Ellsworth and Auchincloss. Also, Silvers let Macdonald know that it was inopportune to publish part two under the shadow of a lawsuit at the very moment when *NYR* was switching from a corporation to a limited partnership. So it was not until six months later (February 3, 1966) that *NYR* rid itself of the Wolfe affair. "They did it as a favor," comments Macdonald.

The institutional motive: Should a writer review an institution with which he is in competition—that is, should the editor of one journal pass judgment on either a representative of another or the other journal itself, without being perfectly plain what he's up to? There is something to be said of the propriety of *Partisan Review*'s co-founder Philip Rahv's giving the shiv to Richard Gilman's *The Confusion of Realms*, since Rahv had quit *Partisan* to found *Modern Occasions* for the same reasons he chose to jump *Partisan* contributor Gilman—just like *PR*, Gilman was too "with it." It would have been far better for Rahv to save Gilman's execution for *Modern Occasions*, where he had been laying booby traps for *PR* and its troopers almost quarterly. In contrast, there is little to be said against *Dissent* editor Irving Howe reviewing *The Partisan Review Reader* in the first issue of *NYR*. Although he closed on a low note, Howe's attack seemed far less open to the suspicion of ideological or personal antipathy.

A hatchet job is the real thing when any combination of these motives is at play in criticism. In the small world of the intelligentsia, natural antagonists will inevitably be pitted one against the other, and this is as it should be, but book review is not always the best place to work off one's literary tensions. As long as the motivational factor is relatively untainted, however, there should be no cause for alarm. *NYR*'s editors and vampire reviewers have drawn their quota of blood, but *their* "lack of character" (a phrase Silvers used to describe his competition) has sometimes shown in the process. And because the motivational ingredient is generally hard to isolate in assessing a reviewer's authoring a hostile notice, the greater burden falls on those in charge of the selection of reviewers to avoid assignments open to the suspicion of *ad hominem* or ideological bias against the author under review. *The New York Review* has, on frequent occasion, failed to shoulder that burden.

The single, sure-shot, beyond-reasonable-doubt instance of editorial complicity at the *Review* is "The Heart's Noodle Caper." "Heart's Noodle" is a perversion of *Heart's Needle*, the title of a Pulitzer prize-winning book of poetry by W. D. Snodgrass. It seems that the perverted title mysteriously appeared in the author's bio, which accompanied Snodgrass' review of Robert Lowell's play *The Old Glory* (December 3, 1964). Victor Navasky attempted to unravel the case of the missing "ee's" in *The New York Times Magazine* by theorizing that Snodgrass had failed to satisfy Silvers' and Epstein's desire for "quotable praises for advertising purposes"[2] and therefore fell victim to typographical sabotage. He was correct in his assumption of premeditation, but all wet on the motive.

"Navasky got it all wrong," spills one of the conspirators, Eve Auchincloss. "Not enough praise? We thought his review of Lowell's play was so obsequious and reverent that we cooked up this silly business while we were at the printer.[3] We thought it was terribly funny while we were doing it. Bob thought I was the culprit, but it was all of us—though obviously Barbara might not

2. "Notes on Cult; or, How to Join the Intellectual Establishment," March 27, 1966.
3. An example of Snodgrass' praise: "This play aims at levels of response most of our plays dream not of. The crux lies in Lowell's mastery of language. Here is none of the bilge Williams or O'Neill call poetry. Here is instead the language of absolute rightness to its speaker which, yet, broadens his range of reference into a universe of discourse."

remember it that way." The case is more complicated, however. For what by pure prank developed into minor hatchetwork seems to have started off as classic case of review puffery.

W. D. Snodgrass was a former student and disciple of Lowell's. They had a mutual admiration for each other's poetry. "He may have influenced me, though people have suggested the opposite," Lowell says in his *Paris Review* interview with Frederick Seidel.[4] The confessional poetry in Lowell's *Life Studies* was indeed inspired by Snodgrass' breakthough in this area. "I mean the poems [of Snodgrass] are about his child, his divorce, and Iowa City, and his child is a Dr. Spock child—all handled in expert little stanzas," Lowell states further in *Paris Review*. "I believe that's a new kind of poetry." So not only did the *New York Review* seek out a putative friendly critic for reviewing its stockholder's play (directed by Silvers' friend Jonathan Miller), but they flew him in from Wayne State in Detroit to fulfill his mission.

Didn't Snodgrass feel a trifle awkward in his assignment? Not at the beginning, anyway. He had not seen Lowell in five years and had long ago escaped his aesthetic domination. After Randall Jarrell told him, "Snodgrass, you're writing the best second-rate Lowell around," he stopped reading his former master altogether, but made a point of reading Lowell's critics. Before agreeing to the commission, he emphasized to Silvers that he would feel free to knock the play if he did not like it. Curiously, by the time the laudatory review was published, Snodgrass and *NYR* had already fallen out. "We had a very serious quarrel," he comments over the telephone from his home in Erieville, New York. "They wanted to take out a sentence or two, and they took it out." The disputed passage had to do with a Yiddish one-liner about a schlemiel and a schlemazzel. Snodgrass was implying that you had to be a schlemiel to expect schlemazzels like the commercial critics, namely

4. Reprinted in *Writers at Work: The Paris Review Interviews* (New York: Viking, 1963).

Walter Kerr and Howard Taubman, to applaud *The Old Glory*. As Snodgrass recollects the episode, Elizabeth Hardwick took the schlemiel position and tried to get him to go after the critics in his review. "I began to worry I was being made use of and got terribly furious." Thus Snodgrass remembers he put in the schlemiel line to disassociate himself from Hardwick. Naturally, he thought Silvers' insistence on removing the oblique reference for stylistic reasons was disingenuous. "If you won't stand with me on one sentence," Snodgrass told Silvers at the time, "take it out, but don't ask me to write for you again." For the sake of one schlemiel and one schlemazzel, Silvers never did.

Snodgrass' memory was shaky on his attitude toward the newspaper reviews. In fact, he did pour oil on the daily critics for one whole column of a five-column piece: "Obviously, we cannot ask that reviewers from the Manhattan dailies know a great play from a bad one," he wrote for openers and closed with a swipe at Hardwick: "Then let not thy heart be troubled. Expect your opponent to act after his nature, or you become victim to your own rage. If you *must* sit down by these people, bring the long spoon. You may get luck and grow strong, whereupon they will come over to join you. Then you *have* got problems." Snodgrass corrected himself in correspondence:

> I had forgotten that I had taken any cracks at the commercial critics, but of course I did. As I recall it, sometime during my visit there, I had talked over the phone with Robert Brustein, who is an old friend—we had taught together at Cornell. I don't remember whether this was before or after the performance and the appearance of the reviews. Though I suspect it must have been after, since the essence of the discussion concerned his anger against the commercial critics and their obtuseness to the excellence of Lowell's work. He encouraged me to join in an attack on them about this, and I was more than happy to do so. So I think I must have

intended to attack them (so joining Brustein) before I ever began the actual writing of my review.

The night of the performance, however, there was a party, first on the stage at The American Place Theater and afterwards at someone's apartment. As I mentioned over the phone, during the party onstage, I got into a quarrel with Randall Jarrell, who seemed determined to force me to agree that this was the greatest play ever written in this country. I didn't think that I felt Jarrell was improperly pressuring me or that he had any political angle to serve—rather I felt that he was personally jealous of Lowell and so overcompensated. Nonetheless, this may have rather put me on my guard. Later in the evening, however, when the party had moved, I would come to feel that Elizabeth Lowell *was* improperly pressuring me. As the reviews appeared in the papers, she became furious with the commercial critics and began to tell me that I simply had to get after them. This at least is what I remember now. As I was to review the play, I thought that was highly improper from someone who was an editor of the magazine and was wife of the author. So I determined to try to thread a course there so that I might attack the reviewers as I had meant to before she said anything, but at the same time divorce myself as much as possible from her position. I wanted to be on Brustein's side and decidedly not on hers.

So much for "the howling puppeteers in the editorial offices."

How Good Is The
New York Review of Books?

How good is *The New York Review of Books*? Good at what? The question must be broken down into several parts before the final reckoning. For in the *Review*'s house there are many mansions and many servants.

As intellectual review. What shall we compare it to when *Partisan Review* (a coterie quarterly), *Dissent* (a pamphlet of democratic socialism), and *Commentary* (Podhoretz's revenge)[1] are not in the same ballpark? *New York Review* has a larger circulation than all of them combined and, as a bi-weekly with just a few days' lead time, beats them to the punch every issue. The foreign competition isn't in the same league either. *New Society*, the *Spectator*, the *New Statesman*, and even the vaunted *Times Literary Supplement*, each with its own periodical specificity, can-

1. *Commentary*'s unflagging backlash was restated in a recent full-page *Times Book Review* ad (September 17, 1972), appealing to people who have "become fed up with chic opinions" and hawking writers like Daniel Moynihan, Nathan Glazer, Alexander Bickel, Midge Decter, James Q. Wilson, Roger Starr, and Samuel McCracken, who, the ad goes, "regularly challenge the conventional wisdom and the fashionable pieties which have been debasing discourse, perverting language, and deadening thought."

not be tossed into the equation haphazardly, however much they
may share common virtues and personnel. *Qua* intellectual
review, *NYR* is unique. No journal in the English language quite
approximates the hypostatic union of its style, diversity, and politics—that is to say, its high, open-ended intellectual journalism,
bearing on catholicity of subjects and allied to a shifting Left
political line, has not a single counterpart.

The New York Review, then, has no measure other than
itself. So how is it doing? Has the *Review* fulfilled its promise to
provide, in its own words, "the sort of literary [in the broad
sense] journal that the editors and contributors feel is needed in
America"? Despite a severe identity crisis in the middle Sixties,
despite the disaffection and dropping of several important writers,
despite a stubborness in not recognizing new talents and sensi-
bilities and, most of all, despite the passage of years, the *Review*
is still champ, still the biggest game in town and, according to
Robert Heilbroner, "the closest thing to intellectual skywriting
we have in the United States." It could not be otherwise with a
murderers' row like AikenArendtGenoveseHampshireHarding
KazinLaschLowellMooreMorgenthauCruiseO'BrienRahvRosenWil-
liams, with spot duty from BerlinBorgesColesEllmannEllsberg
MedawarWoodward. We need not go on with examples of the
Review's pre-eminence. It is a given from which all else here
proceeds.

Those who would challenge the intellectual supremacy of
the *New York Review* must overcome the data contained in "How
to Find the Intellectual Elite in the United States," a fascinating
evaluation of the nation's leading journals written by Charles Kadushin, Julie Hover, and Monica Tichy and published in the
spring 1971 issue of *Public Opinion Quarterly*. In order to put a
scientific fix on the elusive identification of "intellectual elite," the
authors decided on the formula that "influential intellectuals [the
intellectual elite] should be found among writers of journals influ-

ential among intellectuals." Fair enough, but it remained to discover which journals matched the description. To accomplish this task, a select list of thirty-six journals was sent out to 275 editors, authors, and professors,[2] each of whom was asked to choose the three journals which he and his friends most often discussed, which best expressed his opinion on national policy, and on literature, which were probably the most influential among intellectuals regarding national policy and literature. One hundred and forty-seven questionnaires were returned, making 735 (5 x 147 respondents) the total number of selections any one journal could receive.

Unsurprisingly, except for the size of its margin, the *New York Review* swamped not only its Family opponents, but outside competition like the *New Republic, The New York Times Book Review*, and *The New Yorker* as well in the all-important column of total selections. It was first by far with 306; *New Republic* trailed badly in second place with 173, and *Commentary* straggled in third with 129. *Partisan Review* (79) and *Dissent* (35) finished in seventh and thirteenth places. *Modern Occasions*, which began publication in 1970, was not included in the sample. Only *NYR* showed up at least twice on more than half of the respondents' ballots.

The archetypal issue of the *New York Review* would offer one major document like the full text of Fidel Castro's famous confessional speech of July 1970 or a special supplement like Stuart Hampshire's "A New Philosophy of the Just Society"; an extended essay on John Rawls's *A Theory of Justice*; a not-quite-our-class-dearie snub from Elizabeth Hardwick as demonstrated by her review of *Zelda* ("Mrs. Milford is not very forthcoming as

2. The sampling was comprised of 100 randomly selected editors and authors affiliated with the 23 most prominent journals in the list of 36, and 175 professors from the top 10 English, political science, history, sociology, and economic departments as determined by Alan M. Cartlers' *An Assessment of Quality in Graduate Education.*

an analyst, nor is she a particularly interesting writer on her own. However, she has by concentration on her subject, and even perhaps by inadvertence . . .''); an outrageous trial balloon on education like Ivan Illich's "Why We Must Abolish Schooling"; an idiosyncrasy from the late Edmund Wilson; a fiction roundup by a Britisher—V. S. Pritchett's joint review of *Love in the Ruins* and *Being There*; a history review by A. J. P. Taylor, H. R. Trevor-Roper, J. H. Plumb, or Geoffrey Barraclough; an entertainment by Gore Vidal in the mode of his molestation of *Everything You Always Wanted to Know About Sex*; an utterly arcane and incomprehensible throwaway like pianist Charles Rosen's review of three hard-to-get books on music and meter, complete with musical scores; an article that came to the *Review* and nowhere else because of its splendid war record—Daniel Ellsberg's "Murder in Laos: The Reason Why"; a broadside from Izzy Stone, complete with boxed-off paragraphs; an indubitably rational inquiry like Barrington Moore's "On Rational Inquiry in Universities Today"; no poem; no movie or drama review; endless university press advertisements; and a letter from Noam Chomsky protesting the harassment of Catalan intellectuals to which is appended "The Assembly of Montserrat Manifesto." If you've seen one archetypal issue, however, you are in danger of having seen them all. The *Review* keeps bouncing back, fortnight after fortnight, with more of the same, and something for almost everybody and that's why it's Number One in the polls.

Notwithstanding the *Review*'s status and ever mindful of its finitude, the magazine has been delinquent in several fields of scholarship. Dennis Wrong laments the absence of material on linguistics, the study of deviance in sociology, and the spreading influence of phenomenology in American philosophy and social science. To that somewhat specialized complaint, one should add the lack of reviews of theological and religious books. While never large on religion, *NYR* used to throw a religious piece on the pile now and then during the heyday of Pope John's *aggiorna-mento*. But lately, the *Review* has apparently lost the faith. Nine agnostic months separate two abbreviated roundups by W. H. C. Frend.[3] The first was devoted to John M. Allegro's farfetched *The Sacred Mushroom and the Cross* and Malachi Martin's *The Encounter*, which Frend generously describes as "a landmark in contemporary religious writing." The pearl and the swine get equal space—less than a page each! In a second package of five church histories (another truncated two-pager), Frend buries Volume One of Jaroslav Pelikan's colossal *The Christian Tradition* in four paragraphs. Arthur Waskow, dubbed the "Jewish Dan Berrigan" by Garry Wills, was willing to donate material on radical Judaism, but Bob Silvers didn't accept. Despite the Jewishness of Silvers and the Epsteins, Jewish concerns are yet to be bar mitzvahed in the *Review*.

Except for an excerpt from Erik Erikson's *Gandhi*, the venturesome discipline of psycho-history had long gotten the brush-off, as if the research of Kenneth Keniston, Bruce Mazlish, Philip Rieff, Robert Jay Lifton, and Robert Coles was beyond the *Review*'s imprimatur. Actually, Silvers approved and then rejected a major article by Lifton. "It was more psychologically innovative than they were willing to encompass," says Lifton, winner of a 1967 National Book Award for *Death in Life*. An excerpt from Mazlish's psycho-biography *In Search of Nixon* almost saw daylight during the 1972 campaign. Apparently, Silvers was just waiting for a psycho-historian he could trust, and he found him in Robert Coles. A few years ago, he heard that Coles was about a study of political conversions (e.g., former New York Senator Charles Goodell's switch from hawk to dove) and was on the phone in a flash trying to nail it down for the *Review*. Silvers heard wrong but he was able to recruit Coles for future service. His long two-part essay, revealingly titled "How Good Is Psycho-

3. From December 17, 1970, to September 2, 1971.

history?" by *NYR* (February 22 and March 8, 1973), finally gave
the field the attention it deserved.

Sometimes the *Review* gets carried away by its scrupulous insistence on having the last word or no word at all. The better-
late-than-never axiom eventually reverses itself.

Academically speaking, science, anthropology, philosophy,
and scholarly textbooks are relative disaster areas. But these venial
sins of omission are more than compensated for by the *Review*'s
strength in history, foreign and military affairs, law, Latin America, education, economics, and art.

Summing up: as intellectual review, *The New York Review
of Books* is tops—the Colosseum and the Louvre Museum.

All monuments have structural weaknesses, however, which
become more and more visible with age. The *Review*'s main weakness derives from its historic strength. It has avoided variety and
by and large hangs on to a revolving roster of renowned contributors. It is forever Chomsky on resistance, Neal Ascherson on
Eastern Europe, Friedenberg on social mores, Foner on black
history, E. H. Gombrich and Francis Haskell on art, Heilbroner
and Wassily Leontief on economics, Lowell on deceased poets,
Helen Muchnic on Russian literature, Shattuck and John Weightman on French literature, Steel on American foreign policy, Hardwick on theater (when she gets around to it), the same crowd of
British history and fiction reviewers (although Roger Sale, Michael
Wood and Thomas Edwards have interloped in the latter category
of late). Speaking of names, one recent *Review* (November 2,
1972), had pieces by Mailer, Kazin, Hardwick, Lasch, Stone,
Pritchett, Barraclough, and Epstein. That's pouring it on rather
thick. But writing in the very next issue (November 16, 1972)
were unfamiliar *NYR* faces like Harold Acton, Mikhail Agursky,
John Gittings, Max Gluckman, Richard Murphy, and M. K.
Spears. So perhaps the *Review* may forsake its relatively ZPG
policy toward contributors. Silvers feels a certain awkwardness
auditioning new people, especially academics. In many instances,

he's tried them and hasn't liked them or he hasn't tried them because he didn't like them, with the result that *NYR* is getting predictable.

New York Times daily book critic Anatole Broyard catches hold of this diffuse dissatisfaction with *New York Review* when he remarks: "You get the feeling, like in the middle period at *Partisan*, that a *Partisan* syndrome has taken over, that their minds are set."

The *Review*'s reputation among its peers can also be overblown. For example, the *Review* may have won the all-class competition in Kadushin's study (that it was the magazine most frequently discussed among elite intellectuals is trumpeted in *NYR*'s promotion material), but a closer analysis indicates its support is wider than it is deep. Specifically, on the question of whether a journal best expresses the subject's *own* views re national policy, *NYR*'s 17 percent is ranked behind the *New Republic*'s 44 per cent and *Commentary*'s 18 per cent and is just ahead of *Harper's* 16 percent and *The New Yorker*'s 14 per cent. *New Republic* defeats *NYR* a second time but narrowly (44 percent to 39 per cent) on the question of whether the subject thinks a journal is influential among *other* intellectuals re national policy. When Kadushin breaks his statistics down to reveal how the subgroup of professors voted on their own views re national policy, *NYR* was trounced again. English, economics-sociology, and history-political science professors chose *New Republic* over *NYR* by better than 2-1 (it was almost 8-1 in the economics-sociology column); *Commentary* was also preferred to *NYR* in the economics-sociology and history-political science columns. Where *New York Review* picks up points is in the snob appeal questions re influence among *other* intellectuals. Whether or not members of the elite allow the *Review* to influence them re national policy and literature they *think* it influences *other* intellectuals. Although the elite may talk more about the *New York Review*, they act more like *New Republic*—at least when it comes to national policy.

In a follow-up paper based on interviews with 110 elitists, Kadushin and Hover observe: "The curious thing is that most elite intellectuals were opposed to radical politics, but believed that the intellectual community was influenced by these politics. In other words, most of the elite intellectuals we talked with are not influenced by the radical *New York Review* line and do not agree with radical politics, but perhaps, because it appears in print, they assume that other intellectuals are influenced by this line" (*Change*, March 1972).

As literary review. It was never the *Review*'s aspiration to be a literary journal in the strict sense. From the beginning, non-literary matters outweighed criticism. Anyway, no purpose would have been served in duplicating *Partisan*, which is what the *Review* would have done (especially since so many *Partisan* writers were requisitioned at the start) if it had not concentrated in the social sciences. Over the years, however, the *Review* has become less and less literary—with an ever-declining ratio of fiction to nonfiction books reviewed and a spiralling rate of novel roundups as opposed to single reviews. Currently, the novel is so disesteemed in its pages that even the crumbs of a roundup are withheld in many an issue. For example, in the sixteen months from January 1971 through April 1972, *NYR* treated seventy-six nonfiction books in single reviews, whereas only nine novels were accorded similar status. During the same period, seventeen joint reviews were spread over fifty-three novels, and almost one-third of the issues contained no fiction reviews at all—nine out of thirty-one.

Whence this disloyalty to "literature"? "Just when did criticism cease being an influence?" speculated Alfred Kazin in his last *Commentary* piece "Whatever Happened to Criticism" (February 1970) before breaking with Podhoretz. "You cannot say of the *New York Review*," he remarked in passing, "that it is anti-literary in the style of the New Left. But wherever action politics is a pressing ideal, not only to the young who have no other, but to literary men who see it as the counter-weapon to political despair, then literature as a living thing, literature now, literature the ugly duckling gets despised."

F. W. Dupee knows whereof Kazin speaks. "Literary criticism is in the doghouse in this country," he tells his visitor. "I feel the strain myself. Criticism once had an enormous authority. Now it's melted away in proportion to other authority. There's no Susan Sontag flurry today, no new theories of writing developed. Edward Said has been trying to introduce contemporary French criticism, but *New York Review* isn't interested. As regards young people, criticism doesn't have the same prestige." (Halfway through the conversation, Dupee's wife returned bedraggled from a May Day demonstration in Washington—a sign of the times.)

A second, but often unaccounted, factor may have intervened against criticism—simple economic determinism. The university presses gradually became the *Review*'s biggest advertisers (seven out of the first ten among space-buyers), and university presses don't publish fiction. In the book-reviewing business, you tend to follow your advertisers in the allotment of reviews, or you risk losing business. Just as the *Times Book Review* gets zilch in university press ads and returns zilch in reviews of their titles, *NYR* receives plenty money from Chicago, California, Princeton, South Carolina, Oxford, Cornell, and Harvard and knows how (relatively) to please its clients.

Silvers told a marketing seminar of university press people that he was indeed sympathetic to their wishes for more reviews, but that *NYR* was limited by the interests of its reviewers. The university press people understand this, as well as the fact they have no comparable place to go. In 1971, *NYR* reviewed 102 of their books versus 327 trade books. Nevertheless, a one-to-three is no ratio to cry about. It is *New York Review*'s readership, however, that makes it a pearl of great price to the academic presses. "At least 80 per cent of its audience is academically oriented," proclaimed debonair, mustachioed Costello Bishop, when he was Harvard University Press's director of marketing and advertising. "This isn't true of any other magazine. I use *New York Review* both to move merchandise and to show authors that I love their work. The *Review* is the top choice of authors for advertising after the *Times*." Purely as a review medium, how does *NYR* differ from the *Times Book Review*? "You read the *Times* to find out what that reviewer thinks about that book," remarks Bishop. "Readers of the *New York Review* read essays about clusters of books in order to learn something."

Fiction-wise, trade houses hardly pester the *Review* with ads. (Macmillan is so hyped on *NYR*'s academic bias that it won't even buy space for its nonfiction books.) If the trade houses were regularly sticking ads for novels in the *Review*, the *Review* might find itself compelled to respond attentively. But the houses aren't, and the *Review* isn't.

The proportionately small space the *Review* allots for the cultivation of literature is itself a center of dispute: (1) British critics are derided awfully, (2) poetry has been forsaken, and (3) there is *NYR*'s taboo on the "new sensibility."

(1) Pritchett, Jones, Bergonzi, and Enright, the *Review*'s most ubiquitous *littérateurs* from the mother country, seem to suffer in the crossing. Kazin thinks they are a clever crew, but *PR*'s Steven Marcus, who has more legions than Kazin on this one, is bored. "They write after-dinner reviews. It's good cocktail party talk—witty, unserious, fashionable, and stylish—but if you look close, there's very little to them."

(2) The poetry cupboard is just about bare. Poems which appear once a month on the average do better than reviews of poetry books, but overall, *NYR*'s contribution to the American poetry scene isn't worth a pitcherful of warm spit. "No one could possibly deny we're living in an age of good poetry," stresses an angry Stanley Kauffmann. "It's easy to name twenty poets of talent. Yet where's *New York Review* in all this? W. H. Auden writes four dreary pages of Icelandic poetry and sends them right in.[4] Why not four pages on James Wright?[5] *The Times* gave him a page! Where is their review of Stanley Kunitz, a poet who has a very good chance of being an immortal? And who are they kidding being a literary review with this half-baked behavior?"

Robert Lowell apologizes for the half-bakedness by removing Kauffmann's premise: "It [*NYR*] never was primarily interested in the arts, nor pretended to be. It's a review for commentator and reasoner, an epic *New Statesman* [. . .] Poetry reviews are more in the whirl here [in England] than with us [in America]. I wouldn't assert the quality is finer—a true review sinks into the reviewer's mind, causing change and discovery, and can never be anticipated anywhere. We [Americans] assign too many reporters and popularizers to poetry; you [British] save them for plays."[6]

(3) Whatever the "new sensibility" means, exactly, *New York Review* is insensitive to it. Tom Wolfe wasn't being flakey when he observed in *Book World* (January 4, 1971):

Since 1962 *The New York Review of Books* has resisted or ignored almost every literary experiment that has been at-

4. "The Lay of Grimnir," translated from the Icelandic by W. H. Auden and Paul B. Taylor, notes by Peter H. Salus, February 27, 1969.

5. Stephen Spender did not give Wright's *Collected Poems* four paragraphs in a joint review of five poetry books (July 22, 1971): "James Wright is the most academic of the poets under review, beautiful in his way but, in spite of his sensibility and fine intelligence, and in spite of the fact that his poems develop and improve through the collected volume, he never quite breaks the sound barrier."

6. "A Conversation With Robert Lowell," *Modern Occasions*, Winter 1973.

tempted, even Kerouac's and Vonnegut's, and by now virtually ignores new novelists and poets altogether.

And Kazin, who also happens to subscribe to Wolfe's radical chic doctrine, goes along with this, too. "But in the *New York Review*," he stated in that final *Commentary* article, "the mingled voices of Oxbridge and Bedford-Stuyvesant trouble me less than the lack of new names, the lack of concern with new imaginative writing." Conservative to the bone, the *New York Review* won't dance with Andy Warhol, the Living Theater, Jean-Claude Van Itallie, or Richard Gilman, all of whom have been excoriated between its covers. The *Review*'s roster has been swept clean of known intellectual "swingers" like Susan Sontag, Richard Poirier, Richard Gilman, and Albert Goldman, while outsiders like Morris Dickstein and Leslie Fiedler are shunned altogether. What have Hardwick, Richardson, Mazzocco, Rahv, and the other old "sensibilists" at the *Review* got against the new? Rahv, whose split with *Partisan* after thirty-six years involved such matters, says it his way in the inaugural editorial of *Modern Occasions* (Fall 1970): "To our mind, phrases like 'the new sensibility' are pretentious because totally lacking in aesthetic substance. Nor do we intend to participate in the cult of *Now* nor support in any way the obnoxious trendiness that now pervades the literary world. We refuse to be enslaved by the *Zeitgeist*, even if it takes the form of playing up to the real or alleged antics or life styles of 'the kids.' " For Rahv, the villains are not the source of the new, but their promoters. "But the fault may really lie not so much with the creative writers disposed to experimentation as with certain ambitious critics (like Professors Dickstein, Gilman, and Poirier) who are constantly boasting the so-called 'new literature' as nearly the equal of the products of the classic avant-garde." To be abhorred are manifestos like Rémy de Gourmont's "poetry is produced by the genitals." "Such proclamations are mere fugitive expressions of the

Zeitgeist, curiosities of the age, and in no sense contributions to critical theory."

Rahv puts the kids, ambition, and genitals together in so nasty a review of Gilman's *Confusion of Realms* that *NYR* buried it at the end of a summer issue (June 4, 1970) and excused itself with a letter to the editor from Elizabeth Hardwick which protested that Gilman couldn't be that terrible.[7] "What it comes to," Rahv argues in part for all, "is that he [Gilman] is a mere raisonneur of newness *per se*, anxious not to miss out on the very latest permutation of the *Zeitgeist*, however casual or meretricious, whose turgid, laborious prose and graceless conceptual mode attest to the decline of the discipline of criticism in our time."[8] And that's what Rahv, a *Reviewer* regular, Silvers' confidant and the person to whom Hardwick's *A View of My Own* is dedicated, has against the new.

"Their conservatism is a stodgy one," Steven Marcus, a *PR* anti-Rahvian, posits. "It's easy to imagine a strong or powerful literary conservatism like Leavis' or Trilling's. But that means you have to put forward real ideological arguments for literary conservatism. They don't do that. They prefer rather dull ones."

Where does the *Review*'s attachment to the "old sensibility" leave it? In a very uncomfortable position—reclining with both

7. Hardwick testified to the following: "However, I do wish to dissent from the notion of Gilman as 'trendy' and industriously 'with it.' I have read him regularly throughout his career and I have found him independent, unexpected in opinion, rather stubborn, indeed, and generally conservative in taste. I was surprised to find him enthusiastic about Susan Sontag and I felt gratified by this because her work has been so meanly treated by critics here and in England. Rahv seems to suggest that Gilman's praise would not entirely please Miss Sontag, that it is not the kind she would want. If that is true she is really a saint, wed to poverty" (July 2, 1970).

8. Rahv's needle is stuck on Gilman. One year later, Rahv footnoted an editorial bump and run of Susan Sontag with yet another swipe at the poor man: "To me the worst aspect of Miss Sontag's critical forays—and this is even more true of her trendy imitators and followers of the type of Richard Gilman . . ." (*Modern Occasions*, Fall 1971).

cultural conservatism and political leftism. But the editors were disappointed in Richardson's flout of Vonnegut, which was subsequently balanced by Michael Wood's favorable criticism of *Breakfast of Champions* (May 31, 1973), and Brautigan's *Trout Fishing in America* obtained an excellent notice. With her flaming-gay-aesthetic period behind her, Sontag has been invited back and Mailer has returned.[9] So maybe sunnier days are ahead for Rémy de Gourmont and friends.

Summing up: As literary review, *NYR* isn't even trying.

As book review. To its everlasting glory, *New York Review* made book-reviewing an honest profession in America. Before *NYR* showed its stuff, the reviewing business was a gentlemanly affair carried on with charity toward all and malice toward none, or almost none. Reviews were reviews and nothing but reviews. They were kept brief and to the point—ask not what you can do for this book but what this book can do for you. "This dismal atmosphere of literary journalism," was Silvers' assessment, "boring intellectually and without character." However, *NYR*'s get-tough policy and review-essays, which freed the critic from the centuries-old slavery of mere summary and grading, shook things up. Neither the *Times Book Review*, nor *Book Week*, nor *Satur-*

9. Sontag's second coming in *NYR,* apropos the death of Paul Goodman, contains a sentence that attests to a change in her way of thinking. She prefaced the obituary with a description of her bare Parisian study which, she writes, "undoubtedly answers to some need to strip down while finding a new space inside my head" (September 21, 1972).

day Review followed *NYR* into the highbrow, but their middlebrow consciousnesses were raised. Each became a better book
review after the coming of the *New York Review*. The competi-
tive gap, though broad as ever for *Book World* (which was split
in 1972 into two separate Sunday book supplements for the *Washington Post* and the *Chicago Tribune*) and *Saturday Review*
(which was taken over by Norman Cousins' *World* in 1973) is
narrowing in the case of the *Times.*

Bob Silvers no longer has the race all to himself. John
Leonard and his staff of young Turks at the *Times*—Richard
Locke and Roger Jellinek—are gaining on him and from some
angles even appear to be in the lead. Long literary essays on
Proust and Dostoevski have adorned recent *Times* covers, and
their major reviews sometimes go on at *NYR* length—e.g. Kazin
on Revel's *Without Marx or Jesus,* Dickstein on Malamud's
The Tenant, and Richard Locke on Updike's *Rabbit Redux.*
The *Times* no longer considers featuring a bad review of a "big"
book as an ugly breach of etiquette. When Wilfrid Sheed turned
in his distinctly minority report on *Nat Turner* a few years back
(before Leonard became editor), kind editorial hearts fluttered.
Sheed was requested to think his review over, but he changed
nothing. Except for a cosmetic rearrangement of a few sentences,
which saved some Sunday punches for the closing paragraphs, the
Times dutifully but unhappily printed Sheed intact. Now the in-
surgents boldly emblazon their frontispiece with out-and-out de-
tractions. In descending order of pan: Brigid Brophy on Mailer's
Prisoner of Sex, Helen Vendler on McCarthy's *Birds of America,*
and Elie Wiesel on Pierre Joffrey's *A Spy for God.* A comparison
of these latter two reviews with their companions in *NYR* is instructive, for, in both instances, the *Times* was a darned sight
tougher than *New York Review.* Roles have been reversed: *NYR*
seems "boring intellectually and without character," and the *Times*
the very opposite of Elizabeth Hardwick's "puddle of treacle."

Assuming Helen Vendler, a professor of English at Boston University, held no animus toward Miss McCarthy and assuming the *Times* wasn't out to snare *Birds* (a pleasant interview with McCarthy accompanies the review), the motives of both parties are not suspect. Compare this value-free environment with the situation at *NYR*. After what they did to *The Group* and after what she did for them with her Vietnam articles, the *Review* wasn't about to throw *Birds* to the wolves. The novel was sent to V. S. Pritchett instead. "I would guess," one of Pritchett's American cousins at the *Review* remarked, "it's because he's quite capable of being benign for a friend."

Vendler adopted the *Review*'s *oeuvre complète* context by regarding *Birds* in the continuum of McCarthy's fiction. She cites the "very short half-life" of the topicality in the earlier novels, which "fictionally speaking, turns rapidly to lead, its occasion once past." The eye for detail "cannot quite make up for an emptiness at the center—least felt, it is true, when Miss McCarthy is her own heroine and does not try to invent other people." Vendler remembers McCarthy past—McCarthy of *Memoirs of a Catholic Girlhood, The Group*, and *Hanoi*, and brings her to bear on *Birds* in precisely the dredging pattern we have come to expect from *NYR* in these circumstances. From Pritchett's quotesy, pure summary review, however, we would never know McCarthy had written a single word before *Birds*. He guides us on a tour of the novel without the slightest historical aside and then in the last paragraph tacks on the sort of pussyfooting judgment Hardwick warned us about in "The Decline of Book Reviewing": "Everyone is found to have 'filled a need' and is to be 'thanked' for something and to be excused for 'minor faults in an otherwise exemplary work.'" Thus Pritchett reverts to the despised formula:

> *Miss McCarthy has really rediscovered* an old form of travel commentary in giving Peter her own critical detachment and knowledge; but *it doesn't matter* that Peter is too precocious

and, like his mother, too good to be true. *He is a relief* after the showy self-dramatizing confessionals and sexual loud mouths. A late-developer, he enjoys and profits by the virginity that his learned and irresponsible, rational parents have unwittingly loaded him with. *If he is a tame bird, he is very touching* in his dignity. He is too absorbed by what he sees to be self-pitying. Goodness knows how he has missed the morbidity of youth—perhaps that is a loss for him and even *a mistake on Miss McCarthy's part, but one is glad to be spared.* He is just the shy young pedant to keep a topical allegory about intellectual pollution from being a bore. *In a novel he would be thin,* as he is; *but in the Euro-American laboratory he is a ready piece of Puritan litmus.* [Emphasis added.]

Actually, Vendler and Pritchett were not that far apart on the essential merits of *Birds of America*, in spite of their contrary methodologies. Both estimate it something less than a good novel, but of certain value nonetheless. Vendler just doesn't mind saying so in plain English: "[. . .] Mary McCarthy, for all her cold eye and fine prose, is an essayist and not a novelist. But then, if we can have nonfiction novels, why not a new McCarthy genre, the fictional essay?"

The late W. H. Auden admitted to reviewing only books he liked (*The New York Times Magazine*, August 8, 1971). Therefore his lovesong to Joffrey's *A Spy for God*, an account of Kurt Gerstein, the SS gassing expert who tried to alert Allied governments and the Pope to the holocaust, is fully anticipated. "It is very seldom that a book reduces me to tears as this one did," he writes in *NYR*. "It is the story of a man who, if he had not committed suicide in a French prison in 1945, would almost certainly have been hanged at Nuremberg as a war criminal; yet, on finishing it, I find myself sharing Martin Niemöller's conviction that he was a saint." Auden's personal journalism, while most appropriate in reviewing *My Father and Myself* by J. R. Ackerley, since he shared certain affinities with the author, doesn't belong here. For the mysterious

Gerstein could have been a fraud as easily as a saint. "There
are, after all, a number of questions that remain unanswered,"
Elie Wiesel observes unromantically in the *Times*:

> Gerstein joined the Nazi party *at the beginning* of the Hitler
> era. Why? And why did he try to enter the Luftwaffe (which
> turned him down), since it was the SS that carried out the
> crimes he wanted to observe and prevent? And why did the
> SS accept him in spite of his anti-Nazi past? And later? Why
> did he not desert in the years 1943–44? He was certainly in
> a position to do so. If he really wanted to shake the world as
> much as he said he did, why didn't he go to Sweden or Swit-
> zerland and scream and shout his truth at the faces of men?

Next to Vendler's and Wiesel's critical rigor, Pritchett and Auden
sound as soft as Clifton Fadiman, whose tribe the *Review* came to
destroy. The intrepid *Times* also printed Peter Spackman's bloody
attack on Ivan Illich's *Deschooling Society*, chapters of which appeared in *New York Review* (August 11, 1971).

Bob Silvers used to be proud to publish only "critics" and
never "reviewers." Well, the critics, even some of his regulars—
Kazin, Steel, Kempton, Sale, and Elizabeth Hardwick[10]—are
working the other side of the street, while the leprous reviewers
have infected his own house. Silvers had done some raiding himself in the persons of Thomas Edwards, whose review of *Radical
Chic and Mau-mauing the Flak Catchers* pleased Jason Epstein
so much, and Wilfrid Sheed, a *Times Book Review* columnist
as well as John Leonard's favorite critic, who was asked to do
regular movie reviews for *NYR*.

John Leonard's disorderly advance on the *Times* progressed
through Harvard (sophomore dropout), work with migrant apple
pickers (Vermont), Berkeley (B.A.), Pacifica Radio, volunteer

10. Hardwick overcame her reluctance for the *TBR* to review Simone
de Beauvoir's *The Coming of Age* (May 14, 1972).

ghetto tutoring (Roxbury, Mass.), four cleverly executed novels (*The Naked Martini, Wyke Regis, Crybaby of the Western World,* and *Black Conceit*), a staff job on the *Book Review* (1967), and a promotion to daily book reviewer in rotation with Christopher Lehmann-Haupt after Eliot Fremont-Smith's resignation (1969).

Then, after two years of testing by *Times* cardinals, he was consecrated editor of the *Book Review* at the unheard of age of thirty-one. Liberated from the fuddy-duddyism of the past, Leonard's *TBR* swiftly began to win the attention of Wilsonians by upping literary standards and depreciating the book-as-news line. Comparisons with the *New York Review* came automatically, but Leonard isn't looking for such compliments. "Nothing annoys me more than when people say that I'm trying to turn the *Book Review* into *The New York Review of Books*," Leonard told Harry Smith of the lit gossip sheet *The Newsletter* (December 8, 1971). "Nothing could be farther from the truth [sic]. [. . .] I don't agree with half the things I publish." Smith explained that Leonard meant he wasn't about to change the *TBR* to conform to his own politics and quotes him as saying that, in contrast with the *TBR*, "*New York Review* is not a forum and doesn't pretend to be one. It's an ideological publication. Of course, there's nothing wrong with that, but it's not what I want to do."

The *TBR* headquarters are on the eighth floor of the Times Building on West 43rd Street in the heart of the Times Square crime district. In the outer office stalagmites of freshly minted books rise on desks as far as the eye can see. Befitting his status as editor, John Leonard has the only privacy in the cavern—a large, nondescript backroom. It is late Thursday afternoon, several days before the next deadline. Leonard, beer mug in hand, is only too happy to expand on the *Times Book Review-New York Review of Books* bicycle race.

The visitor wonders what effect Leonard thinks *NYR* has had on book reviewing in general and the *TBR* in particular. "Not being wholly facetious, I'd talk about the Hawthorne effect. A bunch of efficiency experts went into this factory in Hawthorne, New York, and were asked how efficiency could be increased through Muzak, colors, times of breaks, etcetera. And what they found was that no matter what they did, production got better. Everybody felt noticed, so everything got better. When the *New York Review* came in, the *Times* was phasing itself out of the shopping list approach, as was *Saturday Review*. I was a charter subscriber to the *Review*. The first issues were the most astonishing. Here was a magazine that was going to treat serious fiction at length and with the proper reviewer that it deserved. But now their fiction coverage is intellectually disgraceful. They aren't interested in fiction. I have to read it now for I. F. Stone. Singlehandedly, the *Review* created a medium for university press ads. I'd like to get some and am in the process of getting some. In the past year, I've run longer, more abstract pieces, not just to get those ads, but because these are the books talking about the most important ideas. Those of us at the *Book Review* all grew up with the *Review* as part of our consciousness, as an alternative—not that we entirely approved of it. We've now come to power. We've got to change. There are a lot of changes I doubt we could have instituted without the *Review*. The essay on Erving Goffman would not have been possible without the *Review*.[11] I don't think the *Times* would have been ready, were it not for their precedent [. . .] The magazine annoys me greatly, but you couldn't conceive of doing the things we've done this year if that magazine hadn't been around for a decade."

Although Leonard believes *NYR* can review some books better than any other journal, he argues that "as a book-reviewing medium, it doesn't even exist." How so? "There is an element of

---

11. A cover review of Erving Goffman's *Relations in Public* by Marshall Berman (February 27, 1972). Goffman is an obscure sociologist at the University of Pennsylvania, whose dense but brilliant academic studies of ordinary people in ordinary jobs makes him, according to Berman, "the Kafka of our time."

perversity in the linking of certain books. Take fiction. They will have one guy review five books, and by the time you've gotten through with the transition sentences, you know an awful lot about the reviewer, but not about the books. You don't put a Malamud and a Hawkes together.

"There's no attempt to really look to find a good young novelist or poet, no sense that this talent might deserve a look by a critic as to what is right, no obligation toward the unformed but gifted up-and-coming writer. The *Review* should be shot full of guilt.

"When *New York Review* looks at a first novel, it's so long after publication that they're depending on other reviews or reviewers to do their job for them. Somebody has said, 'This time we must pay attention.'

"There's no reason why it should consider itself a book-reviewing medium. If it did, I feel it should take into consideration that it's reviewing only famous people in fiction, etc. I say all this with a rather large sense that the *Times Book Review* isn't all I'd like it to be. I've spent the past year putting famous people on my cover."

Leonard suffers no qualms from poaching on *NYR*'s estate, although he admits he was momentarily discomforted when Leonard Ross, whom he published first in *TBR*, popped up over there. "If Bob is publishing someone who's good, I'm not doing my job if I don't ask him. William Gass is an example. He used to appear steadily in the *Review*. If I could get Peter Medawar, I'd do it without a blush. He's a Nobel Prize winner [for medicine and biology in 1960], and I'm ashamed to say I had never heard of him before I read him in the *Review*. I would give him more words than the *Review* and more money. But he wrote me saying, 'No. If I did something like that, I'd do it for the *Review*.' I'd like to create toward the *Book Review* the loyalty Medawar has toward the *Review*."

Leonard is not the only *Review*-watcher who senses that

NYR arranges a good portion of its reviews. He says he is trying
to avoid plants in his own operation. "You never assign someone
you know will hate a book. When anybody calls up and asks for a
book, we put on a mini-FBI investigation. The whole field is volatile. You don't know where the bodies are buried." Nobody's
perfect department: Did Leonard realize that one of his top reviewers was recently assigned a book by an author whom the
reviewer had previously and publicly exposed for plagiarizing the
reviewer himself? (The review, naturally, was vicious.) Leonard
says he didn't know, since the plagiarism charge appeared out of
town. Yet the very same reviewer turned up later praising a book
that listed the reviewer in the acknowledgments. In this instance,
assures Leonard, the acknowledgments page was not sent to the
Times Book Review or the reviewer with the galleys. And what
about the apparent coziness of the following situation which raised
eyebrows at Random House? In consecutive weeks, Elie Wiesel
raved about Meyer Weisgal's *Meyer Weisgal . . . So Far*, and
Charles Silberman raved about Wiesel's *Souls on Fire*.[12] Shouldn't
someone at *TBR* have noticed that both reviewers of these Random
House titles were Random House authors as well and that Silberman and Weisgal shared the same RH editor? "I was aware of the
situation," answers Leonard, "but I assume that both writers are
honest. And besides, not using reviewers from the same house is
not one of our ground rules."

"There are a lot worse examples than these," Leonard admits, "but they involve reviewers we'll never use again."

Leonard, a self-styled "Trilling groupie," has no trepidation
about stepping into the box against the *Review*. "I read them very
carefully," he says with confidence. "I think we're giving them a
run for their money in their own field. Our batting average is getting higher. We're trying several things, and one of the things I'm
trying to do is beat the *New York Review*. A very high standard

12. February 27, 1972, and March 5, 1972.

has been established which I would like to imitate and better. The Goffman piece is something Silvers would have liked to publish. For so long people have been browbeating the *Book Review* as middlebrow and as an adjunct of the Book-of-the-Month Club. But it's always been part of a newspaper and what other newspaper supports a section that doesn't make money? I will never have the space to review all the books *New York Review* chooses to review at the length they choose. I can't win that game. But a lot of their space is wasted. Secretly, I feel I can win it by picking the right books and the right issues. If I did my job perfectly, every front page would have a review of a great book."

NYR never intended to become an Alice's Restaurant, where you could find anything you wanted in the way of reviews. "Coverage" was the beast that devoured other book media. "Serious discussion of important books," as the second issue stated in editorial, was their motto. Even so, tons of notable books which are right up the *Review*'s alley are habitually neglected. To name a few: Theodore Roszak's *The Making of a Counter Culture*, Charles Reich's *The Greening of America*, Norman Mailer's *The Prisoner of Sex*, Germaine Greer's *The Female Eunuch*, Kate Millet's *Sexual Politics*, Robert Coles' *Erik Erikson*, Charles Silberman's *Crisis in the Classroom*, Alvin Toffler's *Future Shock*, Robert Brustein's *Revolution as Theater*, Stokely Carmichael's *Stokely Speaks*, K. S. Karol's *Guerrillas in Power*, Hugh Thomas' *The Pursuit of Freedom*, John Campbell's *The Foreign Affairs Fudge Factory*, Jules Witcover's *The White Knight*, and Daniel P. Moynihan's *Maximum Feasible Misunderstanding*, and through the years a standing-room crowd of National Book Award nominees. (But room was made for Carlo Ginzburg's *Il Nicodemismo: Simulazione e disimulazione religiosa nell' Europa del 1500*.) Movie books didn't seem to attract the slightest attention until 1973. Before then, not a single work by Pauline Kael, Andrew Sarris, John Simon, or lesser-known film critics had been the object of *NYR* treatment. Is this any way to run an outfit that Silvers now maintains is primarily a book review?

Naturally, these omissions are cause for resentment. One discontented author gave voice to some of the anti-*NYR* themes abroad in academia in a letter to a fellow author:

"Richard Kostelanetz has done a tricky piece of analysis, which suggests that the *NYR* is a Jewish plot ["Militant Minorities," *The Hudson Review*, Autumn 1965].[13] I'm pretty naïve about what goes on inside the New York literary world, but I don't think that's correct. When you come from the West Coast, as I do, you see things differently. What you see in the *NYR* is a plot to saw the United States off just west of the University of Pennsylvania and then marry the eastern portion to Oxbridge, England. I've picked up copies of the *NYR* which are more than half done by mediocre British academics, who often have no idea what they're talking about when they address the American scene. But I guess they add a kind of old world luster and exotic gentility. On the other hand, the number of 'Westerners' who make it into the *NYR*'s pages is infinitesimal [. . .] and most of these are East Coast academics who are touring the great wilderness. The *NYR*'s reports on Berkeley have often been done by visiting profs from Harvard or Brandeis.

"I only happen to live in California (most of the time) and have no regional chauvinism about the matter. I guess I have no loyalties to any real estate anywhere. But I must say this project the *NYR* is pushing seems irritatingly bizarre. I have been told that the reason I don't get any attention is simply because I'm not East Coast and Ivy League and the *NYR* is out to restore America's proper cultural balance. What comes from west of the Appalachians just *can't* measure up. If that's so, it sounds like a crazy

---

13. Truman Capote endorses this notion, too. In his *Rolling Stone* interview (April 12, 1973) he spoke of the "goddamned Jewish Mafia working tooth and tong on *The New York Review of Books*."

operation to me. But I know I have heard this kind of talk from New Yorkers whenever I pass through: To wit, the New York analysis is the only one that gets it straight—whatever *it* is. (I recall Mary McCarthy saying in one of her reports from Vietnam that she always sought to talk to soldiers from New York, because they were 'wised up' about things; and all the rest were sort of boobs. I also recall hearing from a friend at *Life* a few years ago that as long as student rebellion was happening at Berkeley, it was just fun and games, but when it arrived at Columbia and Harvard, it had to be taken seriously as 'a social phenomenon,' and that was why they had decided not to use a review of mine which seemed too indulgent toward these dangerous kids. This was just after a flare-up at Harvard.)"

An Oxbridge-Bowash strategy at *NYR*? Yes, and the *Review* can get away with it, since more than 50 per cent of its subscribers are crammed into the mid-Atlantic states. Who knows what talents are going unmined in them thar hills? Bob Silvers sure doesn't.

Our California correspondent is partially right: Silvers' fussiness can be blamed for some of the *Review*'s lapses in coverage. For example, Silvers admitted to a friend that he hasn't been able to find a reviewer whose stuff he likes on the psychoanalytic tradition except Britain's Charles Rycroft. Rycroft can write for *NYR*, but no one is trusted to review *him* there. Then there is the ideological factor. Neither *American Power and the New Mandarins* nor *At War With Asia* by Chomsky was reviewed there. (Hans Morgenthau did the latter for the *TBR.*) Are we to presume there is no one in the trans-Atlantic community capable of judging these books in the *Review*? Why not reach out for a different viewpoint on Chomsky and have Howe or Harrington criticize him in his own ballpark? The *Review* need not be so famous for protecting its own side. Robert Heilbroner on Barrington Moore, Jr.'s *Reflections on the Causes of Human Misery and Upon Certain Proposals to Eliminate Them*, Wassily Leontief on

Heilbroner's *Between Capitalism and Socialism*, Martin Bernal on Frances FitzGerald's *Fire in the Lake*, or FitzGerald on Mary McCarthy's *Hanoi* contained few, if any, surprises. And neither did Jason Epstein on *Teachers Strike* by his arch-enemy on this issue, Martin Mayer. To the extent the *New York Review* is a captive of its own ideology, it fails as a review of books.

The most frequent apolitical murmur one overhears about *New York Review* has to do with the length. Why do *NYR's* reviewers run on so? Put yourself in Silvers' shoes. Say the late Edmund Wilson rang you up and said he'd like to do something on Tolstoy. What would you have said? "Beautiful, Bunny, but keep it short"? "The day Bob Silvers says cut to Wilson," remarked an associate of Wilson before his death, "is the day Wilson stops sending copy to the *Review*. Bob hasn't got the muscle to cut five hundred words from Wilson. He's working with one hand tied behind his back." And Wilson was just one of many. When a journal pays so little for a lot of work and time, it has to concede something. "All the space you want" is an offer many intellectuals can't refuse.

Great length is not the only gamble Silvers takes with great critics. He also risks having to carry them in the late rounds of their careers. Leonard Kriegel, author of the critical study *Edmund Wilson*, suggests that Wilson was not up to par toward the end: "Wilson's work in *New York Review* depicted a critic who more and more was content to play the role of the grand old man of American letters. And God knows, Wilson deserved that right. On the other hand, for a review that prides itself on its intellectual incisiveness, Wilson's writing there seemed to me rather self-indulgent and essentially minor in the particular concerns he evinced. Even when he wrote about a figure like T. S. Eliot, as he did in a review of the original drafts of *The Waste Land*,[14] his

14. *The Waste Land* by T. S. Eliot, A Facsimile and Transcript of the Original Drafts Including the Annotations of Ezra Pound, edited by Valerie Eliot, November 18, 1971.

remarks lacked in the kind of critical perception he brought to Eliot's work in the past—for example, the chapter on Eliot in *Axel's Castle* and the long essay on Eliot in *The New Yorker* in 1958. What I saw of Wilson in *New York Review* was decidedly inferior to the critical standards Wilson himself once set in the *New Republic* in the Twenties and Thirties and even in *The New Yorker* in the Forties and Fifties. One didn't come away from reading Wilson in the *Review* with the impression that this is the foremost American critic." Margot Hentoff, in just about the *Review*'s only concession to mass-cult books, has appeared too infrequently with some pointillist comments on Vidal's *Myra Breckinridge*, Buckley's *The Governor Listeth*, Jimmy Breslin's *The Gang That Couldn't Shoot Straight*, and Joe Flaherty's *Managing Mailer*. What the *Review* lacks, according to Ronald Steel, is a slick like Alan Pryce-Jones, former editor of the *TLS* and book reviewer for the late *Herald Tribune*, to liven the operation.

Summing up: as book review, neither as good nor as necessary as it once was, but still the repository of selected magnificent reviews.

As New Left Movement review. NYR has been so identified with the New Left that Dennis Wrong unconsciously slipped into calling it the "New Left Review" during the author's interview with him. Just where does the *New York Review* stand? To the left of Carnegie Hall (looking uptown) and, with the exception of Vietnam and university politics, to the right of most of what was commonly associated with New Left politics, whatever this term means at the turn of the decade. The *Review*'s leftism has almost always been of the thoroughbred kind, sympathetic yet temperamentally apart from the grittier Movement writers and causes, which are relegated to the back of the magazine—to the letters columns. Except for Tom Hayden and Jerry Rubin, who appeared in *NYR* only once, Rennie Davis, who co-authored a single article, and the departed Kopkind, what other streetwalking New Left critics have they published? I. F. Stone, Noam Chomsky, Jason Epstein, Murray Kempton, Edgar Z. Friedenberg, and the late Paul Goodman are class. They pass the cultural test. But where are the Movement journalists, the blue collar reporters of the revolution who keep the fires blazing at *Ramparts*, the *Village Voice, Liberation*, and the *Guardian*? Paul Cowan, Jack Newfield, Nat Hentoff, Dave Gelber, Sol Stern, James Ridgeway, Dave Dellinger, Karl Hess, David McReynolds, Jimmy Breslin, and Andrew Kopkind are a credit to their race, but need not apply to the *Review*. *Pas de cachet*? Yet there's room for Elizabeth Hardwick in Watts, Francine du Plessix Gray at the Panther Rally in New Haven, and Leslie Fiedler on *his* pot bust—this is the stuff of radical chic that Wolfe didn't pick up. Long ago, Silvers was begged by former assistant Janet Coleman to publish Carl Oglesby, a young New Left theoretician, but no go. Silvers rejected Dan Berrigan's Hanoi reportage in 1967 and didn't use him until he went underground in 1970. The radical scholarship produced at places like The Institute for Policy Studies and the Cambridge Institute has been dipped into only sparingly, leaving Marcus Raskin, Richard Barnet, Arthur Waskow, Gar Alperowitz, and their colleagues practically untouched. Herbert Marcuse, Howard Zinn, and Staughton Lynd have not only never written for the *Review*, but in the case of Marcuse and Lynd, their books have been consistently savaged in its pages. The permutations of liberation—concerning women, gays, abortion, welfare, drug and prison reform, and anything remotely connected with rock culture—seem to draw a blank with *NYR* editors. "If anybody came here from

another planet and just read the *New York Review*," says Richard
Poirier, "he'd never even know there was anything going on in
popular, much less a counter-culture."

"We're not hippies," Elizabeth Hardwick insists, and her mo-
tion is seconded by Robert Lowell's sonnet "Marching," which
closes:

> *Revolution*
> *dragging her terrible premenstrual cramps*
> *marches with unbra'd breasts to storm the city*[15]

Recent articles on health and consumer affairs, however, do
indicate a stirring in the direction of what Jack Newfield hails as
the "new populism."

The slippery nature of the *Review*'s politics has damaged its
credibility in some pockets of the Movement. An editor of one
Left weekly goes as far as saying, "Despite their attention to
Vietnam, the *New York Review* is apolitical, essentially unliterary,
and therefore Philistine. They've been political in intention. Their
politics are against the war. But that's no politics. If that's all you
have, then you get right into the next war. You're not stopping
the machine." Jason Epstein might agree with him. When an
interviewer asked him recently to explain the *Review*'s politics,
he replied, "There is no political line. We go from issue to issue."

It is this attitude that worries Gar Alperowitz of the Cambridge Institute, who thinks the *Review* should be entering into a
second phase in this postwar period, but doesn't see the signs yet.
"Will the *Review* become like the liberal professors who stuck
their toes into radicalism with the war, but who are now drawing
back into the tower? I believe there's a possibility they can move
out of that. Their Paul Goodman trend should be pushing out to
new Paul Goodmans—to Murray Bookchin, Garry Wills, Todd

15. *Modern Occasions*, Fall 1970.

Gitlin, Carl Oglesby." And perhaps a trend is in the works: Wills, an uncommonly learned journalist as well as a master prose stylist, reviewed several books on the 1972 campaign for *NYR* last fall (October 4, 1973). And Oglesby has been asked for a review.

Jimmy Breslin isn't anxious about the politics of the *Review*; he just ignores the magazine. "I read Kempton," he snorts, "but the rest is a lot of shit." *Village Voice* columnist and co-author of *The Populist Manifesto* Jack Newfield is of two minds. "Certainly, on the war the *Review* has been marvelous," he comments. "At a time when other publications are moving to the Right— *Commentary, Harper's, New York, The New York Times Magazine*—particularly on the question of racism, the *Review* has stayed its ground. My trouble with them is their sense of fashion. Certain writers like Hayden and Kopkind are dropped. It's like Stalin's Russia. I also don't think Murray [Kempton] has done his best stuff for them. He was better in the *Post*.

"They are missing this whole thing on popularism, too. They are late on the ethnics and the blue collar revival. Personally, I don't look to the *Review* to learn something. They're not at the frontier of consciousness. If you're not writing about Attica or the working class, then you're not there. I believe that Pete Hamill, Wicker, and Studs Terkel are there more than the academics."

A scary thing happened on the heels of Dennis Wrong's "Case." A month or so after Wrong blitzed the *Review* from the Right, the *Review* itself published an issue (January 7, 1971) packed with pieces critical of various Left forms. Elizabeth Hardwick spanked the films *Gimme Shelter, Trash,* and *The Groupies;* Murray Kempton trashed Tom Hayden's book *Trial;* James Baldwin gently chided Angela Davis' unhistoricity in an open letter; and Wassily Leontief exposed the troubles of Cuban socialism. None of these articles, except for Kempton's, would be cause for a double-take all by itself. But squeezed together in a Dagwood sandwich so close to Wrong, they tripped alarms all over the Eastern seaboard. "One *Commentary* is fine," said a former buddy of Podhoretz at the time, "but two is horrible." Naturally, Silvers disparages the idea of being affected in any way by *Commentary*.

Kempton's review of *Trial*, however, is open to suspicion of having sprung from pique. Kempton, who usually reviewed what books Silvers assigned for his monthly spot, volunteered for *Trial*. Hayden had accused him of copping out on the Movement, and now it was Kempton's turn at bat. "It was an act of pure malice, lacking even the justification that Mr. Kempton had a particular axe to grind," complained Richard Flacks in a long letter to the editor (May 6, 1971), which went unanswered save for a begging off paragraph about not wishing to intrude on the professor's space. "As originally written, it could have appeared comfortably in *Commentary*," states Kempton. "I wasn't terribly pleased by the piece. I could have been more fair to Tom." Silvers engaged Kempton in a protracted conversation to get him to think through the tone of his dislike. Says Kempton: "It is perhaps true, even after Silvers had performed so nobly, that the piece might better have not been written; no piece conceived in animus can be entirely redeemed; and I hope it is not just a weakness in character and a desire to be liked that makes me always a little sorry when I attack private men. I really do prefer celebration. Still, the point remains that whatever meanness of spirit entered the piece was mine alone and whatever gentleness finally intruded was Silvers' inspiration—to which, I am, as so often, most grateful—and any inference that the whole package was produced by some *New York Review* direction to clean our skirts is, in this case, unjustified."

Indications that *New York Review* is winding down its war are not always best sought in the magazine. What isn't published can be as significant as what is in plotting *NYR*'s political curves. The fate of Roger Wilkins' review of *Seize the Time* by Black Panther Party Chairman Bobby Seale may tell something of where the *Review* was at the dawn of the Seventies. White man Tom Wicker of *The New York Times* was approached to do the review

first, but he declined, recommending Wilkins, a black and a
former Assistant Attorney General in Ramsey Clark's office who
is now with the *Washington Post*. Jason and Barbara Epstein
partied with Wilkins one evening in the summer of 1970. Would
he consider reviewing *Seize the Time*? "We'd really like you to do
this," said Jason Epstein very casually. (The more casual the
better, since the book was edited by John Simon at Random.)
Wilkins wasn't sure. He would read it and let Barbara know. Well,
he was quite excited about Seale's badass history of the Panthers.
He would review it with pleasure. But *NYR* never published the
piece. After months of circumlocution and delays at the *Review*
office, Wilkins withdrew his manuscript in a rage.

Wilkins was not eager to spread around his past troubles with
the *Review*. He eventually talked in the drawing room of Jean
Stein's Central Park West apartment. Wilkins, handsome in a
greying, modest Afro, had been collaborating with Stein on an
Angela Davis interview for *Life*. He rose from a table set up
in front of the French windows and sat down on a small couch
in the center of the well-appointed room. Help arrived with a plate
of shrimp as he began the story of his review, which was full, he
said, "of traumatic tension that white people, some white people,
can't understand."

"The real drama in the review was a black guy who was an
Assistant Attorney general saying that Bobby Seale was our kins-
man. It was a very passionate piece, in which I tried to show a link
in heritage between guys like Seale and guys like me. The differences weren't very great. The review turned out to be very pro-
Panther." Wilkins gave his 10,000-word manuscript to Barbara
Epstein in July. Then negotiations went on for the next five
months. Wilkins admits he responded to the book emotionally and
that his review needed tightening, but he couldn't seem to nail
Epstein down. He would make corrections, and she wouldn't say
whether they satisfied her. "It's an important and powerful piece,

and let's get on with it," she told Wilkins in the early innings, yet she never got on with it herself, according to Wilkins.

"I finally went to them in November and said, 'Look, you guys put down points that you feel need to be made or corrected, and I'll see if I can do it.'" Epstein responded with a request for several clarifications which Wilkins interpreted as fundamentally racist. He wrote Epstein immediately to recall the manuscript. But instead of sending his letter off in the heat of the moment, he sat on it for a few days while he tested his reaction on three white friends. "Yes, you're right," they all commented on Epstein's memorandum, "that's racist."

What was "racist" about the document? "It didn't say, 'You niggers is vituperative,'" Wilkins kidded. "I would characterize it as a strong effort to have me as a black man deviate from what I thought was a perfectly proper position—that is, viewing the Panthers from the black establishment perspective, to viewing them from their perspective with issues whites thought were important." Silvers had come a long way from Ronald Steel's "Letter from Oakland." Too many pigs had been offed in the interim not to deal directly with Panther rhetoric. But, for Wilkins, that was the man's problem. "If I am turned on more by the issues of Panther leadership of the black *lumpen proletariat* and in the ghettos than their devotion to Kim il Soong, that's my prerogative. It was a subtle racism—an inability to accept the intellect and hence the validity of a black man's view of what they know about. If they asked an Indian writer to write about the Pakistan war, they wouldn't assume they knew more than he did. It's a bunch of capable A students who continued to be A students throughout life."

The Roger Wilkins affair doesn't mean the *Review* is phasing itself out of the New Left. That could happen only over Chomsky's, Stone's, and rows of other limp bodies. Some who read Wilkins' article deemed it "unsalvageable" for editorial rather

than political reasons. But, according to the author, the objections
of the editors were purely political. Without access to the various
drafts and memos of requested changes, no one lacking privy to
the Wilkins-*Review* dossier can say for certain whether the problems were primarily aesthetic or, as the author claims, political.
But one thing seems clear: The *Review* is demonstrably cooling
off. Its former revolutionary extravagance is being curtailed.
Nevermore provo pieces by Andrew Kopkind, nevermore Jerry
Rubin raving "No, I am Spartacus, No, I am Spartacus,"[16] and,
apparently, no Roger Wilkins doing a softshoe with Bobby Seale.

Summing up: unbeatable as *haute* New Left review with
Chomsky, Stone, and others, but unfulfilling where New Left and
the counter-culture converged in the Sixties.

As "chief theoretical organ of Radical Chic." The phrase is
Tom Wolfe's, and at first glance it appears to make sense. The
Review is both radical and chic, but is it host to radical chic in
that term's most pejorative connotations? Wolfe explains himself
in the essay of the same title:

> The chief theoretical organ of Radical Chic, *The New York
> Review of Books*, regularly cast Huey Newton and Eldridge
> Cleaver as the Simon Bolivar and José Marti of the black
> ghettos. On August 24, 1967, *The New York Review of
> Books* paid homage to the summer urban riot season by
> printing a diagram for the making of a Molotov Cocktail on
> its front page. In fact, the journal was sometimes referred to

16. "An Emergency Letter to My Brothers and Sisters in the Movement," February 13, 1969.

goodnaturedly as *The Parlour Panther*, with the *-our* spelling of *Parlour* being an allusion to its concurrent motif of anglophilia. The *Review*'s embracing of such contradictory attitudes—the nitty-gritty of the ghetto warriors and the preciosity of traditional English Leavis & Loomis intellectualism—was really no contradiction at all, of course. It was merely the essential double-track mentality of Radical Chic—*nostalgie de la boue* and high protocol—in its literary form.

And what is *nostalgie de la boue*? Translated it means "nostalgia for the mud." As employed by Wolfe, it serves as a code word for aping avant-garde fads and lower-class tastes. In society, mud nostalgia is a tool of *arrivistes,* who are compelled to certify their superiority over the hated bourgeoisie by shocking them. During the 1960s in New York, mud nostalgia was twisting at the Peppermint Lounge,[17] pop art, camp, digging the Rolling Stones and boxer José Torres (who did three rounds with Norman Mailer on Dick Cavett). That's cultural *ndlb*. Political *ndlb* operates on the same premise:

> [. . .] i.e. the styles of romantic, raw-vital, Low Rent primitives are good; and *middle class*, whether black or white, is bad. Therefore, Radical Chic invariably favors radicals who seem primitive, exotic and romantic, such as the grape workers, who are not merely radical and 'of the soil,' but also Latin; the Panthers with their leather pieces, Afros, shades, and shout outs; and the Red Indians, who, of course, had always seemed primitive, exotic, and romantic.

Wolfe grants that the impulses undergirding radical chic are sincere. "On the first track—well, one *does* have a sincere concern for the poor and the underprivileged and an honest outrage against discrimination. On the other hand—on the second track of one's mind, that is—one also has a sincere concern for maintain-

17. Eldridge Cleaver was on to this phenomenon in *Soul on Ice*: "They were swinging and gyrating and shaking their dead little asses like petrified zombies trying to regain the warmth of life, rekindle the dead limbs, the cold ass, the stone heart, the stiff, mechanical disused joints with the spark of life."

ing a proper East Side life style in New York Society." If this be hypocrisy, then Wolfe has made the most of it.

Since he was doing a book on the case, then *Review* columnist Murray Kempton knew the hairy legal status of the 21. Through his intervention, a pre-Bernstein fund and consciousness raiser was thrown at the New York apartment of movie director Sidney Lumet (with the Bernsteins as guests). Wolfe wasn't there, but he pieced together a flashback scene starring one of his favorite targets. "Murray Kempton cooled things down a bit," he wrote with obvious relish. "He stood up and, in his professorial way, in the tweedy tones of a lecturer who clicks his pipe against his teeth like a mental metronome, he summed up the matter. Dependable old Murray put it all in the more comfortable terms of Reason Devout, after the manner of a lead piece in the periodicals he worshipped, the *New Statesman* and the *Spectator*."

Kempton returns contempt for ridicule. "Who is Wolfe to judge these people's morality?" he wonders rhetorically. "He's a fashion writer. When they were on Andy Warhol, he took him seriously! He has no social purpose in his writing. If that's all there is in life, then I pity him."

At stake here is not the coexistence of Bob Silvers the courtier visiting Jackie at Lake Como with Bob Silvers the revolutionary sweating bullets in a Catholic resistance meeting on the night of Dan Berrigan's capture; the issue is not the conflict between a man who would not sign the Writers and Editors War Tax Protest in 1968 and a man who put his John Hancock on the Petition for Redress of Grievances in 1972,[18] but whether *New York Review* is indeed "the chief theoretical organ of Radical Chic."

18. See *The New York Review of Books*, June 15, 1972. Silvers and Barbara Epstein sat down in the Capitol building on May 24, 1972, with 100 or so radical-liberals from the petition-oriented *Redress* organization. Ninety-four in their group were arrested for "unlawful assembly," but the editors of the *Review* had left the scene before the police moved in. They told people they had to get back to New York to put out an issue. "It was like wild horses getting them to come in the first place," said one of their companions on the trip.

Wolfe abuses his license on his radicalism rap. The *Review* has not "regularly [if ever] cast" Newton or Cleaver in the role of black messiah. Jack Richardson gave Cleaver's *Soul on Ice* a calm literary treatment, and Harold Cruse's review of *Post-Prison Writings and Speeches* was anything but a rave. Ronald Steel's rhapsody of the Panthers is about the only evidence, apart from that worn-out exhibit A—the Molotov Cocktail cover—that Wolfe might have dredged up from mud nostalgia. And when was the last time you read a Chicano or Red Indian piece in the *Review*? *NYR* is radical, all right, but its radicalism is not as totally puerile as Wolfe's hypothesis demands. You didn't have to be poor and black to be radicalized by Lyndon Johnson. Even some of the chic drew the line at genocide.

Mud nostalgia is even more inappropriate as a description of the *Review*'s cultural side. Its editors have always been above such *ndlb* favorites as rock, camp, and pop art. That's because they're too chic, Wolfe would riposte. But it was the chic who put the Peppermint and Warhol and camp on the Sixties map. Wolfe fails to distinguish well enough between the *lived* radical chic of the Bernsteins and the *literary* radical chic of *NYR*, as if the two species could be compared at all. While, for the sake of argument, both parties might share roughly similar politics, the middle category of chic cannot be meaningfully distributed to include lunch at the Running Footman for Felicia and Lenny and an interview with Igor Stravinsky in *NYR*. The seeming incongruity —the radical chic—of the Bernsteins having the Panthers in for cocktails is not of the same order as having Stravinsky and Stokely Carmichael back to back in a magazine. There is no earthly reason or ethical imperative why anyone of intelligence and morals should not be interested in both at once or why appreciation for the former on one track must blunt one's solidarity with the latter on the other track. The aesthetic realism in the back pages of *Ramparts* and the *Guardian* are a drag. There is nothing in the *New York Review* that promotes the marvelous

lives of Bernsteins' guestlist. Set a copy of *New York Review*
before most of them, and they would probably say, repeating the
words of Mrs. Peter Duchin as she was about to meet a Panther
chez Bernstein: "This is a first for me."

You want to read a real organ of radical chic? Then read
The New Yorker. Start with its morally indignant short-takes on
Nixon's diabolism in "Talk of the Town," leaf through war pieces
by Seymour Hersh, Frances FitzGerald, Mary McCarthy, and
William Woodward, and then check the Porsche, Lord and Taylor,
Bill Blass, and the John Baldwin ads, especially the John Baldwins
(*"More patrician peasantry* . . . A spin of shawl, a fling of fringe
—tossed over an ankle-length dress of white-flowered black Bell-
seta nylon jersey, by Mr. Dino. $100" [emphasis added]). If
it's going to be "Up against the wall!" then *The New Yorker*
goes first.

Summing up: as "the chief theoretical organ of Radical Chic"
—Almost, but not quite. But that lived radical chic never dies,
it fades into "Suzy Says" (The New York *Daily News*, February
29, 1972):

> The all-time drop-dead New York apartment is the just-
> finished flawlessly functioning Faberge box of a flat of
> Valerian Rybar, the international interior designer who does
> things for the Patinos, the Schlumbergs, the Wiley Buchanans,
> the Graham Mattisons and others too utterly everything to
> mention.
>
> What Valerian has done for himself is design and decorate
> an apartment that is a working jewel in a glowing setting. It
> looks like something Salvador Dali could conceivably have
> had a hand in—with an assist from maybe Raymond Loewy.
> But it's the apotheosis of Valerian Rybar alone. [. . .]
>
> Supping and sipping were the Baron and Baroness Guy de
> Rothschild, Betty and Francois Catroux, the Baron Alexis de
> Rede, Andre Oliver, the designer, and Etienne de Montpezat,
> the Queen of Sweden's brother-in-law, all from Paris. Then

there were Mary McFadden, the magazine editor, in yards of pale yellow chiffon, blonde Berry Berenson in black platforms, Anne Slater in butterscotch jersey, Francoise and Oscar de la Renta, Lady Dudley with Robert Silvers, Annette and Sam Reed, John Radziwill, Lady Dudley's tall good-looking son, and others too esoteric to mention. It seemed about as good a way as any to break in an interior designer's masterpiece.

As house organ of Random House. The architect of this argument is Richard Kostelanetz, thirty-three, a once precocious littérateur who has authored or edited over twenty books. Having run into a losing streak with publishers lately and having heard similar down-and-out stories from scores of talented contemporaries, he concluded that there must be a conspiracy afoot. For Kostelanetz, this revolting development presages "the end of intelligent writing"—which is also the title of his book, due to be published in the spring of 1974. *The End* purports to do to the "lit mob" what *The Valachi Papers* did to the real one. It is a detailed indictment of alleged shenanigans in the upper reaches of the literary world. Kostelanetz excavates a lot of ground and appears to turn up several corpses. But because this canary, unlike Valachi, is looking outside-in, he really can't be sure of his body count. An almost absolute reliance on circumstantial evidence and reading of minds robs Kostelanetz of final authenticity. Kostelanetz can be persuasive in alleging a close relationship between the *New York Review* and Random House. In 1969, he fed Harry

Smith's lit gossip *Newsletter* some of his research into the
Epstein-Epstein-Silvers combine. Here's how the *Newsletter*
handled it (March 5, 1969):

*THE NEW YORK REVIEW OF BOOKS GIVES STRONG
PREFERENCE TO THE RANDOM HOUSE GROUP*, a
Newsletter study reveals. Reviewing *NYR*'s full 1968 record,
researchers found *RH & its subsidiaries, Knopf & Pantheon,
dramatically outdistanced any comparable group of competitors* in books reviewed and authors accepted:

1/ *Led* with seventeen of the seventy-three *books singled
out* for separate review (more than 23 per cent)—more than
Macmillan, Farrar Straus & Giroux, Houghton Mifflin,
Atheneum, Little, Brown, Dutton, Norton and Holt, Rinehart
& Winston COMBINED.

2/ *Led in total number of books reviewed*—forty-one (no
other publisher having as many as the nineteen for the Knopf
imprint alone, firms such as Scribner's, Simon & Schuster,
Bobbs Merrill, Morrow and Putnam's getting less than five).

3/ *Received favorable reviews in three out of every four
cases*—half being highly favorable and only several highly
unfavorable—although *NYR* is reputed to be tough on books,
an establishment where, as Norman Podhoretz observed, "a
book is assumed to be guilty until it proves itself innocent."

4/ *One of every four reviewers were RH authors with
books in print, 37 per cent of them reviewing books by other
RH authors.*

5/ *RH accounted for nearly half of the other essays and
well over half (57 per cent) of those contributed by authors
with books in print.* Many of the articles were from forthcoming books.

6/ *RH led with at least thirty-nine contributors to* NYR,
many with several pieces each, in the twenty-four issues year.

(Futher statistical information will be provided on request.)

*The picture emerges of the Random House team with top
billing in* NYR, *in the spotlight issue after issue.*

The combine is the chief advertiser, with more than twice as many ad pages as any competitor. *NYR* co-editor Barbara Epstein is the wife of Random House vice president & editor Jason Epstein.

The *Newsletter* began its investigation after hearing a leading critic's complaint that *NYR* is "in effect, a house organ of Random House." He charged "there is a deal" whereby RH publishes "the lit mob of Left-Wing writers centering about *NYR*, with the review, in return, acting to promote RH books." Queries to other knowledgeable persons elicited similar opinions. *Despite the intimate relationship, however, it was discovered that* NYR *is not really a house organ of Random House.*

"It is absurd to allege any kind of deal," NYR editor Robert B. Silvers responded. *"There is no conscious intention"* to give favors to Random House. He contended it is "unfair to consider them as one publisher." (Even considered as separate publishers, however, the RH & Knopf imprints each have more books individually reviewed than any other publisher, individually lead in the other important categories as well.) Moreover, Silvers objected, "Individual reviews are not a meaningful category." (*TN*, however, believes it is safe to generalize that books singled out for review are, in fact, singled out.)

Declaring "we have never chosen books for review on the basis of who published them—nor reviewers," Silvers said he has *no intention of correcting any disparity or changing his policy in any way.*

In *The End of Intelligent Writing*, Kostelanetz goes into greater detail. After combing through the cumulative index of the *Review*'s first six years (1963–68), he came up with further data on the *NYR*-Random House axis. (N.B. By Random House: Kostelanetz means Random House as well as wholly-owned divisions Knopf, Pantheon, and Vintage Books.) For example: (1) four of the five most featured poets (four or more poems) in

NYR appeared in Vintage Books; (2) sixteen of the twenty-three most featured essayists (three or more essays) were Random House authors; and (3) twenty-three of the forty-five most featured reviewers (ten or more reviews) have been Random House authors. To Silvers' rebuke that the *Review* is blind to the brand names of publishers and inclinations of reviewers, Kostelanetz responds: "The governing assumption is that the commissioned reviewers would want to satisfy their editors (as most do) and thus be invited to contribute again. And with so many Random House-Vintage authors reviewing Epstein's books, one could also count on a measure of intellectual likemindedness . . ." But beyond all this *a fortiori* fiddle, Kostelanetz argues that the *Review*'s setup was a magnificent indiscretion from the beginning. "It was, after all, indubitably improper for a manufactureer to found in his personal residence a public medium supposedly scrutinizing both his own and his competitors' produce and then installing his wife to co-manage it. . . ." For those who don't get the "indubitably," Kostelanetz spells it out by saying that the husband and wife relationship is too close to pass off possible conflict of interest as nothing more than similar editorial enthusiasms. "However," he closes his case, " 'that this operation was anything but covert,' to use a Murray Kemptonism, and yet so scarcely exposed, remains one of the most devastating indictments upon American cultural life. *Quod erat demonstrandum.*"[19]

True enough, no one in the publishing community has ever publicly inveighed against the *New York Review*-Random House pair bond. Irving Kristol, formerly executive vice president at

19. On hearing of this critique when it was called to his attention by The Media Industry Newsletter, Jason Epstein called Kostelanetz "an ambitious little hustler who has no talent and has been rejected by everyone. He's a bad writer who used to hang around the *New York Review*, and I used to throw him out" (Media Industry Newsletter, May 6, 1971). Kostelanetz's reply was carried in *The Newsletter*: "[. . .] One more thing, isn't it characteristically duplicitous that Epstein should claim to be bouncer in an office where he elsewhere states he has no policy-making role."

Basic Books, never gave it a thought. "Really, it's very tricky," he says when the ethical dilemma is posed. "It's quite common in France for book publishers to found their own journals. The assumption is that this is done for literary motives and not for commercial advancement." Kristol forgets that *NYR* and Random have always denied consanguinity and would be appalled by his well-meaning analogy.

The *Review*'s relative impotence in affecting the sale of trade books probably explains the industry's indifference to the arrangement. "The percentage of *Review* readers on college faculties is forty," states the head of one of Random's leading competitors, who is bothered by the *NYR* arrangement, "and these people are the worst [hardback] book buyers in the world. They get their library to buy the book or bum a copy—and that's a long way from lunch. A review in *New York Review* is useful, but not compelling, although it has a good deal of cachet in regard to foreign rights. [. . .] If the *Review* were a more potent factor, they [publishers] would resent it." Or, as the executive editor of a large trade house says in answer to Kostelanetz's plea: "It just doesn't count for all that much for me to look for conspiracy. Only a small portion of the books we publish lives or dies by the *New York Review*. If I worked for Basic Books or Praeger, maybe I would care."

Yet an official of Basic Books doesn't care, either. "If the *New York Review* reviews one of our books close to publication date," he reveals, "it helps us. But it reviews so late—after the books are virtually off the bookstore shelves—that it has minimal impact. Its review is simply for the record." He contrasts *NYR*'s sorry record in moving books with the goldmine effect of the *Times Book Review*: Basic's and Erving Goffman's *Relations in Public* was proceeding with sales of 1,200 a month for six months before *TBR* gave it front-page coverage; immediately thereafter, sales went up to 1,400 a week. In the opinion of the man from Basic, as well as most other entrepreneurs in the book trade, *New York Review* has no such clout.

Kostelanetz's 1968 statistics were not challenged by either Random or the *Review*—excepting Silvers' qualification that Random House, Knopf, and Pantheon ought to be considered separate and distinct houses in any accounting. How sporting is it to make Knopf and Pantheon guilty by corporate association? Surely Knopf's editor-in-chief, Robert Gottlieb, and Pantheon's managing director, André Schiffrin, are as independent of Jason Epstein as Roger Straus of Farrar, Straus & Giroux. But Farrar, Straus & Giroux is by no means a beneficiary of the *Review*'s largesse, nor does it happen to be a Random subsidiary. Knopf and Pantheon are both. Statistical evidence strongly suggests the possibility of an editorial predisposition toward Random-Knopf-Pantheon on the part of the *Review*—unless one uncritically accepts the tacit rebuttal that the Random House combine puts out books so far superior to the competition that they warrant the disproportionate review attention. Undeniably, their output is of a high order, but whether high enough to leave all competitors trailing in the dust is surely debatable.

Is *NYR*'s favoritism toward the Random House combine still in working order? That depends on your measure. In 1971, for example, Random-Knopf-Pantheon kept apace of its 1968 standings in the category of "books singled out for separate review"— sixteen out of sixty-nine for 23 per cent—again besting the aggregate totals of Macmillan (1), Farrar, Straus & Giroux (1), Houghton Mifflin (2), Atheneum (2), Little, Brown (1), Dutton (1), Norton (1), and Holt, Rinehart and Winston (3). Harcourt, Brace and Jovanovich's four separate reviews actually beat Random House, which garnered only three. Knopf got eight and Pantheon five. In 1971, the Random House imprints were also way ahead of the field in the total number of books reviewed with forty-nine. No other publisher came near that figure.

Impressionistically, *New York Review* no longer seems as intimately bound up with the Random House conglomerate as it has been in the past. Death, decline, and shifts in houses are breaking up that old gang of *NYR*/Random writers. Goodman, Hofstadter, Wilson, Auden, and Stravinsky are dead, and Morganthau, Lowell, and Macdonald (since moved to Viking) aren't as prolific as they once were. Politically, *NYR* and Random no longer need to look to each other for solace. Random's radical line of books and authors, which received so much play in the *Review* in the Sixties, is no more. The *Review*'s political horizon is now, and probably forever, beyond Random House.

Is it corruption when Bob Silvers asks *NYR* regular Robert Heilbroner whom *he* would recommend to review *his own Random House book*? Cronyism might be a more apt description of the query put to Heilbroner and the situation that obtains between *NYR* and Random. Cronyism not only avoids the murky region of intent, which corruption does not, but it covers cases outside the strict Random circle. For instance, Karl Miller, editor of *The Listener*, reviewed V. S. Pritchett's *Midnight Oil* with Graham Greene's *A Sort of Life* (July 20, 1972). Pritchett is one of Epstein's authors at Random, but Miller has no formal relations with Random. He was, however, Pritchett's editor at the *New Statesman* for years. His review opens: "Perhaps *The New York Review of Books* is not too austere to allow me to begin with a simple-hearted reminiscence. Some years ago, I had lunch with these two writers in London's most congenial restaurant . . ." That's cronyism.

Finally, how good is the *New York Review of Books*? There is a sign over the bar in a Dublin pub that says: "When sex is good, it's the most beautiful thing in the world. But when sex is bad, it's still pretty good." That's how good is *The New York Review of Books*.

8

In Search of the Review:
An Epilogue

S ix months after the initial rendezvous with the author, Bob Silvers still doesn't want to talk about the *New York Review*. He reckons the people the author visited and doesn't cotton to some of the research. Elizabeth Hardwick has undoubtedly had his ear. He says it is the poison of our age that one should be characterized not by what one does but by other measures and that the author should call him back in a week. "He's so serious about the *Review*'s survival," says a friend, "that he doesn't want it reviewed." Silvers consents to a second meeting, however.

It is almost twilight in the city. Silvers and Barbara Epstein are working late when the visitor arrives. Silvers excuses himself for a few seconds while he brings his co-editor a manuscript. The office is more kempt now than it was the previous winter. The tide of books has receded between publishing seasons, and on a clear summer's night Silvers can see across the room. He returns in a trice, sits down at his desk, and actually leans forward to discuss the magazine. He hates the idea of publicity, he says. There's too much seizing on the notion that one can understand things better if one understands the personality.

Silvers' strike zone is so narrow that it is useless to ask him questions about editorial operations, his relations with authors, and the politics of the *Review*. Roger Wilkins' complaint is floated in his direction, and it floats right back with a shrug. Wilkins can believe the disputed *NYR* memorandum was racist if he wants to. Then does he publish only articles he agrees with? He indicates that one can see in certain terms that an article can be challenged, but still one may think that it is worth publishing. All he can say is that "we stand on what we have published, and one hopes that if they read one issue, they'll read another."

Without the markings of editorials, however, it is not always clear where the *Review* stands, e.g., their treatment of Martin Luther King. In the summer of 1967, Andrew Kopkind defiled King shamelessly, portraying him as a leader out of step, "shuffling between Chicago and Cleveland." A year later, Elizabeth Hardwick went down to Atlanta herself for King's funeral and resurrected his reputation in and for the *Review*: "Perhaps what was celebrated in Atlanta was an end, not a beginning—the waning of the slow, sweet dream of Salvation, through Christ, of the Negro masses." The *Review* rushed to the aid of King's memory once again in 1970 with an ambush of John Williams' exposé *The King God Didn't Save*—a slight gossip charging that King's sex life was monitored by the FBI and used by Hoover to blackmail the Nobel laureate into cooling his activism. A friend of King's, Pastor Richard Neuhaus of Brooklyn, was the un-neutral reviewer.

Was this change of heart the *Review*'s way of making amends? Silvers say no, they're just three different views of King. "Everyone will have his own interpretation, and I don't want to comment." *New York Review*, too, means never having to say you're sorry.

The visitor recites the passage from Podhoretz's anti-Americanism column, where he declares the *Review*'s radicalism "consists entirely of preserving and enlarging the heritage of hatred for America to which both groups, [backers and editors], each for reasons of its own, have dedicated their lives and their fortunes and their sacred honor." Silvers is not bowled over by the sweep of Podhoretz's analysis. A silly statement, he remarks calmly. He notes that *NYR* published Frank Donner's "Spying for the FBI," Francis Carney's "Radical Takeover at Berkeley," and Schorske's "The Weimar Analogy." These are about the possibilities of this country, he feels. If one read these articles and then read Podhoretz, one would see how silly it is. If people read Podhoretz and agree, says Silvers, then *tant pis!*

Will the *Review* admit to no mistakes? "Oh sure, we've made mistakes, but I don't think it's meaningful for me to . . ." The interview has exhausted itself. Silvers has no more answers to give. He has sipped enough of the poison of our age.

Contrary to Silvers' project, we would know more about *The New York Review of Books* if we could seize the personality of its editor—the only kid on Long Island who conscientiously objected to being a plane-spotter during World War II, the grown-up who enjoys breakfasts with McGovern, and whose favorite intellectual is, in Robert Heilbroner's view, the learned and detached Barrington Moore.

The visitor pans the office in search of personal effects, Silvers' "Rosebud." Cut to a psychedelic poster of glorious Che taped to his door. Pan back across the room and stop on the United States seal painted on the front of his desk, a former television studio prop. Pan up and left along the wall where a photo of the wizened Ezra Pound stares blindly into the void. The Red guerrilla and the fascist poet. America in the middle. When Silvers' time is up, and this debris is thrown into the fire, maybe they will find, though no one will notice, the Spanish legend inked into his blotter—*Vivir bien es la mejor venganza.*

Author's Note

This book originated in a humble twenty-page magazine assignment, but in the course of researching the history of *The New York Review of Books*, one lead led to another until I wound up with a manuscript ten times the commissioned length. After one hundred interviews and much reading and correspondence during the spring and summer of 1971, I had fashioned something much larger than intended. Still, I did not have a book, since the perimeters of magazine writing had unconsciously bounded my inquires. I began a second round of research in January of 1972. Further additions and updates were incorporated during the greater part of 1973.

As a biweekly, *New York Review* can and sometimes does effect abrupt shifts in policies and contributors which may in turn change long-standing attitudes toward the journal among the intelligentsia and other interested parties. So it is impossible to freeze forever the views of the persons I have cited, My chronicle, however, records what was happening as the *Review* entered and passed through its first decade.

September 27, 1973
NEW YORK, NEW YORK

Index

Humphrey, Hubert, 73, 201, 215
Huntington, Samuel, 169

I. F. Stone's Bi-Weekly, 163, 164–165
I. F. Stone's Weekly, 33, 65, 167
Illich, Ivan, 254, 268
"Impotence of Victory, The" (Talmon), 181
In Search of Nixon (Mazlish), 255
"Industrial Work and Leisure in the United States" (Riesman and Bloomberg), 112
"Influential Intellectual Journals" (Hover and Kadushin), 80, 101
Inside the Third Reich (Speer), 184
Intellectual Origins of American Radicalism, The (Lynd), 242
"Interview with Hagib Bourguiba, An," 112
Ionesco, Eugene, 204
Israel Among the Nations (Talmon), 181
Israel and World Politics (Draper), 177
"Issue at Ocean Hill, The" (Epstein), 92
"Issues" (Podhoretz), 150, 151, 157, 160

"Jack Richardson in Las Vegas" (Richardson), 222
Jackson, Henry, 138
Jackson, Jonathan, 172, 189
Jackson, Katherine Gauss, 115
Jacobs, Jane, 87
Jarrell, Randall, 246, 248
Javits, Marion, 69
Jefferson, Thomas, 72
Jellinek, Roger, 265
Jews, 37, 46, 48, 55, 56, 60, 128, 134, 146, 150, 151, 160, 167, 168, 191, 203, 204, 212, 255, 274
Joffrey, Pierre, 265, 267
Johns Hopkins Univ., 23
Johnson, Lyndon B., 31, 33, 34, 36, 71, 144, 146, 155, 157, 165, 183, 212, 287
John Updike (Samuels), 191
Jones, D. A. N., 30, 204, 260
Journal from Ellipsia (Calisher), 191
Journal of International Affairs, 75
Joyce, James, 94

Kadushin, Charles, 7, 80, 101, 252, 257, 258
Kael, Pauline, 273
Kahn, Herman, 41
Kallman, Chester, 221
Kandy-Kolored Tangerine-Flake Streamlined Baby, The (Wolfe), 242
Karol, K. S., 273
Kauffman, Stanley, 261
Kaufman, Irving, 164
Kazin, Alfred, 21, 32, 38, 115, 117, 189, 191, 197, 200, 252, 256, 259, 260, 262, 265, 268
Kefauver, Estes, 62
Kemble, Penn, 34
Kempton, Murray, 29, 32, 50, 60, 117, 120, 129, 130, 134, 139–140, 147, 169, 185, 240, 241, 268, 278, 280, 281, 286, 292
Keniston, Kenneth, 255
Kennedy, John F., 31, 51, 118, 119, 144, 162, 196, 214
Kennedy, Robert, 14, 46, 48, 55, 73, 128, 214
Kermode, Frank, 30
Kerouac, Jack, 262
Kerr, Walter, 247
Khan, Yahya, 117
Kibel, Alvin, 193
Killings at Kent State, The (Stone), 64
King, Martin Luther, 14, 48–49, 55, 72, 73, 300
King God Didn't Save, The (Williams), 300
Kirkus Service, Inc., The, 66, 67, 219
Kissinger, Henry, 41, 169, 184
Koestler, Arthur, 114
Kohl, Herbert, 65
Kolin, Grace, 122, 289
Kolin, Dr. Michael, 122
Kopkind, Andrew, 4, 14, 46, 48–49, 50, 72, 121, 131, 143, 162, 185, 205, 209–211 214, 239, 278, 280, 284, 300
Korean War, 133, 138, 164, 166
Kostelanetz, Richard, 274, 292, 294
Kosygin, Aleksei, 215
Kotlowitz, Robert, 229
Kozol, Jonathan, 59
Kraft, Joseph, 33, 36
Kramer, Hilton, 240
Kriegel, Leonard, 276–277
Kristol, Irving, 5, 32, 41, 42, 43–44, 54, 64, 87, 114, 129–130, 169, 184, 292–293
Kronenberger, Louis, 148
Kropotkin, Peter, 163, 164
Krupnick, Mark, 149
Kunitz, Stanley, 261

Lacoutre, Jean, 33, 35
LaFeber, Walter, 174, 175, 176
Lane, Sir Allan, 87
Laqueur, Walter, 132, 177
Lasch, Christopher, 14, 40, 65, 72, 127, 129, 130, 142, 252, 256
Last Tango in Paris, 202
"Last Word, The" (Leonard), 121
Lawrence, D. H., 85, 98
"Lay of Grimnir, The," 261
Leavis, F. R., 225, 263, 285
Lehmann-Haupt, Christopher, 269
LeMay, General Curtis, 35
Leonard, John, 121, 149, 227, 265, 268–273
Leontief, Wassily, 256, 275, 280
Lerner, Max, 138, 166
"Letter From Havana" (Steel), 55, 182
"Letter to My Brothers..." (Rubin), 74–75
"Letter from Oakland" (Steel), 75, 183, 283
"Letter to a Pakistani Diplomat" (Ahmad), 117
"Letter from the Vatican" (Rynne), 202
"Letter to a Young Man About to Enter Publishing, A" (Silvers), 121
Levine, David, 28, 32, 33, 36, 46, 50, 199, 211–216
Lewis, Oscar, 87
Liben, Meyer, 192
Liberal Imagination, The (Trilling), 85, 161
Liberated Woman and Other Americans, The (Decter), 141
Liberation, 178, 278
Libman, Lillian, 228
Lichtheim, George, 30, 130, 145, 155
Life, 275, 282
Life Studies (Lowell), 246
Lifton, Robert Jay, 22, 117, 255
Line, Lemuel, 51
Lippmann, Walter, 181, 183
Listener, The, 30, 295
Little, Brown, and Company, 290, 294
Little Foxes, The (Hellman), 105, 106, 241
"Living in New York" (Epstein), 158–159
Locke, Richard, 265
Lolita (Nabokov), 86
London, Jack, 163
Lonely Crowd, The (Reisman), 85, 131
Looking Glass Library, 20, 26

307

308

310

311